STADIA

In this fully updated and redesigned edition of the essential and long-established *Stadia*, the authors offer their unrivalled expertise to all professionals who commission, plan, design, and manage high-quality sports venues.

Ideas about the design and use of stadiums continue to evolve and this fifth edition includes the latest developments in the field. With updated chapters on sustainability, masterplanning and services, a new chapter on branding activation, and new global case studies, *Stadia 5th edition* is the ultimate guide to all aspects of stadium design, from local club buildings to international showpieces.

In addition to a wide array of international case studies, the authors draw on the experience of the design firm Populous who in recent years delivered the 2010 Yankees Stadium in New York, the 2010 Aviva stadium, Dublin, the 2004 Benfica stadium, Lisbon, the 2010 Soccer City FNB Stadium, Johannesburg, the 2012 Marlins Park, Miami, and the 2012 new Olympic Stadium, London.

GERAINT JOHN
RIBA Dip Arch (UCL) CISRM
MILAM FRSA
Honorary Life President of the UIA
(International Union of Architects)
Sports and Leisure Programme
Former Chief Architect at GB
Sports Council

ROD SHEARD
Dip Arch (QUT) RIBA ARAIA FRSA
Stadium designer and Senior
Principal of Populous
Author of *The Stadium: Architecture
for the New Global Culture*

BEN VICKERY
RIBA BA Dip Arch FRSA
Senior Principal of Populous and
co-author of the SGSA guide on
concourses

The authors: Ben Vickery, Geraint John and Rod Sheard

STADIA: THE POPULOUS DESIGN AND DEVELOPMENT GUIDE

FIFTH EDITION

Geraint John, Rod Sheard and Ben Vickery

Routledge
Taylor & Francis Group

LONDON AND NEW YORK

Fifth edition published 2013
By Routledge
2 Park Square, Milton Park, Abingdon, Oxon OX14 4RN

Simultaneously published in the USA and Canada
by Routledge
711 Third Avenue, New York, NY 10017

Routledge is an imprint of the Taylor & Francis Group, an informa business

First edition published by Elsevier Limited 1994
Second edition published by Elsevier Limited 1997
Third edition published by Elsevier Limited 2000
Fourth edition published by Elsevier Limited 2007

British Library Cataloguing in Publication Data
A catalogue record for this book is available from the British Library

Library of Congress Cataloging in Publication Data
John, Geraint.
Stadia : the design and development guide / Geraint John, Rod Sheard and Ben Vickery. -- Fifth edition.
pages cm
Includes bibliographical references and index.
1. Stadiums--Design and construction. 2. Stadiums--Management. I. Sheard, Rod. II. Vickery, Ben. III. Title.
GV413.J64 2013
796.06'8--dc23
2012034158

ISBN: 978-0-415-52271-7 (hbk)
ISBN: 978-0-415-52270-0 (pbk)

Typeset in Gotham by Commercial Campaigns commercialcampaigns.co.uk
Cover and page design by Deep www.deep.co.uk
Publication project management by Alma Media International www.almamedia.co.uk

Publisher's note
This book has been prepared from camera-ready copy provided by the authors.

CONTENTS

Foreword by Jacques Rogge, President of the IOC   ix

Preface and acknowledgements   x

Picture credits   xi

1. **The stadium as a building type**   **01**
   1.1   A venue for watching sport   01
   1.2   History   02
   1.3   Current requirements   15

2. **The future**   **21**
   2.1   The importance of the stadium as
        a building type   21
   2.2   Economics of stadia   21
   2.3   Stadium technology   23
   2.4   Ergonomics and the environment   24
   2.5   What is the future for the stadium?   24

3. **Masterplanning**   **27**
   3.1   The need for a masterplan at all
        sports grounds   27
   3.2   Orientation of play   29
   3.3   Zoning of the venue   30
   3.4   Event overlay – what needs to be added
        to hold the event   32
   3.5   Security against terrorism   34
   3.6   Stadia in the city   34

4. **External planning**   **37**
   4.1   Location   37
   4.2   Transportation   39
   4.3   Provision of parking   40
   4.4   Stadium landscaping   45

5. **Form and structure**   **49**
   5.1   The stadium as architecture   49
   5.2   Structure and form   50
   5.3   Materials   53
   5.4   The playing surface   55
   5.5   Foundations   56
   5.6   Seating tiers   56
   5.7   Concourses, stairs and ramps   57
   5.8   Roof   58

6. **Security and anti-terrorism measures**   **71**
   6.1   Introduction   71
   6.2   The threats from terrorism   71
   6.3   Authorities   72
   6.4   Implications for management and operation   72
   6.5   Responses by the design team   72

    6.6   Conclusion   74

7. **Activity area**   **77**
   7.1   Playing surfaces   77
   7.2   Pitch dimensions, layout and boundaries   83

8. **Sports and multi-purpose use**   **99**
   8.1   Introduction   99
   8.2   National sports traditions   100
   8.3   Financial viability   100
   8.4   Catering for different sports   103
   8.5   Catering for non-sports performances   106

9. **Crowd control**   **109**
   9.1   General   109
   9.2   Perimeter fences   110
   9.3   Moats   112
   9.4   Changes of level   114

10. **Providing for disabled people**   **119**
    10.1   Equal treatment   119
    10.2   Sources of information   120
    10.3   Design process   121

11.	**Spectator viewing**	**127**
11.1	Introduction	127
11.2	Ground capacity	127
11.3	Viewing distances	132
11.4	Viewing angles and sightlines	137
11.5	Obstructions to viewing	143
12.	**Spectator seating**	**145**
12.1	Basic decisions	145
12.2	Seat types	146
12.3	Seat materials, finishes and colours	151
12.4	Choice	152
12.5	Dimensions	152
12.6	Seat fixings	154
12.7	Seating for spectators with disabilities	155
13.	**Private viewing facilities**	**157**
13.1	Introduction	157
13.2	Trends	159
13.3	Design	160
13.4	Multi-use	164
14.	**Circulation**	**167**
14.1	Basic principles	167
14.2	Stadium layout	168
14.3	Access between Zone 5 and Zone 4	168
14.4	Access between Zone 4 and Zone 3	170
14.5	Overall design for inward movement	171
14.6	Overall design for outward movement	175
14.7	Elements	176
14.8	Facilities for people with disabilities	180
15.	**Food and beverage catering**	**183**
15.1	Introduction	183
15.2	Automatic vending machines	186
15.3	Concessions	188
15.4	Bars	189
15.5	Self-service cafeterias, food courts and restaurants	190
15.6	Luxury restaurants	192
16.	**Toilet provision**	**195**
16.1	Toilet provision generally	195
16.2	Toilets for spectators	196
16.3	Scales of provision for spectator toilets	196
16.4	Location of spectator toilets	200
16.5	Detailed design	200
17.	**Retail sales and exhibitions**	**203**
17.1	Introduction	203
17.2	Advance ticket sales	203
17.3	Programme sales	204
17.4	Gift and souvenir shops	204
17.5	Museums, visitor centres and stadium tours	205

18.	**The media**	**207**
18.1	Basic planning	207
18.2	Outside facilities	209
18.3	Press facilities	209
18.4	Radio broadcast facilities	210
18.5	Television broadcast facilities	210
18.6	Reception, conference and interview rooms	211
18.7	Provision for disabled people	213
19.	**Administrative operations**	**215**
19.1	Basic planning	215
19.2	Facilities for permanent management	216
19.3	Facilities for temporary events management	218
19.4	Facilities for visitors	218
19.5	Provision for stewards	218
19.6	Facilities for police and security officials	219
19.7	Toilets	221
19.8	First-aid facilities for staff and spectators	221
19.9	Provision for disabled people	222
20.	**Facilities for players and officials**	**225**
20.1	Basic planning	225
20.2	Players' facilities	226
20.3	Team management facilities	229
20.4	Officials' facilities	229
20.5	Medical examination facilities	230
20.6	Ancillary facilities	230
20.7	Provision for disabled people	231
21.	**Services**	**233**
21.1	Lighting systems	233
21.2	Closed-circuit television systems	240
21.3	Sound systems	242
21.4	Heating and cooling systems	246
21.5	Fire detection and fighting systems	246
21.6	Power supply and event continuation	247
21.7	Water supply and drainage services	248
21.8	Information technology	249
22.	**Maintenance**	**255**
22.1	Introduction	255
22.2	Pitch maintenance	255
22.3	Stand maintenance	257
23.	**Operation and funding**	**261**
23.1	Stadium finances	261
23.2	Capital costs	261
23.3	Operating costs	268
23.4	Income generation	269
23.5	Controlling costs and revenues	271
23.6	Conclusion	272
24.	**Sustainable design**	**275**
24.1	What is sustainable design?	275
24.2	Re-use	277
24.3	Reduce	278
24.4	Recycle	282

VI

24.5 Planting and green roofs   283
24.6 Certification   283
24.7 Future technologies   283

25.   Brand activation   **287**
25.1   Maximising revenue   287
25.2   Time, not space   287
25.3   Brand activation through integration:
       The fan experience   288
25.4   Marrying team brand with
       commercial identities   288
25.5   The process   288

Appendix 1: Stadia briefing guide   **291**

Appendix 2:
Video screens and electronic scoreboards   **297**

Appendix 3: Case studies   **301**
01.   Allianz Arena, Munich, Germany
02.   Amsterdam Arena, Amsterdam, Netherlands
03.   ANZ Stadium, Sydney, Australia
04.   Arizona Cardinals Stadium, Phoenix, USA
05.   Ascot Racecourse, Ascot, UK
06.   Astana Stadium, Astana, Kazakhstan
07.   AT&T Park, San Francisco, USA
08.   Aviva Stadium, Dublin, Ireland
09.   Braga Municipal Stadium, Braga, Portugal
10.   Cowboys Stadium, Dallas, USA
11.   Donbass Arena, Donetsk, Ukraine
12.   Emirates Stadium, London, UK
13.   Forsyth-Barr Stadium, Dunedin, New Zealand
14.   Greenpoint Stadium, Cape Town, South Africa
15.   Heinz Field, Pittsburgh, USA
16.   Marlins Park, Miami, USA
17.   Melbourne Cricket Ground, Melbourne, Australia
18.   Telstra Dome, Melbourne, Australia
19.   Nanjing Sports Park, Nanjing, China
20.   Oita Stadium, Oita, Japan
21.   Olympic Stadium, London, UK
22.   The Oval, London, UK
23.   Reliant Stadium, Houston, USA
24.   Salzburg Stadium, Salzburg, Austria
25.   Soccer City, Johannesburg, South Africa
26.   Soldier Field, Chicago, USA
27.   Stade De France, Paris, France
28.   Stattegg Sports And Leisure Facility, Graz, Austria
29.   Wembley Stadium, London, UK
30.   Westpac Stadium, Wellington, New Zealand
31.   Wimbledon AELTC: Centre Court, London, UK

Bibliography   334

Index   336

VII

INTERNATIONAL
OLYMPIC
COMMITTEE

**Foreword by the President of the International Olympic Committee,
Jacques Rogge**

For the Fifth Edition of *Stadia: The Populous Design and Development Guide*

Stadia are the homes of sport. Each one is designed to effectively respond to the special requirements of its use; be it sport specific, multi-sport, or multi-purpose. They can also be highly symbolic, reflecting the mindset of the times and the culture of the team, city or event with which they are associated.

For the Olympic Games, stadia are the visual icons and the backdrop to the memorable images of the competitions. The concept, the design, and the choice of materials, must guarantee the best conditions for the athletes. In the spirit of the Olympic Games, the Stadia should embody culture and art as well as sport.

Stadia design is continually developing to keep pace with changing technology and with the social, economic and environmental standards of society. It is clear that neither stadia, nor sport, can live in isolation: they have to be part of everyone's life and society. The Stadia should be integrated into an urban development plan that respects the city's post-Games requirements in order to ensure a responsible and positive legacy. Their design and construction must reflect the increasing importance of sustainability.

Designing and developing sports stadia, both new and the upgrading of existing, is a demanding task for architects and their design teams. I am grateful to the authors for their valuable contribution to this endeavour, by creating a new fifth edition of this established reference book.

Jacques Rogge

IX

PREFACE

This is the fifth edition of our guide to the commissioning, planning, design and management of high-quality sports venues. First published in 1994, the book has been through regular revisions to reflect the changing technical knowledge and ideas about the viewing of sport.

The content is borne of the many years' experience embedded in Populous as a global design agency. Populous has been involved in the design of some of the world's most significant sports venues. These include the Forsyth Barr Stadium, in Dunedin, New Zealand, which is the only stadium in the world to feature a natural grass pitch under a fully fixed roof; the Nanjing Sports Park, in China, not only an integrated sports destination but a catalyst for urban development; the UK's most successful entertainment venue, the O2 Arena, in London; and New York's Yankee Stadium, a design that acknowledges and reflects years of American sporting history.

The authors themselves have between them over 60 years' experience in designing, procuring and reviewing sports stadia around the world. Populous Senior Principal Rod Sheard played a leading role in modernising and creating a new grandstand for Ascot Racecourse, in the UK. He was also the key member of the Populous team that upgraded the All England Lawn Tennis Club, at Wimbledon, in London.

Populous' most recent work has concerned the London 2012 Olympic Games. As well as designing the main stadium itself and masterplanning the Olympic Park, the agency was appointed official Architectural and Overlay Design Services Provider to the London 2012 Olympic and Paralympic Games. Ben Vickery, Senior Principal and co-author of this book, was a lead on this team. He has also worked on the rebuilding of Wembley Stadium, in London, and the Aviva Stadium, in Dublin.

Geraint John, visiting professor at various universities, and Honorary Life President of the International Union of Architects Sports and Leisure Programme, is another of the book's co-authors.

The book aims to share Populous' hard-won expertise for the benefit of all who love sport, participate in sport and produce sporting events. Like its preceding volumes, it is intended to be a comprehensive, authoritative and practical guide that will help designers, managers, owners, investors, users and other interested parties to understand one of the most exciting and rewarding types of building today. We hope that this book will inspire the creation of venues that are practical, elegant and a real asset to their communities.

ACKNOWLEDGEMENTS

The contents of this book represent the combined experience and views of the three authors, but they owe a great debt of gratitude to the many experts without whose help this work would have been much the poorer.

The International Association of Auditorium Managers (IAAM), the Sports and Play Consortium Association (SAPCA) and the International Association for Sports and Leisure Facilities (IAKS), in the person of Johannes Buhlbecker, are among the organisations which gave valuable assistance.

Andrew Szieradzki of Buro Happold provided information for Chapter 6, and Jeff Perris of STRI for Chapter 7. Michael Abbott Associates on behalf of SAPCA gave major assistance on Chapters 7 and 22, as did Jim Froggatt of the Football Licensing Authority on Chapters 10, 11, 12 and 15. Ed Raigan and his colleagues at ME Engineers reviewed and re-wrote Chapter 21, Barry Winterton and Peter Gray of Franklin and Andrews reviewed Chapter 23, and Henrik Henson of Daktroniks provided information for Appendix 2. The architects of the projects in the case studies have contributed information about their designs.

Within Populous there were contributions from Michele Fleming, Philip Johnson and Damon Lavelle.

Finally the authors wish to acknowledge the major contribution made by Tony Richardson and his colleagues at Alma Media for picture research, editing and graphic design.

PICTURE CREDITS

Cover	Getty Images – Ben Stansall		309	Peter Barrow
			309	Donal Murphy
ii	Pierre Sheard		309	Donal Murphy
viii	Getty Images – David Eulitt		310	Luis Ferreira Alves
			311	HKS
viii	Ed Massery		311	HKS
4	Bannister Fletcher		312	Corbis – Photomig
20	Populous		313	Hufton + Crow
26	Olympic Development Authority		313	Getty Images – Michael Regan
33	Populous		314	Chris Sullivan
36	Patrick Bingham-Hall		315	GMP
48	Getty Images – German Images		315	GMP
67	AELTC		316	Ed Massery
70	Getty Images – Stuart Franklin		317	Rod Mar
76	Chris Gascoigne		318	Getty Images – Allan Baxter
98	Getty Images – Neil Lupin		319	Patrick Bingham-Hall
108	G4S Group 4 Securicor		319	Patrick Bingham-Hall
118	PA Photos		320	Xu Xing, Nanjing Sports Park
126	Populous		321	Kisho Kurokawa architect & associates
144	Donal Murphy		321	Kisho Kurokawa architect & associates
156	Hufton + Crow		322	Populous
166	Fisher Hart		323	Populous
182	James Pearson-Howes		324	Hufton + Crow
194	Populous		324	Hufton + Crow
202	Getty Images – Andy Kropa		325	Ed Massery
206	Getty Images – Thomas B. Shea		326	Red Bull Photofiles
214	Getty Images – Lali Masriera		327	Pete Boer
224	Getty Images – Victor Decolongon		327	Chris Gascoigne
232	Getty Images – Lars Baron		328	mkoff@cz-studio.com
254	Arsenal FC – Stuart MacFarlane		329	Getty Images – Stephane de Sakutin
260	Donal Murphy		329	Getty Images – Joel Saget
274	Getty Images – Jamie McDonald		330	Hohensinn Architektur
286	Simon Warren		331	Nigel Young, Foster+Partners
290	Getty Images – Mark Cunningham		332	Patrick Bingham-Hall
296	Getty Images		333	Getty Images – Julian Finney
300	Christy Radecic			
302	Duccio Malagamba			
302	Getty Images – Altrendo Travel			
303	Sander van Stiphout			
304	Patrick Bingham-Hall			
305	Populous			
305	Populous			
306	Corbis – Leo Mason			
307	Sembol Insaat			
307	Sembol Insaat			
308	Hawkeye Aerial/Joel Avila			

01

1.1	**A VENUE FOR WATCHING SPORT**
1.2	**HISTORY**
1.3	**CURRENT REQUIREMENTS**

1.1	**A VENUE FOR WATCHING SPORT**	1
1.1.1	**ARCHITECTURAL QUALITY**	

A sports stadium can be seen as a huge theatre for the exhibition of heroic feats. It is this combination of dramatic function and monumental scale that leads to powerful civic architecture.

The first great prototype, the Colosseum of Ancient Rome, did indeed achieve this ideal, but unfortunately very few stadia since then have succeeded as well. The worst are rather brutal, uncomfortable places, casting a spell of depression on their surroundings for the long periods when they stand empty and unused, in sharp contrast to the short periods of extreme congestion on event days. However the best are comfortable, safe and inspiring; they offer their patrons an enjoyable afternoon's or evening's entertainment. Few, however, achieve a level of architectural excellence.

Blending the tiers of seating, the ramps or stairs, and the immense roof structures into a single harmonious and engaging architectural ideal is a challenge that sometimes seems almost beyond solution. The result is that sports stadia tend to be lumpy agglomerations of elements that are out of scale with their surroundings and in conflict with each other, and often harshly detailed and finished.

This book cannot show the reader how to create great architecture. But by clarifying the technical requirements as much as possible, and by showing how these problems have been solved in particular cases, it hopes at least to help designers with difficult briefs to create fine buildings. If this process is done well, the rewards are great.

1.1.2   FINANCIAL VIABILITY

In the 1950s, when watching live sport was already a major pastime for millions, sports grounds around the Western world were filled to bursting point at every match. But in the decades following this post-World War II boom, those same venues struggled to attract large audiences and many were fighting for financial survival. Fortunately, owners and managers have been creative in finding solutions. There are now clear

Heinz Field in Pittsburgh, Pennsylvania, home of the Pittsburgh Steelers NFL team. Architects: Populous signs at the beginning of the 21st century that audiences are returning to traditional sports, and new events are helping to fill stadia beyond their previous event schedule.

The reality is that, for a sports stadium to be financially viable, some form of subsidy is still often required, whether open or covert. With this in mind, there are usually three factors at play:

- Other revenue streams for the stadium should ensure the subsidy is not impossibly large.
- The project should be sufficiently attractive to justify investment from the public purse.
- It should be sufficiently attractive to private sponsors.

Some may feel that the above statements are too pessimistic. Consider the North American experience, however. The USA and Canada have highly affluent populations, totalling around 350 million. They are keen on sport and have energetic leisure entrepreneurs and managers very skilled at extracting the customer's dollar. Of all the world's countries, the USA and Canada should be able to make their stadia pay. They have seemingly explored every avenue – huge seating capacities, multi-use functions, adaptable seating configurations, total enclosure to ensure comfort, retractable roofing to protect from the elements – and yet they still struggle to make a profit, particularly when the huge initial costs of development are taken into account.

Just as there are no hard and fast rules for producing great architecture, there are no magic formulae to guarantee profitable stadia. Teams of experts must analyse the costs and potential revenues for each individual case and find a viable solution; or, at least, leave a gap that can be bridged by private sponsors or public support.

This book identifies the factors that need to be considered. But before getting into such technical details, we should make the most important point of all: sports and entertainment venues are one of the great historic building types, representing some of the very earliest works of architecture (Ancient Greek stadia), some of the most pivotal (Roman amphitheatres and thermae), and some of the most beautiful (from the Colosseum in Ancient Rome to the Olympic Park in Munich 20 centuries later). Therefore we will start with a brief historic survey.

1.2   HISTORY
1.2.1   ANCIENT GREECE

The ancestral prototypes for modern sports facilities of all kinds are the stadia and hippodromes of Ancient Greece. Here, Olympic and other sporting contests were staged, starting – as far as we can tell – in the eighth century BC.

STADIA

Greek stadia (foot racecourses) were laid out in a U-shape, with the straight end forming the starting line. These stadia

Figure 1.1
The U-shaped sunken stadium at Athens, first built in 331 BC for the staging of foot races, was restored and used for the first modern Olympics in 1896.

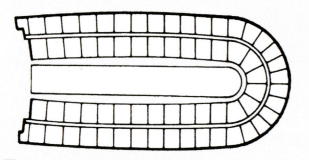
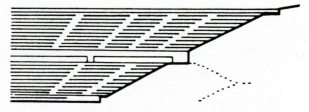

varied somewhat in length, the one at Delphi just under 183m long, the one at Olympia about 192m. Such stadia were built in all cities where games were played. Some, following the pattern of Greek theatres, were cut out of a hillside so that banks of seats with good sightlines could be formed naturally, while others were constructed on flat ground. In the latter case the performance area was sometimes slightly excavated to allow for the formation of shallow seating tiers along the sides.

Stadia built on the flat existed at Ephesus, Athens and Delphi. The latter – almost 183m long and 28m wide – had a shallow bank of seats along one side and around the curved end. The judges' seats were at the midpoint of the long side, very much like a modern facility. The stadium at Athens was first built in 331 BC, reconstructed in AD 160 and reconstructed again in 1896 for the first modern Olympic Games. In its latest form it can still be seen accommodating up to 50,000 people in 46 rows (Figure 1.1).

Hillside stadia existed at Olympia, Thebes and Epidauros, and their similarity to Ancient Greek theatres is unmistakable: these are essentially elongated theatres for the staging of spectacular physical feats. From them runs a direct line of development, firstly to the multi-tiered Roman amphitheatres, and ultimately to modern-day sports stadia.

The civic importance of such sporting facilities in Ancient Greek life is demonstrated particularly well at Olympia, on the island of Peloponnesus. The site housed a great complex of temples and altars to various deities and, at the height of its development, was a rendezvous for many across Ancient Greece. There was a sports field situated adjacent to an enclosed training gymnasium, and along the edge of the field, a colonnade with stone steps to accommodate the spectators. As the track became more popular, two stands were constructed, facing each other on opposite sides of the activity area. The fully developed stadium consisted of a track 192m long and 32m wide with rising tiers of seats on massive sloping earth banks along the sides. These seats ultimately accommodated up to 45,000 spectators. The stadium had two entrances, the Pompic and the Secret, the latter used only by the judges.

Adjacent to the stadium at Olympia was a much longer hippodrome for horse and chariot races, and in these twin facilities one clearly discerns the embryonic forms of modern athletic stadia and racing circuits. The stadium has been excavated and restored and can be studied, but the hippodrome has not survived.

While modern, large-capacity, roofed stadia can seldom have the simple forms used in Ancient Greece, there are occasions when the quiet repose of these beautiful antecedents can be emulated by modern architects. Unobtrusive form is important, as is the use of natural materials which blend closely with the surroundings so that it is difficult to say where landscape ends and building begins.

HIPPODROMES

These courses for horse and chariot races were between 198m and 228m long, and 37m wide. They were also laid out in a U-shape. Like Ancient Greek theatres, hippodromes were usually made on the slope of a hill to give rising tiers of seating. From them developed the later Roman circuses, although these were more elongated and much narrower.

1.2.2   ROMAN AMPHITHEATRES

The militaristic Romans were more interested in public displays of mortal combat than in races and athletic events, and to accommodate this spectacle they developed a new amphitheatrical form: an elliptical arena surrounded on all sides by high-rising tiers of seats enabling the maximum number of spectators to have a clear view of the terrible events staged before them. The word arena is derived from the Latin word for sand, or sandy land, referring to the layer of sand that was spread on the activity area to absorb spilled blood.

The overall form was, in effect, two Ancient Greek theatres joined together to form a complete ellipse. But the size of the later Roman amphitheatres ruled out any reliance on natural ground slopes to provide the necessary seating profile. Therefore the Romans began to construct artificial slopes around the central arena – first in timber (these obviously have not survived) and, starting in the first

3

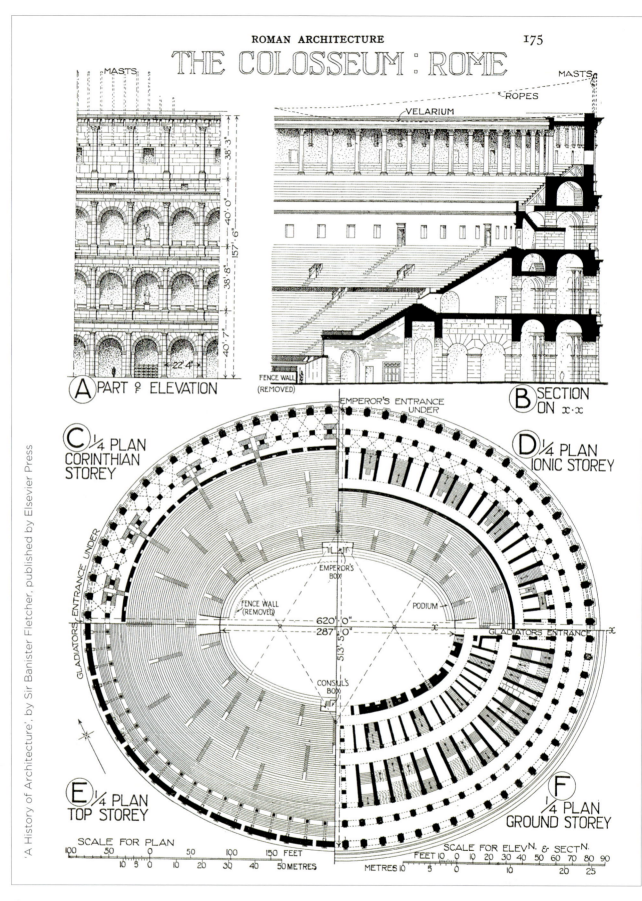

THE COLOSSEUM : ROME

A PART OF ELEVATION

B SECTION ON x·x

C ¼ PLAN CORINTHIAN STOREY

D ¼ PLAN IONIC STOREY

E ¼ PLAN TOP STOREY

F ¼ PLAN GROUND STOREY

EMPEROR'S ENTRANCE UNDER

EMPEROR'S BOX

FENCE WALL (REMOVED)

PODIUM

620' 0"

287' 5"

513' 5"

CONSUL'S BOX

GLADIATORS ENTRANCE UNDER

GLADIATORS ENTRANCE

FENCE WALL (REMOVED)

MASTS

VELARIUM

ROPES

MASTS

SCALE FOR PLAN

SCALE FOR ELEVᴺ. & SECTᴺ.

Figure 1.2
The Colosseum of Rome (AD 82) was built for gladiatorial combat and not for races. It therefore took the form of a theatre in which rising tiers of seats, forming an artificial hillside, completely surrounded an area. The great stone and concrete drum fused engineering, theatre and art more successfully than most modern stadia.

century AD, in stone and an early form of concrete. Magnificent examples of the latter may still be seen in Arles and Nimes (stone), and in Rome, Verona and Pula (stone and a form of concrete). The amphitheatre at Arles, constructed in around 46 BC, accommodated 21,000 spectators in three storeys. Despite considerable damage in the intervening centuries – the third storey which held the posts supporting a tented roof has gone – it has been used recently for bullfighting. The Nimes amphitheatre, dating from the second century AD, is smaller but in excellent condition and also in regular use. The great amphitheatre in Verona, built in about 100 AD, is world famous as a venue for opera performances. Originally it measured 152m by 123m overall, but very little remains of the outer aisle. It currently seats about 22,000 people and measures 73m by 44m.

The Flavian Amphitheatre, in Rome (Figure 1.2), better known as the Colosseum from the eighth century onwards, is the greatest exemplar of this building type and has seldom been surpassed to this day as a rational fusion of engineering, theatre and art. Construction began in AD 70 and finished 12 years later. The structure formed a giant ellipse of 189m by 155m and rose to a height of four storeys, accommodating 48,000 people. It was a stadium capacity that would not be exceeded until the 20th century. Spectators had good sightlines to the arena below, the latter being an ellipse of roughly 88m by 55m, bounded by a 4.6m-high wall. There were 80 arched openings to each of the lower three storeys, with engaged columns and encircling entablatures applied to the outer wall surface as ornamentation. The openings at ground level gave entrance to the tiers of seats. The structural cross-section (Figure 1.2B), broadening from the top down to the base, solved three problems at one stroke:

- It formed an artificial hillside, giving spectators a theatrical view of the action.
- It formed a stable structure. The tiers of seats were supported on a complex series of barrel-vaults and arches which distributed the immense loads via an ever-widening structure down to foundation level.
- The volume of internal space suited the numbers of people circulating at each level – fewest at the top, most at the

base. The internal aisles and access passages formed by the structural arcades were so well-planned that the entire amphitheatre could, it is thought, have been evacuated in a matter of minutes.

The arena was used for gladiatorial contests and other entertainments. It could be flooded with water for naval and aquatic displays. Beneath the arena was a warren of chambers and passageways to accommodate performers, gladiators and animals. The spectator tiers could be covered by stretching canvas awnings across the open top using a system of ropes and pulleys.

All these diverse functions were smoothly assimilated into a great drum shape that stands magnificently above the townscape. It is functional in layout, rational in appearance, yet rich and expressive in its surface modelling. Present-day designers could do worse than to spend some time contemplating the achievements of the Colosseum before tackling their own complex briefs. It is interesting to compare the footprint of this ancient building with the London Olympic Stadium.

CIRCUSES

As the theatres of Ancient Greece led to the Roman amphitheatres, so their hippodromes led to the Roman circuses. These circuses were U-shaped equestrian racecourses with the straight end forming the entrance and accommodating the stalls for horses and chariots. The starting and return courses were separated by a spina – a low wall decorated with carvings and statues. Seats rose in tiers along the straight sides of the U and round the curved end, the lower seats in stone and reserved for members of the upper classes, the upper seats made of wood.

A notable early example was the Circus Maximus, in Rome (fourth century BC), followed in 46 BC by a successor of the same name. This was possibly the largest stadium ever built. It was about 660m long and 210m wide, and offered all-seating accommodation for spectators in three tiers parallel to the track.

Other Roman examples include the Circus Flaminius (third century BC) and the Circus Maxentius

5

(fourth century AD), the latter being the only Roman circus still surviving today. Outside Rome were the Byzantium Hippodrome of the second century AD (based on the Circus Maximus) and the Pessimus Hippodrome which was unique at the time since it featured a Greek theatre and a Roman hippodrome linked at the centre of the hippodrome via the theatre stage. Two events could be staged separately in theatre and hippodrome, or the whole structure could be used in combination for a single grand event. This building was an obvious ancestor of the modern, multi-purpose stadium complex.

1.2.3   MEDIEVAL AND AFTER

As Christianity swept through Europe, religion became more important, and architectural effort was turned to the building of churches rather than places of recreation and entertainment. No major new sports stadia or amphitheatres would be built for the next 15 centuries.

Sports buildings inherited from the Roman era became neglected. Some were converted to new uses as markets or tenement dwellings. The amphitheatre at Arles, for instance, was transformed into a citadel with about 200 houses and a church inside it, built partly with stone from the amphitheatre structure. Many others were simply demolished.

During the Renaissance and after, competitions on foot or horseback were held in open fields or town squares, sometimes with temporary stages and covered areas for important spectators, rather along the lines of the first Greek hippodromes. But no permanent edifices were built, even though deep interest was taken in classicism and in the architecture of stadia and amphitheatres. The Colosseum was particularly closely studied, but only for its lessons in façade composition and modelling, which were then transferred to other building types.

1.2.4   THE 19TH CENTURY

The stadium as a building type saw a revival after the industrial revolution. There was a growing demand for mass spectator events from the public; there were entrepreneurs who wished to cater for this demand; and there were new structural technologies to facilitate the construction of stadia or enclosed halls.

A particularly important impetus came from the revival of the Olympic tradition at the end of the 19th century. At the instigation of Baron Pierre de Coubertin, a congress met in 1894, leading to the first modern Olympic Games being staged at Athens in 1896. For this purpose, the ancient stadium of 331 BC, which had been excavated and studied by a German architect and archaeologist called Ernst Ziller, was rebuilt to the traditional Greek elongated U-pattern, its marble terraces accommodating about 50,000 spectators (Figure 1.1). Thereafter, Olympic Games were held every four years, except when interrupted by war. Those which produced notable changes or advances in stadium design are noted below.

1.2.5   20TH-CENTURY OLYMPIC STADIA

In 1908 the Games were held in London. The White City Stadium, designed by James Fulton, was built for the purpose. It was a functional building, with a steel frame, accommodating over 80,000 spectators – the first purpose-designed modern Olympic stadium. The arena was gigantic by the standards of today (Figure 1.3), accommodating a multitude of individual sports and surrounded by a cycle track. It was subsequently decided to reduce the number of Olympic sports, partly to give a smaller arena. In later years White City Stadium became increasingly neglected and was finally demolished in the 1980s.

World War I meant the 1916 games did not take place, but a stadium with a capacity of 60,000 had been built in 1913 in Berlin in anticipation of these games. Its interest lies in its pleasantly natural form. Like the theatres and stadia of Ancient Greece, it is shaped out of the earth, blending quietly into the surrounding landscape and making no monumental gestures. The architect was Otto March, and this stadium formed a prototype for the numerous sport parks built in Germany in the 1920s.

In 1936 the city of Berlin did finally host the Olympic games. The Nazis had recently assumed power and used the occasion to extend the stadium of 1913 to a great oval structure accommodating 110,000 spectators, 35,000

Figure 1.3
White City Stadium in London (1908) was the first modern Olympic stadium and accommodated over 80,000 spectators. Its athletics field was encircled by a cycle racing track which made the arena larger than later examples.

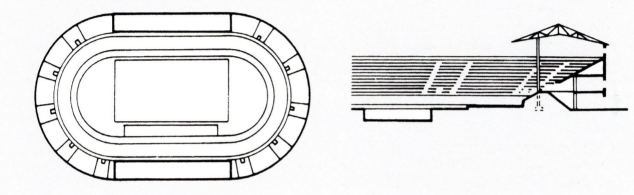

Figure 1.4
The Berlin Olympic stadium of 1936 accommodated over 100,000 people in a rationally planned elliptical layout.

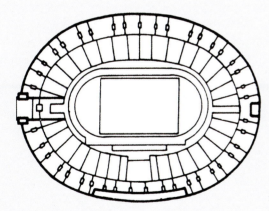
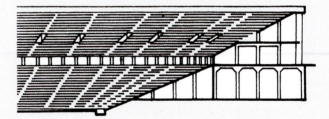

of them standing in 71 rows (Figure 1.4). The monumental stone-clad stadium was, unfortunately, used not only for sporting functions but also for mass political demonstrations. In spite of these unpleasant associations, the Berlin stadium, with its rational planning and powerful, columned façade, is a highly impressive design, renovated and a roof added for the 2006 FIFA World Cup. The architect was Werner March.

The 1948 Olympics returned to London, where the 24-year-old Wembley Stadium was renovated by its original designer Sir Owen Williams.

The 1960 Olympiad in Rome marked a new departure. Instead of staging all events on a single site, as before, a decentralised plan was decided upon, with the athletics stadium in one part of the city and other facilities

Figure 1.5
The Rome Olympic stadium of 1960, also a colonnaded oval bowl, bears a family resemblance to that of Berlin.

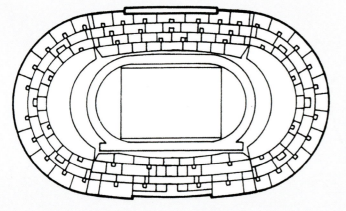

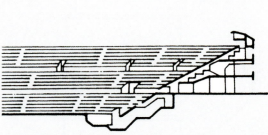

8

some distance away on the urban outskirts. This was to remain the preferred approach for decades to come. The main stadium, by architect Annibale Vitellozzi, was an uncovered three-storey structure (Figure 1.5) which bore some similarities to the Berlin stadium. It has an orderly and handsome limestone-clad façade wrapped around its oval shape, to which a roof was added in 1990 when Rome hosted the FIFA World Cup competition. Two of the fully enclosed smaller halls dating from 1960 are architecturally significant: the 16,000-capacity Palazzo dello Sport (designed by Marcello Piacentini and P.L. Nervi) and the 5,000-capacity Palazzetto dello Sport (designed by Annibale Vitellozzi and P.L. Nervi, Figure 1.6). Both are circular, column-free halls which combine great visual elegance with functional efficiency. Pier Luigi Nervi was the structural engineer on both.

In 1964 the Olympics were held in Tokyo. The Jingu National Stadium, first built in 1958, was extended for the occasion (Figure 1.7) but, as in Rome, two smaller fully-enclosed halls caught international attention. These were Kenzo Tange's Swimming Arena and Sports Arena, seating 4,000 and 15,000 respectively. The Swimming Arena

building was justifiably called 'a cathedral for swimming' by Avery Brundage, the International Olympic Committee (IOC) president. Here, 4,000 spectators could sit under one of the most dramatic roof structures ever devised: steel cables were draped from a single tall mast on the perimeter of the circular plan, and concrete panels hung from the cables to form a semi-rigid roof structure. The roof forms of the two gymnasia may look natural and inevitable, but both were the result of very extensive testing and tuning on large-scale models, not merely for structural efficiency but also for visual composition.

In 1968, Mexico City was the Olympic host and rose to the occasion with several notable stadia. The University Stadium, built in 1953 for a capacity of 70,000 spectators, was enlarged in 1968 to become the main Olympic stadium with 87,000 seats (Figure 1.8). Its low, graceful form is notable. Like the 1913 stadium in Berlin, it is what might be called an 'earth stadium' because it barely rises above the natural landscape, it uses hardly any reinforced concrete, and it blends smoothly into its surroundings. It also uses splendid sculptural decoration to enhance its exterior form. More impressive in scale is the Aztec Stadium (architect

Figure 1.6
A smaller enclosed stadium with column-free interior and of exceptional architectural merit: the Palazzetto dello Sport for the Rome Olympics of 1960. It has a concrete shell roof resting on 36 pre-cast perimeter supports.

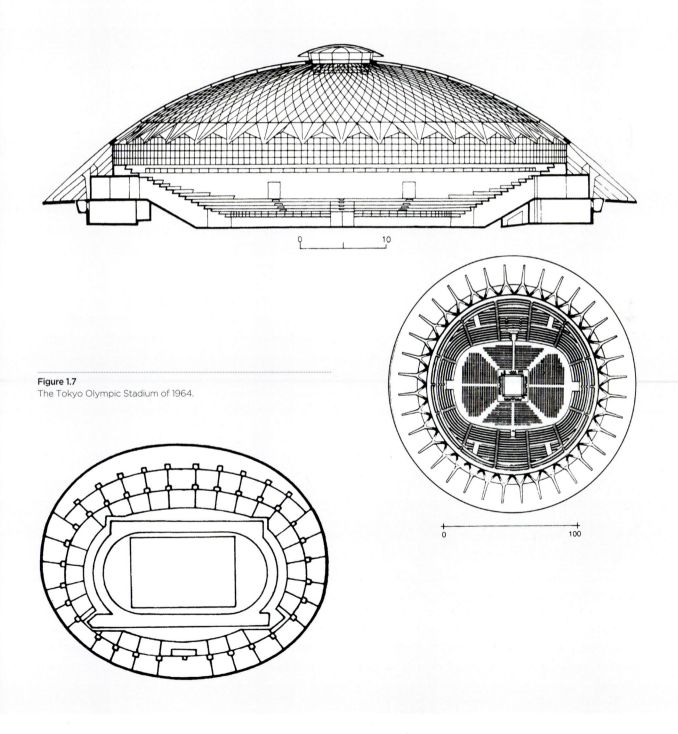

Figure 1.7
The Tokyo Olympic Stadium of 1964.

Figure 1.8
The Mexico City Olympic Stadium of 1968 seated spectators in a low, graceful shape sunk into the landscape.

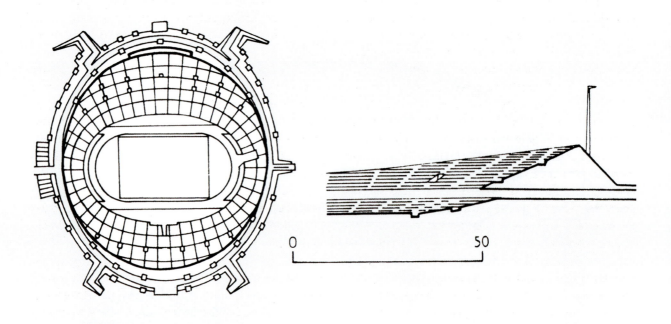

Figure 1.9
The Munich Olympic Stadium of 1972 brought the series of architecturally outstanding stadia of the preceding decades to a climax.

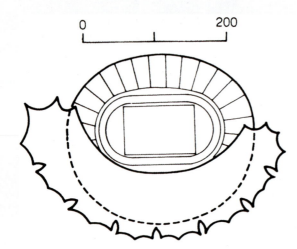

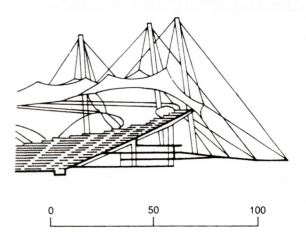

Pedro Ramirez Vasquez), accommodating 107,000 seated spectators. Most viewers are under cover, and while some are a very long way from the pitch, it is a wonderful experience to see this number of cheering fans gathered under one roof. This is said to be the largest covered stadium in the world. Finally, as at Rome in 1960 and Tokyo in 1964, there was a fully enclosed indoor arena also worthy of note.

In 1972 the Olympics returned to Germany. The site, formerly an expanse of nondescript land near Munich, was converted with exemplary skill into a delightful landscape of green hills, hollows, meadows and watercourses. Perhaps in a conscious attempt to erase memories of the heavy monumentality of the 1936 Berlin stadium, a very expensive but delightfully elegant lightweight roof was thrown over one side of the stadium (Figure 1.9 and the frontispiece to Chapter 5) and extended to several other facilities, creating an airy structure that still holds its age well many years later. The arena is embedded in an artificially created hollow so that the roof, which consists of transparent acrylic panels on a steel net hung from a series of tapered masts, seems to float above the parkland, its gentle undulations mirroring those of the landscape below. It must be said that environmental problems have been experienced under the pool section of this plexiglass canopy and that a PVC-coated polyester parasol was suspended under the arena section to shade the area below from the sun. Nevertheless, the roof, which is further described in Section 5.8, remains an outstanding achievement. As well as being beautiful, it is the largest to date, covering 8.5 hectares. The stadium designers were architects Günter Behnisch and Partners, and engineers Frei Otto and Fritz Leonardt.

In 1992, the Olympics went to Barcelona where the Montjuic stadium for the 1929 Barcelona International Exposition was extensively remodelled by architect Vittorio Gregotti. To cater for the majority of track, field and pitch sports, only the Romanesque façades were left intact. Everything inside the perimeter walls of the stadium was removed, the playing area was lowered to allow twice the previous seating capacity, and a new tunnel system was installed around the nine-lane running track so that members of the press could circulate freely without interfering with the

events above. Outside the old gate to the stadium is a new piazza, from which access is gained to four other facilities: the 17,000-seat Palau Sant Jordi gymnasium (architect Arata Isozaki), the Picornell swimming complex, the University for Sport, and the International Media centre. The site is very compact compared to most other recent Olympic games.

Following concerns about the long-term viability of huge stadia built just for Olympic athletic events – most notably in the case of the Montreal stadium built for the games in 1976 – later host cities have constructed stadia with their post-Olympic life in mind. The stadium at Atlanta for the 1996 Games was designed to be converted afterwards into a baseball stadium, and that for the Sydney Olympics in 2000, by Populous, was designed with 30,000 temporary seats that were removed after the Games so the building could be reduced in size to host a mixed programme of sports.

The best of the above structures rise to the level of great architecture. Very interesting and innovative stadia were also built for the Games of 1976 (Montreal), 1980 (Moscow), 1988 (Seoul). In Athens in 2004, the existing Stadium was modernised by the engineer Calatrava.

This tradition of innovation in Olympic stadia has continued. The Beijing Olympics, in 2008, had a spectacular design by architects Herzog and DeMueron. For the 2012 London Olympics a design by sports architects Populous and structural engineers Buro Happold created a light and elegant composition designed to be reconfigured after the Games to accommodate other events. Organisers have now recognised that the legacy of Olympic buildings has become as important as their use during the actual Games.

1.2.6   20TH-CENTURY SINGLE-SPORT STADIA

As the above Olympic stadia were being created, increasingly ambitious facilities were also evolving for specific sports such as soccer, rugby, American football, baseball, tennis and cricket.

SOCCER

Soccer stadia predominate in Europe and much of South America, owing to the popularity of the sport in these countries. But different traditions in these different regions have led to a variety of architectural types. In the UK, the typical pattern is for each stadium to be owned by a particular soccer club, and to be used only by that club. This dedication to a single sport, combined with very limited income, has helped create a feeling of community between fans. There are two reasons for this.

There is a tradition in the UK of standing terraces where fans stand closely together. This is no longer acceptable at top division clubs on safety grounds, and all standing terraces in the Premier and First Divisions have been converted to seats. (See Chapters 11 and 12.)

British soccer stadia have long been designed to accommodate spectators very close to the pitch. This allows intimate contact with the game but makes it difficult to incorporate an athletics track around the perimeter of the pitch. This intimate social atmosphere is a much admired aspect of the British soccer stadium, and one which most clubs would wish to retain.

In mainland European soccer there is a very different pattern: stadia are typically owned by the local municipality and used by a large number of sports clubs. The soccer clubs run their own lotteries, ploughing the profits back into the sport; many stadia are also used for other sports, particularly athletics. For all these reasons, European stadia have in the past tended to be better funded than British examples and somewhat better designed and built – examples are Düsseldorf, Cologne or the FIFA World Cup venue at Turin. But an athletics track encircling the pitch pushes spectators away from the playing area. This loss of intimacy must be weighed against the advantage of better community use.

The most notable British soccer stadia are those of the Premier League clubs. Elsewhere there is, sad to say, a depressing tendency for clubs to settle for the cheapest and quickest solution, with little or none of the vision one occasionally finds on the Continent. Exceptions in the UK are Huddersfield, Bolton, and the Arsenal Emirates stadium in London.

Soccer is very popular in South America, where there is a liking for very large stadia. The largest in the world is the Maracana Municipal stadium in Rio de Janeiro, Brazil which has a normal ground capacity of 103,000 spectators,

of whom 77,000 can be seated. It contains one of the first examples of the modern dry moat separating spectators from the field of play. This moat is 2.1m wide and about 1.5m deep. This is rather small by current standards (see Section 9.3), but it did establish a trend in player-spectator separation which has been used around the world including, for instance, in the 100,000-capacity Seoul Olympic stadium of 1988. The stadia built for the 1990 FIFA World Cup in Italy, and the 2002 FIFA World Cup in Japan and Korea, set very high design standards.

RUGBY

One of the most important British examples is Twickenham Rugby Football Ground, in London, dating back to 1907. The 10-acre site has undergone considerable development since then. The East, North, West and South stands are linked by a single, 39m-deep, cantilevered roof sweeping round all four sides of the field. Total ground capacity is 82,000, all seated and all under cover. Because the stands shade the natural grass turf for part of the day, they have translucent roofs to allow some transmission of sunlight, including ultraviolet radiation, to the pitch.

Other British rugby stadia worth studying are the Millennium Stadium at Cardiff Arms Park, in Wales (designed by Populous, and successfully used for international rugby and soccer), and the Murrayfield Stadium in Edinburgh. Other leading rugby stadia include the Sydney Football Stadium, in Australia, the Stade de France, in Paris, and Ellis Park, in Johannesburg. The most spectacular rugby venue is Aviva Stadium in Dublin which has been rebuilt on the site of Lansdowne Road and is used by both the Irish Rugby Football Union and the Irish Football Association. Designed by Populous, it is a spectacular, curvaceous, transparent shell which accommodates 52,000 spectators (see Case studies). Rugby has moved increasingly towards stadia shared with football. Examples in the UK include Watford, Huddersfield, and Queens Park Rangers. Greater attention has to be paid to the grass pitch to permit joint use.

AMERICAN FOOTBALL AND BASEBALL

After World War I, the USA broke new ground with a series

Figure 1.10
In the Harry S Truman complex in Kansas, the Kauffman (originally called the Royals) Stadium is designed specifically for baseball. Architects: Howard Needles Tammen & Bergendoff (HNTB).

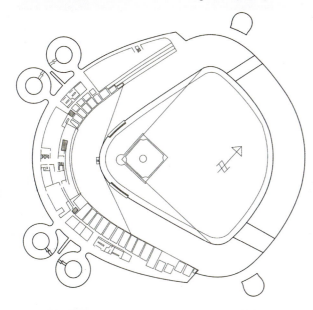

Figure 1.11
The Arrowhead Stadium for American football is a separate entity, in recognition of the very different seating geometries required for good viewing of the two games. Architects: Charles Deaton, Golden in Association with Kivett & Myers.

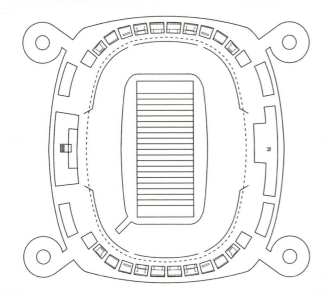

of pioneering stadia built particularly for the two burgeoning national sports: American football and baseball.

To cater for the growing popularity of American football there evolved a new type of single-tier elliptical bowl of vast capacity surrounding a rectangular football pitch. The first was the Yale Bowl at New Haven (1914, capacity 64,000). It was followed by the Rose Bowl at Pasadena, California (capacity 92,000), the Orange Bowl, in Miami (1937, capacity 72,000), Ann Arbor stadium, in Michigan (capacity 107,000) and others. Stands in the largest of these were up to 90 rows deep, the more distant spectators being so far from the pitch that they could not see the ball clearly.

Baseball became the second great popular sport. Because it requires a pitch and seating configuration very different to football, a series of specialised baseball stadia were built, including the famous Yankee Stadium, in New York (1924, capacity 57,000).

Typically, the stadia for these two sports were urban, built in the midst of the populations they served, and normally open or only partly roofed. After World War II there was a new wave of stadium building, but the typology shifted gradually towards multi-purpose facilities, often fully roofed, and often situated out of town, surrounded by acres of car parking. Between 1960 and 1977, over 30 such major stadia were built, the most impressive being the Oakland Coliseum, Shea Stadium, in New York (1964, baseball and football, demolished 2009), and the Busch Stadium, in St Louis (baseball). More recent examples are the Comiskey Park Baseball Stadium, in Chicago (1991), seating 43,000 spectators on five levels, and the Minute Maid stadium, in Houston, seating 41,000 spectators, and with a closing roof.

The Louisiana Superdome, in New Orleans, opened in 1975, and is the largest of this generation of stadia. It has an area of over five hectares, is covered by one of the world's longest roof-spans with a diameter of 207m, is 83m tall and has a maximum capacity of 72,000 for football. One of its most interesting features is a gondola suspended from the centre of the roof, comprising six huge television screens, showing a range of information including instant action replays.

Many of these great stadia catered for both American football and baseball (and usually other types of

13

activity) in an attempt to maximise revenue. However, as already mentioned, the shapes of football and baseball pitches are so different that it is difficult to provide ideal seating configurations for both, even with movable seating systems, as in the John Shea dual-purpose stadium of 1964. The Harry S Truman Sports Complex, in Kansas, of 1972 therefore separated the two sports: the Royals Stadium overlooks a baseball pitch (Figure 1.10), and its sister Arrowhead Stadium a football field (Figure 1.11), each of them being shaped to suit its particular sport. Each stadium has its own facilities for its particular group of patrons.

TENNIS

14

The world's most famous tennis venue is the All England Lawn Tennis and Croquet Club, at Wimbledon, in London, home since 1922 to The Championships. The two-week tournament

Figure 1.12
Plan of the Rod Laver Arena, which seats 15,000 spectators.
Cox Architects & Planners.

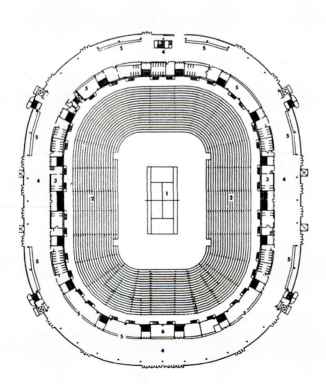

now attracts about 45,000 people each day. The tournament facilities comprise 18 grass courts, five red shale courts, three clay courts, one artificial grass court and five indoor courts. In addition to these tournament facilities there are also 14 grass practice courts in the adjacent Aorangi Park.

To many people, Wimbledon means the Centre Court. The stadium surrounding this famous patch of grass was built in 1922 and has been gradually upgraded and renewed ever since. The stadium does in many ways give the most satisfying tennis experience in the world: the tight clustering of spectators round the grass court, under a low roof which reflects the buzz of sound and applause from the fans beneath, creates an intimate theatrical atmosphere and an intensity of concentration which are missing from most other venues. To prepare the club for the future, a master plan for the site was prepared and implemented. It includes a new No.1 Court designed to replicate the intimate Centre Court atmosphere. Recently Wimbledon has had its most innovative addition, a moving fabric roof over the Centre Court (see Case studies). Designed by Populous, it can retract during fine weather and stack at one end of the court to minimise shade on the precious grass. During inclement weather the roof can expand to cover the entire playing surface and adjoining spectators so that play may continue.

There are three other Grand Slam tennis venues, all comparable in scale and complexity to Wimbledon: Flushing Meadows, in the USA, Flinders Park, in Australia, and Roland Garros, in France. They all vary greatly in terms of atmosphere and tradition.

Flushing Meadows is home to the US Open Championship where the spectators' attitude to viewing is much more casual than at Wimbledon. This is reflected in the design of the principal court, Arthur Ashe Stadium, where the spectators sit out in the open under a busy airport flight path, with the outermost seats too distant to offer good viewing. The sense of detachment seen here is quite characteristic of US stadia which tend to be very large and to be patronised by spectators not averse to wandering around for refreshments while a game is in progress.

Australia's National Tennis Centre, in Melbourne Park (formerly Flinders Park), was constructed on derelict land between 1986 and 1987. It can seat a total of around 29,000 spectators on 15 courts which include the Rod Laver Arena (Figure 1.12). In addition to these there are five indoor practice courts.

The front rows of the Rod Laver Arena, also known as the Centre Court, are at a greater distance from the court than at Wimbledon or even Flushing Meadows, on the theory that a ball travelling at over 100mph cannot be seen properly by viewers who are too close to it. It is a theory contested by some who insist that spectators want to be close to the action, even if that means the ball is occasionally a blur. The 15,000 seats are fed by 20 entrances, and the stadium has a sliding roof which takes 20 minutes to close. Unlike Wimbledon, the court has a Rebound Ace, hard acrylic surface which has the advantage of allowing intensive, multi-purpose year-round use for other sports and concerts. Around 120 events are staged per annum. However, it is thought by some to be visually dead compared to the Wimbledon grass courts.

Since completion of the Melbourne Park venue, there has been an increased demand, not foreseen at the time, on the hospitality, catering and press facilities. An expansion plan is therefore being undertaken which would double the site area and include a number of new facilities, a merchandising centre, a sports medical centre and more car parking. There would also be an additional moving roof over the Margaret Court Arena, making a total of three moving roofs on site.

In France, the French Open venue is the Roland Garros stadium, in Paris's Bois de Boulogne. It was established in 1928 and has been gradually upgraded ever since. The 15-acre site contains 16 championship courts, all clay-surfaced. In atmosphere, the Centre Court is closer to Flushing Meadows than Wimbledon, being open to the sky and with greater viewing distances than the tight clustering found at Wimbledon. As at Wimbledon and Flinders Park, an expansion plan is underway.

CRICKET

Lord's Cricket Ground, in London, has been the home of the Marylebone Cricket Club (MCC) since 1814 and is the symbolic centre of world cricket. The five-acre site accommodates spectators in a variety of open and roofed stands which have gradually grown up round the playing field. The site development policy is to deliberately build on this pattern of individual buildings surrounding a green, instead of unified stadia built to a single architectural style. The policy is clearly reflected in the 1987 Mound Stand which replaced an earlier stand on the same spot; and the 1991 Compton and Edrich Stands. The Mount Stand designed by Hopkins Architects seats 5,400 spectators in two main tiers – 4,500 at terrace (lower) level and 900 at promenade (upper) level, the upper seating level being sheltered by a translucent tented roof. The most recent addition to the grounds was on the North Side, designed by Grimshaw & Partners.

The Oval ground in south London, home of the Surrey County Cricket Club, is as well known as Lord's and the site has been masterplanned for the future by Populous. Also in Britain, a new cricket ground has been built for County Durham by architect Bill Ainsworth. In Australia, the leading venue is Melbourne Cricket Stadium (see Case studies) which has recently been rebuilt.

| 1.3 | **CURRENT REQUIREMENTS** |
| 1.3.1 | **THE SPECTATOR** |

For all of these sports, stand design begins and ends with the spectator. At the outset of a project the first questions to be asked, and answered, must be: who are the spectators? What are they looking for in the facility? How can their numbers be maximised? Only when these questions are answered is it possible to examine the technical solutions and do the necessary calculations. This simple methodology should be used for all sports projects.

It must be understood that different people have different motives, and that any crowd will contain a variety of sub-groups with different reasons for attending. Some have a primarily sporting interest; some a social reason for attending; some combine the two.

The sporting-interest spectators are found in the stands and on the terraces for every game. For them, live sport at its highest level has an almost spiritual quality, an attitude aptly expressed in a statement once made by the great Liverpool soccer manager Bill Shankly: 'Football is not a matter of life and death; it is more important than that.'

These fans are knowledgeable. They respond instantly to every nuance of the action, they offer advice to the players, and they recognise the form, fitness and style of individual players, and the effectiveness of strategies and tactics. Such issues form the basic topics of conversation before, during and after the game in the car, the pub or the train. The motivation and the behaviour of this group sometimes attracts negative comment, but you could say this of any group of people sharing some passionate interest – evangelical churchgoers, for instance.

The social-interest spectators are found in the clubhouse, dining rooms and private boxes, entertaining or being entertained. The game is interesting to them, but interrupts the personal or business conversations and only briefly becomes the topic of interest. At the end of a game, a short post-mortem takes place so that all parties can hint at the depth of their sporting knowledge before resuming the business conversation. This group is usually well dressed because its members will be interacting with other people to whom they must present themselves appropriately, whereas the sporting-interest spectators dress casually because their interaction is with the event.

A third group contains elements of the previous two and tends to be fickle: these are the casual supporters who can be persuaded to attend if the conditions are right, but equally easily deterred. When England hosted soccer's World Cup, in 1966, attendances in the UK reached about 29 million per annum, declining to around 20 million over the following years. Clubs lose supporters when the team plays poorly, as some spectators attend only when standards of play are perceived to be high or when star names are playing. These fans are also deterred by discomfort, a perceived risk of violence or lack of safety. Studies carried out well before the disaster at the Hillsborough Stadium, in Sheffield (see below), found that soccer fans in the UK perceived violence from other fans, and the risk of being crushed by crowds or mounted police as serious threats. All these perceptions have their effect on attendances.

It should be noted that under the UK's Disability Discrimination Act, around a fifth of the people in each of the above groups may come within the legal definition of disabled people. This definition is surprisingly wide, and goes far beyond the traditional concept of people in wheelchairs. By law, all such people must be fully catered for in both the design and management of the venue, as outlined in Chapter 10.

1.3.2 THE PLAYER OR ATHLETE

After the spectator the next most important person in the stadium is the player or athlete: without these people there is no game or event. Players' and athletes' needs are covered in Chapters 7 and 20. The UK's Disability Discrimination Act (and similar acts in other countries) requires full provision to be made for disabled players in events such as the Paralympics.

One matter must be mentioned at this stage because it will influence the proposed stadium in a fundamental way. Sometimes players require a natural grass pitch, but other design requirements (such as the need for a multi-use surface, or for a roofed stadium) make a grass surface unviable. In this case very difficult choices must be made about design priorities.

For some sports a natural grass surface is obligatory – for instance rugby and cricket. For others it may not be obligatory, but is still very much the preferred option for players. In all these cases it is not merely the provision of the grass pitch that is important, but also its condition at time of play. The playing surface is a small ecosystem which actively responds to changes in the environment: it fluctuates in rebound resilience, stiffness and rolling resistance, and can alter the trajectory of a bounce or roll so that players talk of the ball 'skidding through' or 'standing up'. All of these minute but critical variations can occur in a relatively short space of time, even during a game. Such uncertainties tend to widen the players' range of skills, both technically and tactically, because they must be sufficiently inventive and responsive to cope with changing conditions. In this way, a natural surface may well raise the standard of play, and allow for the display of individual talent. But it may be almost impossible to provide a natural grass surface if the brief requires a fully roofed stadium, or if the facility requires a multi-use pitch. The Forsyth Barr

16

Stadium, in the New Zealand city of Dunedin, may point the way forward since it is the world's first permanently-roofed, grass-pitch rugby stadium. It was designed by Populous for the New Zealand Rugby World Cup in 2011 (see Case studies).

Such problems are more pressing in Europe than in North America, partly because the traditional European games of soccer, rugby and cricket are based on a vigorous interaction between the ball and the playing surface, so that the latter becomes critical. In American football and baseball, however, the ball is kept off the ground at the critical stages of play, thus allowing a more tolerant choice of playing surface. American players tend also to be well padded and less likely to suffer injury when falling on a relatively hard surface, whereas lightly clad European players are more vulnerable and have a preference for natural grass. But it is interesting that a preference for natural grass pitches seems to be returning in American football.

For athletics, a synthetic rubber track has become the normal surface, with the centre field in grass.

1.3.3   THE OWNER

Assuming players and spectators can be brought together, it falls to the stadium owner to ensure that the physical venue continues to be financially viable. As stated in Section 1.1.2, very few stadia produce profits for their owners simply on their sporting functions. In most cases it will be necessary for the planning team to devise a development that will enable owners to:

- Come as close as possible to profitability simply on sporting functions (i.e. gate income).
- Narrow the shortfall by exploiting non-sporting market income (non-gate income).
- Close any remaining gap through public funding or other forms of direct subsidy or grant.

GATE INCOME

It will seldom be possible to recoup all costs from gate revenue, but this has traditionally been the most important single source of income and needs to be maximised. Investors will require a guaranteed target market of known size and characteristics, a guaranteed number of event days, and a guaranteed cash flow from these sources. To this end:

- An analysis of the market must be made as outlined in Section 1.3.1. It must be established who the stadium is catering for, how many of them there are, how much they will pay, how often they will attend, what factors will attract them, and what factors will deter them.
- Gate revenue can be enhanced by various forms of premium pricing, for instance sale or rental of private boxes at high prices.
- It must be decided which sports types the stadium will cater for. This requires a careful balancing of factors. A facility catering for, say, both soccer and athletics will offer the possibility of more event days than one catering for a single sport. But, by trying to accommodate other functions, the facility may be less suitable for its major use, as discussed in Section 1.2.6 above and in Chapter 8. This is partly because different sports require different pitch sizes, surfaces and layouts; partly because they require different seating configurations for good sightlines.

NON-GATE INCOME

Options for increasing non-gate income include sale or rental of hospitality boxes, catering concessions, merchandising concessions, advertising and event sponsorship, media studio rentals and parking rentals. While these can make a vital financial contribution, the planners must not lose their sense of priorities: such forms of income must always be supportive, never primary. Increasingly, such supportive factors will have a direct influence on stadium design because, for instance, a game watched by 15,000 people from the stands may be watched by 15 million on television – with great cost implications for a sponsor – and these millions must be satisfied. But, at the same time, the stadium must not lose its attraction to its primary patrons – those entering by the gate.

SUBSIDY

After all the above methods of revenue maximisation have been built into the project, there may still be a funding shortfall. A final element of support will probably be required from the local municipality, a national grant scheme or elsewhere.

GETTING IT ALL TOGETHER

The key to a successful outcome is clarity of understanding between all concerned. Stadium developers must have a clear understanding of the spectators and players they are aiming for, and how to attract them. The stadium users must be clear about the uses to which the stadium might be put and their compatibility with the stadium design. Public or private investors must share the same view of the purpose of the stadium and how it will benefit the local community. If any of these matters are fudged or left unresolved, or if priorities are put in the wrong order, the stadium is likely to have a very clouded future. Chapters 8 and 23 deal with some of the above aspects in more detail.

1.3.4 STADIUM SAFETY

Safety is such a crucial aspect of the successful stadium that a few paragraphs must be devoted to this subject. Wherever crowds gather, particularly in a context of intense emotion, as is the case with sport, mishaps are possible. The wooden stands of the Constantinople Stadium, home to Roman chariot races, were burnt down by spectators in 491 AD, 498 AD, 507 AD and finally in 532 AD, when Justinian the Great lost his patience and called in the army to restore order, leading to an estimated 30,000 deaths.

A partial list of recent disasters includes the following:

1996:   83 people were killed and between 127 and 180 people were injured in a stadium in Guatemala City when soccer fans stampeded before a FIFA World Cup qualifying match. Angry fans kicked down an entrance door, causing spectators inside to cascade down onto the lower levels.

1992:   17 people were killed in Corsica when a temporary grandstand collapsed in a French Cup semi-final match between Bastia and Marseille.

1991:   One person died and 20 were taken to hospital after a stampede when 15,000 fans were allowed into the grounds without tickets just after kick off at Nairobi National Stadium, in Kenya.

1991:   40 people died and 50 were injured after a referee allowed an own goal at a friendly soccer match in Johannesburg, in South Africa.

1989:   95 people died and many were injured during a crowd surge into a restraining fence after kickoff at Sheffield's Hillsborough Stadium, in the UK. The Lord Justice Taylor Report followed, with a subsequent new edition of the Safety at Sports Grounds Act 1990 and additional tightening of the certification system under the Football Supporters Act 1989 which established the Football Licensing Authority. The soccer administrators also reacted by setting up the Football Stadia Advisory Design Council in 1991.

1985:   38 people died and 100 were injured in a crowd riot at the Heysel Stadium, in Belgium.

1985:   10 people died and 70 were injured in a crush when crowds tried to enter after kickoff through a tunnel which was locked at Mexico University Stadium, in Mexico.

1985:   56 people died and many were badly burnt in a fire at Valley Parade Stadium, in Bradford, UK. The Popplewell Inquiry followed, with a subsequent increase in powers under the existing Safety at Sports Grounds Act.

1982:   340 people were reported to have died in a crush at Lenin Stadium, in Russia.

1979:   11 people died and many were injured after a surge into a tunnel at a pop concert at Riverfront Stadium, Cincinnati, USA.

1971:   66 people died after a soccer match at Ibrox Park Stadium, in Glasgow, UK. The Wheatley Report followed, with the subsequent Safety at Sports Grounds Act 1975 based upon its findings.

1964:   340 people died and 500 were injured after a referee disallowed a goal by the home team in a soccer match in Lima, Peru.

02

THE FUTURE

2.1   **THE IMPORTANCE OF THE STADIUM AS A BUILDING TYPE**

2.2   **ECONOMICS OF STADIA**

2.3   **STADIUM TECHNOLOGY**

2.4   **ERGONOMICS AND THE ENVIRONMENT**

2.5   **WHAT IS THE FUTURE FOR THE STADIUM?**

The village stadium concept from Populous reinterprets the typical cityscape of hot dry countries to include a stadium as a cultural hub. Combining modern technology and traditional ideas it creates a low-energy arena that responds to the climate, culture and evolving city. Architects: Populous

2.1   THE IMPORTANCE OF THE STADIUM AS A BUILDING TYPE

Stadia are amazing buildings. They can shape our towns and cities more than almost any other building type in history, and at the same time place a community on the map. They have become an essential ingredient of the urban matrix that binds our cities together. They are arguably the most viewed building type in history thanks to the Olympics and other global sporting events. They can change people's lives and often represent a nation's aspirations.

They can be very expensive buildings, but equally they can generate substantial revenues. In the 21st century, the global financial power of sport in general is increasing as sport becomes the world's first truly global cultural activity. Stadia, the buildings that accommodate sport, are becoming among the most important buildings any city of the future can build, partly because of their power as an urban planning tool.

In the last 150 years, sport has been codified and professionalised. At the same time there has been a dramatic process of urbanisation, with populations moving from the country to the city. With this social shift there has been an equally dramatic rise in the popularity of sport, perhaps as a consequence of this new urban society.

Stadia are also a key ingredient in the marketing of cities and even nations. Look at the tourist impact on Athens for the 2004 Olympic Games, for example. It was reported there were as many as 1.9 million overnight stays during the event.

Stadia have evolved into a building type with all the elements needed to sustain independent city life, including residential, commercial, retail and leisure. These all work together with the other services and transport infrastructure required to make these stadium cities thrive.

2.2   ECONOMICS OF STADIA

Despite their huge public profile, stadia are not without their problems. Owners and operators are very aware of the shortcomings of past generations of stadia: how they have sometimes been difficult to manage without a huge and expensive workforce,

Playing area		Support facilities		Additional facilities	
Primary	Secondary	Primary	Secondary	Primary	Secondary
Soccer	Concerts	Restaurant	Banquets	Health club	Offices
Tennis	Conventions	Bar	Parties	Other sports	Retail
Rugby	Exhibitions	Private box	Meetings	Hotel	Cinemas
Cricket	Other sports	Lounges	Conventions	Sports retail	Residential

Note: The above are only broad indications of options to be investigated. For actual design it will be necessary to undertake detailed studies using specialist advisers.

Table 2.1   Possible multi-purpose uses of sports stadia

and how they have been limited in their flexibility. More recently, many of these issues have been resolved. There are now few major stadia under development which don't include experienced people in their design teams.

To spread the construction and maintenance costs across more than one sport or club some stadia have dual owners or tenants. Ownership issues resulting from this co-habitation have been addressed – sometimes very successfully. In the UK town of Huddersfield, for example, soccer and rugby combine happily in the Galpharm Stadium. Even London's new Wembley Stadium (see Case studies) has been designed for soccer, rugby and athletics, as well as music concerts. The facilities in huge stadia like Wembley, with its extensive private suites, corporate boxes and large restaurants, allow financially lucrative events to be staged. More recently, Aviva Stadium, in Dublin, was made possible when rugby and soccer agreed to jointly use the venue.

In the USA, the idea of multi-purpose, rather than sport-specific stadia is not very popular, mainly because the principal sports – American football and baseball – are so different in pitch form and layout. There are also economic factors at play. Sponsorship and naming rights revenues are so high in the USA that it makes business sense to have different stadia for different sports. How else could a developer justify building a stadium for American football that features as few as eight home games per season?

It is possible that clubs wishing to improve their grounds might act more aggressively as developers. They may finance new facilities by selling surplus land or by becoming more commercial, as Arsenal Football Club, in London, did when they developed Emirates Stadium (see Case studies). Recently, some sports clubs have joined forces with non-sports tenants so that sport becomes just one element in a mix of activities. Good management of these mixed venues can increase revenue by exploiting each part of the facility for more than one purpose, a strategy sometimes referred to as multi-use. Table 2.1 shows some possible combinations of sports and commercial uses.

The key to all these approaches, if they are to be successful in the long term, is creative management. Stadia management is becoming recognised as a specialist field all over the world, and sporting venues are now beginning to attract the very best employees. New ideas are emerging such as added-value tickets which encourage the whole family to attend by including meals, bus rides to the stadium, and signed programmes. Family enclosures, which have gained popularity in the UK, are also a relatively new but important trend. Child-minding facilities, baby-changing rooms, family cinemas, museums, cafés, restaurants and children's play areas are also finding their way into the modern stadium.

The bottom line is that any facility which attracts a wider cross-section of spectator, and keeps them entertained for longer, should eventually reap financial rewards. It is through a policy of inclusion that the spectators of tomorrow will be created.

2.3   STADIUM TECHNOLOGY

In the global village, sport is becoming a common social currency that everyone, everywhere can trade in and understand. Technology is helping to revolutionise this global village, particularly sport. We expect races to be timed to hundredths of a second, blood samples to be analysed down to particles per million, instant video play-backs, optional camera positions on television, and computer-generated images to determine if a ball is in or out.

However, what we have seen so far is just the tip of the technological iceberg. Sport is benefiting from improved, faster, and safer construction techniques, allowing lightweight opening roofs, moving seating tiers and playing fields, and replaceable grass cricket wickets. The dividing line between natural grass and synthetic playing surfaces is becoming blurred. A hybrid of both types is now possible thanks to plastic-mesh root reinforcement, plastic turf support, and plastic granular growing surfaces with computer-controlled nutrient injection. New hybrid grass types require less light, grow faster, and are far more robust. The quality of synthetic grass is now so high that it has been accepted under certain conditions for top-class soccer. These advances allow a greater number of different types of events to take place on the same pitch, making the venue more financially viable and able to justify greater capital cost.

Sightlines, crowd flows and environmental comfort for the 21st-century stadium are all calculated and designed on computer, and the creation of three-dimensional virtual models of these buildings is critical. The latter are now an indispensable tool allowing design teams to communicate effectively with owners and future spectators, showing them the exact view they will enjoy from certain seats.

Advances in technology allow officials to measure results extremely accurately, but also to communicate these results to the stadium spectators just as quickly as if they were watching on TV at home. There is no guarantee that future generations will find live sport as attractive as the present generation, and the move to provide better information to spectators is essential to maintain attendance at live events. Ticket prices are increasing, and there is more competition for our leisure time. It is possible to sit at home and watch sports events on TV, often free of charge. The old argument that only the major events are televised is no longer true; cable and satellite television have changed that theory forever as more and more sport is televised. Sport is still comparatively cheap to produce for TV and almost always finds an audience. It is now possible to broadcast channels dedicated to one sports club. Digital streaming over the internet is also having an impact.

Live sport needs to compete with TV on equal terms. As well as offering facilities at the stadium that are as comfortable, convenient and safe as those in spectators' homes, it must also offer information equal in range and quality to that provided by professional broadcasters. Replays and information about athletes and previous matches should be automatic, but so should highlights of other events, match statistics, expert commentary, and perhaps even revenue-generating advertisements. Called narrowcasting, this information can be broadcast via the stadium's closed-circuit television (CCTV) network, not just to large video screens, but also individually to each spectator. It was once thought these receivers would become part of the stadium fabric by being built into seat-backs, but now many people can receive the same broadcasting through their smart phones. Press the button marked 'statistics', and key in your favourite player's name; press 'action', type in the date of the match, and see the highlights of his match-winning performance two years ago. The horse-racing industry already uses this technology, possibly because of the large betting revenues at stake. Interactive websites are also developing quickly. Wimbledon has worked closely with IBM to establish one of the most sophisticated websites in sport, including interactive apps for spectators that guide them around the club grounds.

Technology is also revolutionising the management of stadia. Conventional turnstiles are evolving into more user-friendly control systems, but still have some way to go before they are likely to be considered welcoming. The ideal would be an entrance linked to the stadium computer system, looking more like an airport X-ray machine. Details on the spectators' tickets would be scanned, giving them access to different areas of the grounds and entitling them to other benefits. Monitors would then scan the ticket at each access or sales point. If the pass was invalid for any reason, a warning would sound and the ticket-holder would be advised where to go to seek help. Automatic barriers would close if the unauthorised spectator attempted to proceed any further. The stadium's computer would also store key information on the spectators attending, including age, sex, address and event preferences. From this database of information, the stadium management could then form a precise profile of who attends which events, allowing them to target exact socio-economic groups for future events. This demographic information is essential for future marketing and critical for the economic survival of the venue.

2.4   ERGONOMICS AND THE ENVIRONMENT

Technology is being used to improve spectators' comfort levels when they are at the stadium, controlling aspects of the environment such as temperature, humidity and air movement more accurately. The increasing use of retractable roofs (see Section 5.8) forms part of this trend.

The design of the seats themselves is also more focused on the ergonomics of spectators. Padded seats and arm-rests are becoming more common. The size of the average spectator is also increasing. Seat spacing and access to seating rows must cater for this. There are now extra facilities for all the family to enjoy as well as other entertainment areas for those not committed to the game. Stadia will eventually include every type of facility from business centres to bowling alleys, similar to the facilities found in international airports or shopping malls. Attractions will be designed to encourage spectators to arrive early and stay on after the match has finished – perhaps even sleeping overnight in the stadium hotel.

Tomorrow's stadia will be places of entertainment for the family where sport is the focus, but not the complete picture. It will be possible for five members of a family to arrive and leave together, but to experience five different activities in the intervening period. While the parents watch the live game, their children might experience it in the virtual-reality studio where images from pitch-side cameras provide immediate action. One concept under development is a flexible village stadium where the traditional town square, with all its cafés, restaurants and shops, can be converted into a stadium using retractable, folding seating tiers. These would be moved out of the way for most of the year, and only brought out for event use, allowing the stadium and the heart of a town centre to share the same space (Chapter frontispiece).

2.5   WHAT IS THE FUTURE FOR THE STADIUM?

Will the stadium be the ideal forum for sport in the future? Or will new sports emerge that are better suited to other building forms? In recent years a number of sporting events have evolved that do not require a stadium at all; extreme sports, for example, that require outdoor spaces and which are ideal for TV broadcast. Completely new sports have emerged such as the Ironman triathlon.

However, for all the popularity of events that do not require a stadium, there is no indication that the public is losing its appetite for attending live sport. The majority of professional sports are continuing to grow, leading to a continued growth in investment in new venues of increasing comfort and sophistication.

03

MASTERPLANNING

3.1 THE NEED FOR A MASTERPLAN AT ALL SPORTS GROUNDS
3.2 ORIENTATION OF PLAY
3.3 ZONING OF THE VENUE
3.4 EVENT OVERLAY – WHAT NEEDS TO BE ADDED TO HOLD THE EVENT
3.5 SECURITY AGAINST TERRORISM
3.6 STADIA IN THE CITY

3.1 THE NEED FOR A MASTERPLAN AT ALL SPORTS GROUNDS

3.1.1 BASIC PRINCIPLES

Sports complexes are often constructed over a period of years (or even decades) for reasons of finance, natural growth or land availability. To ensure that the ultimate development is consistent both aesthetically and functionally, and to avoid abortive work, a comprehensive plan for the entire development should be completed at the very outset. This allows successive phases of the development to be carried out by different committees or boards over a period of time in the safe knowledge that their particular phase will be consistent with the whole.

Figure 3.1 shows a plan of the masterplan for the London Olympics as it was during the 2012 Games, which can be compared to the frontispiece showing the proposed reconfiguration after the Games are over. These diagrams show how important it is to think ahead and plan for the legacy of all venues.

The art of planning large stadium sites hinges on the correct zoning of the available land and the various facilities that have to be accommodated within the site boundaries. These facilities include not only the direct sporting functions, but also very substantial parking areas, pedestrian and vehicle routes, etc.

3.1.2 SEQUENCE OF DECISIONS

All design decisions on the site layout should be set out using the following determining factors.

PITCH, PLAYING AREA, CENTRAL ZONE

The starting point of design is the central playing field – the performance area. Its shape, dimensions and orientation must enable it to fulfill all the functions required of it. Surprisingly, not all established sports have clearly defined dimensions to work to (see Chapter 7).

27

The London Olympic Park as it will look after the Games. Much of the installation for the Games is temporary and after the event this will be replaced by permanent housing. Masterplan designed by Populous, EDAW, Allies and Morrison, Foreign Office Architects, Hargreaves, LDA design.

Hackney Marshes

Waltham Forest

Eton Manor Gate

Eton Manor

Velodrome

BMX

Hockey

Basketball

Car park

Warm up

Olympic Village

MPC

IBC

Catering Village

Stratford International

Hackney

Copper Box

Westfield

Hackney Wick Station

Stratford Gate

Stratford

Water Polo

Victoria Park

Aquatics Centre

Newham

Olympic Stadium

Orbit

Greenway

STRATFORD HIGH STREET

Figure 3.1

The masterplan for the London Olympics as it was during the 2012 Games. Masterplan designed by Populous, EDAW, Allies and Morrison, Foreign Office Architects, Hargreaves, LDA design.

Warm up

Tower Hamlets

Pudding Mill Lane Station

28

SEATING CAPACITY

Next comes the seating capacity. If the pitch is to be of variable size in order to cater for very different activities, then the design capacity should be stated as two figures: the number of seats around the maximum pitch size (perhaps soccer or athletics) and the maximum capacity around the smallest space user (perhaps the performers in a pop concert, or a boxing ring). The stadium owners will have very strong views on seating capacities as these form the basis of their profitability calculations.

ORIENTATION OF PLAY

Pitch orientation must be suitable for the events to be staged (see Section 3.2), and the masterplan must be structured around this. Whilst there are established norms for the orientation of playing areas, there are many exceptions to the rule, so exploring a number of options is always worth the effort.

ZONING

Finally, all the elements of the stadium – from the pitch at the centre, to the parking spaces outside – must be planned with safety zoning in mind, as explained in Section 3.3. This helps define activities in what will eventually become a complex layout of buildings and functions.

3.2   ORIENTATION OF PLAY

3.2.1   DESIGN FACTORS

The orientation of the playing field will depend on the sports hosted there. The following factors need to be considered:

- The hemisphere in which the stadium is located.
- The period of the year in which the designated sports will be played.
- The times of day these events will be played.
- Specific local environmental conditions such as wind direction as well as the amount of enclosure surrounding the playing field.

All the advice below applies to open stadia in temperate zones in the northern hemisphere, and readers should make the necessary adjustments for stadia in other situations.

Stadia that are completely roofed or with large closing roofs can obviously be more flexible in their orientation.

3.2.2   SOCCER AND RUGBY

In Europe, soccer and rugby are played during the autumn and winter months, usually in the early afternoon. This means the sun is low in the sky and moving from south-south-west to west. An ideal orientation for the playing area is to have its longitudinal axis running north–south, or perhaps northwest–southeast. In this way, the sun will be at the side of the stadium during play, and the early morning sun will fall on the greatest area of the pitch, thus helping thaw any frost in the ground before play commences. Figure 3.2 summarises the situation.

The sun should be at the side of the pitch during play. This suits the players, the spectators and the TV camera-men, none of whom wish to look directly into a low, setting sun.

3.2.3   ATHLETICS

In Europe, track and field sports take place mostly during the summer and autumn months. Runners and hurdlers approaching the finishing line should not have the sun in their eyes; nor, ideally, should spectators. The ideal orientation in the northern hemisphere is for the longitudinal axis of the track to run 15 degrees west of north (Figure 3.2). The same applies to the stadium which should be situated on the same side as the home straight, and as close to the finish line as possible.

Sometimes it is difficult to achieve the above track orientations while also conforming with the requirements for wind direction. Where possible, alternative directions should therefore be provided for running, jumping and throwing events. If world records are to be considered, shielding from winds may be a necessity.

3.2.4   TENNIS

The longitudinal axis of the court should run in a north–south direction. A divergence of up to 22 degrees in either direction is acceptable; 45 degrees is the absolute limit. If matches are to be played in early morning or late evening, the orientation becomes more critical.

Figure 3.2
Recommended pitch orientations in northern Europe for principal sports. The underlying principle is that runners in athletics and sportsmen in ball games should never have late afternoon sun in their eyes.

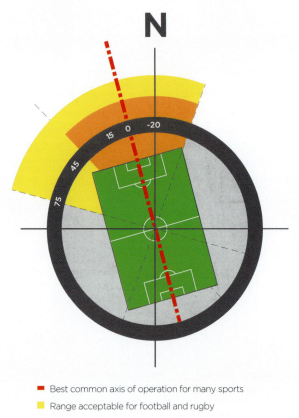

■ Best common axis of operation for many sports
■ Range acceptable for football and rugby
■ Best range of track and field pitch games

Zone 1:   The activity area: the central area and/or pitch on which the sport takes place.

Zone 2   The spectator terraces.

Zone 3:   The concourses surrounding the activity area.

Zone 4:   The circulation area surrounding the stadium structure and separating it from the outer security line.

Zone 5:   The open space outside the outer security line, separating it from the car parks.

The purpose of such zoning is to allow spectators to escape from their seats in an emergency to a series of intermediate safety zones, leading ultimately to a place of permanent safety outside. It provides a clear and helpful framework for design, not only for new stadia, but also for the refurbishment of existing facilities.

A tragic example is provided by the fire which took 56 lives at the Valley Parade Stadium in Bradford, UK, in 1985. The stand was an old one, built of timber framing and steps. On May 11th, 1985, a fire started in the accumulated litter under the steps and spread rapidly through the structure. Most spectators fled from the stands (Zone 2) to the open pitch (Zone 1), and were safe. However, many made their way back through the stand towards the gates by which they had entered. Because there was no Zone 3 or 4 in the stadium, these gates formed the perimeter between the stadium and the outside world. Management had taken the view that these gates needed to be secure – therefore the escaping spectators found them locked. Many people were trapped here, killed by the fire and smoke.

Two lessons came out of this experience, one for managers and one for designers:

• Managers must ensure that gates offering escape from the spectator terraces to places of safety are manned at all times when the stadium is in use, and easily opened to allow spectators to escape in an emergency.

• The stadium needs to be designed on the assumption that management is not foolproof. There should, where possible, be a Zone 4 within the outer perimeter to which spectators can escape and where they will be safe even if the perimeter gates are locked.

3.3   ZONING OF THE VENUE

3.3.1   PLANNING FOR SAFETY

The next priority is to plan the position of the stadium on the site, and to start thinking about the relationship between its main areas. This is best done by identifying the five zones which make up the safety plan (Figure 3.3). The size and location of these zones are critical to the performance of the stadium in an emergency.

Careful preparations are needed for disabled spectators – particularly those in wheelchairs – in case of emergency. They are by far the most onerous user group in these circumstances. See Chapter 10.

More detailed design notes follow below.

3.3.2   ZONE 5

The stadium will often be surrounded to a certain degree by car parking, bus parking and access to public transport. The car parks (well-designed, to avoid bleakness and confusing layout) should ideally be evenly distributed around the stadium so that spectators can park their cars on the same side of the stadium as their seats.

Between this ring of transport areas and the stadium security perimeter there should be a vehicle-free zone, usually described as Zone 5, which can serve several useful purposes:

- This area is deemed to be a permanent safety zone to which spectators can escape from inside the venue via Zones 3 and 4. They can safely remain there until the emergency has been dealt with. It should be possible to accommodate most of the stadium population here at a density of around four to six people per square metre. Surrounding roads can also be used as part of this calculation, provided direct and easy access is possible.
- From the point of view of everyday circulation, Zones 4 or 5 provide a belt of space in which spectators can circumnavigate the stadium to get from one entrance gate to another, assuming their first choice of gate was wrong (see Section 14.3.1). Every effort should be made to ensure that people are directed from their cars (or other points of arrival) to the appropriate gate for their particular seat, but mistakes will always be made and there should be an easy route round the stadium to allow for this. Modern stadium management tends to allow spectators into any gate at the venue. More circulation inside the stadium minimises the need for external circulation.
- Retail points, meeting points and information boards can also very usefully be located in this zone of open space.

Figure 3.3
Zoning diagram showing the five safety zones which form the basis for a safe stadium.

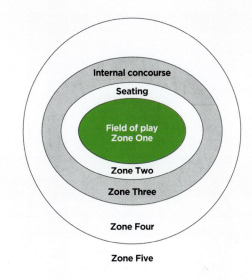

Zone one: The playing field

Zone two: The spectator seating and standing areas

Zone three: The internal concourses, restaurants, bars and other social areas

Zone Four: The circulation area between the stadium structure and the perimeter fence

Zone five: The open space outside the perimeter fence

To serve this social function, and to maximise the revenue generation, the surface and its fittings (kiosks, information boards etc) should be pleasantly designed. Clients now recognise how important it is to welcome their spectators with appropriate facilities.

- Zone 5 can also serve as a pleasantly landscaped buffer zone between the event and the outside world. Stadium performances – whether they are sport, music or general entertainment – are essentially escapist. Their enjoyment can be heightened by visually disconnecting the audience from the outside world.

31

3.3.3   ZONE 4

The stadium perimeter forms a security line across which no one can pass without a valid ticket. Between this line of control and the actual stadium structure is Zone 4, which may have two functions:

- It is a place of temporary safety to which spectators can escape directly from the stadium, and from which they can then proceed to permanent safety in Zone 5. It is therefore a form of reservoir between Zones 3 and 5. If the pitch (Zone 1) is not designated as a temporary safety zone, then Zone 4 should be large enough to accommodate most of the stadium population at a density of four people per square metre. But if Zone 1 is a temporary safety zone, Zone 4 may be reduced appropriately. In all cases, the number of exit gates, and their dimensions, need to allow fast, easy access from one zone to another (see Section 14.6).
- When it comes to everyday circulation, Zone 4 is the main circumnavigation route for people inside the stadium perimeter – those who have had their tickets checked at control points. Urban stadia that sit within the tight constraints of a city grid will sometimes need to consider special management techniques when this zone is not of the ideal size.

3.3.4   ZONE 3

This comprises the stadium's internal concourses and social areas (restaurants, bars etc.) and is situated between Zones 2 and 4. Spectators must pass through this zone in order to reach a final place of safety (Zones 4 or 5). For this reason, this zone, or the circulation areas within it, are often designed with a good level of fire safety so that large numbers of people can move through them without risk.

3.3.5   ZONE 2

This comprises the viewing terraces around the performance area. In many cases the greatest danger comes from the building behind the terraces, so the seating terraces are seen as a place where spectators can stay in relative safety.

There may be a ticket check between Zones 2 and 3, where stewards guide people to their seat. There will often be a barrier at the edge of the arena (Zone 1) to prevent people entering the field of play, but this barrier must not impede people needing to flee from a fire or other emergency. This must be designed with both crowd control and free movement in mind.

3.3.6   ZONE 1

The pitch or event space forms the very centre of the stadium. Along with Zone 4 it can serve the additional purpose of being a place of temporary safety, under the following conditions:

- The escape routes from the seating areas to the pitch must be suitably designed. For example, escape will not be an easy matter if there is a barrier separating pitch and seating terraces (see Chapter 9).
- The surface material of the pitch must be taken into account. The heat in the Valley Parade Stadium fire (mentioned above) was so intense that the clothing of police and spectators standing on the grass pitch ignited. Had the pitch been covered with a synthetic material, that too might have ignited. These matters must be discussed with the fire authorities at design stage. It is crucial that management do not change the pitch surface years later without being aware of the safety implications.

3.3.7   BARRIERS BETWEEN ZONES

In all cases, the number of exit gates, and their dimensions, must allow quick and easy access from one zone to another. Fortunately, the advent of digital wireless technology now allows control points within a venue to be automated where they are left permanently open unless a valid ticket is not received. The principles of gate design are discussed in a later section.

3.4   EVENT OVERLAY – WHAT NEEDS TO BE ADDED TO HOLD THE EVENT

At stadia there is normally a regular schedule of events throughout the year. Sometimes, in addition to these, infrequent but larger events are hosted. For example, a club soccer ground will stage its annual league matches, but it might also bid to hold an international cup final that comes to the stadium once every few years. Such a match will attract more spectators, more media and more sponsors for whom it is not worth constructing permanent accommodation. Temporary arrangements need to be made; this is called an overlay (see Section 5.2.2).

In order for the overlay to be accounted for in the masterplan, designers need some idea of the events to be hosted. In general, an infrequent event at a stadium is likely to require more space, certainly outside the building and possibly also inside. Some of the temporary areas that might be needed are:

- Additional space for larger crowds to arrive at the stadium. This might be more car parking, wider access routes, more bus drop-off areas and increased ticket checking, possibly including bag searching.
- Sponsors' advertising, additional catering, sales areas and visitor attractions. Some major events even feature activities for visitors who come along but do not actually watch the main event.

- Additional security. High-profile events often require greater security measures, and more space to search spectators, for example.
- Temporary media areas with space for TV broadcast vehicles, journalists, associated dining, electrical generators etc. TV satellite vehicles require a view of the sky where the satellite is located.
- Additional back-of-house areas. The need for facilities such as extra offices, waste rooms, storage and ticketing should not be forgotten.

These areas will require space around the stadium. The best method is to keep the areas partly flexible and non-specific so that they do not constrain the layout of temporary accommodation. Every major event has different requirements, and the overlay for each event is likely to change over time.

33

Figure 3.4
An aerial view of the proposed masterplan of the Youth Olympics in Nanjing, China.

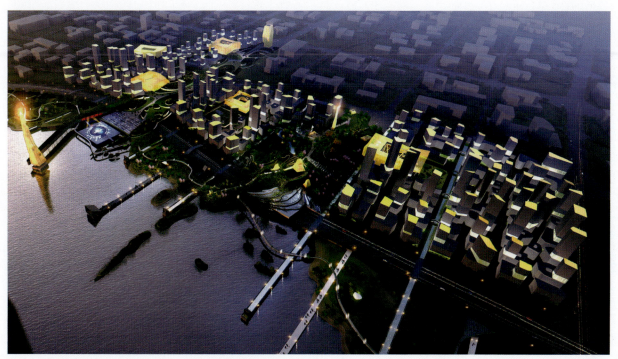

3.5 SECURITY AGAINST TERRORISM

Unfortunately, in recent years it has become necessary to consider that high-profile sports activities might become the target of terrorists. The actual likelihood of a terrorist attack, and the possible methods employed, are best known by the police who should be consulted at an early stage. The security arrangements of the building should be tailored around their advice.

In general, lines for security cordons can be drawn around the sports building, firstly for vehicles further away from the stadium, and secondly for spectators as they have their tickets checked. The cordons will require space for searching of spectators and their belongings.

For more detail on these matters, see Chapter 6.

3.6 STADIA IN THE CITY
3.6.1 PLANNING A CITY AROUND SPORT

At an early stage, as well as the stadium layout, it is important to consider the place the venue occupies in its town or city. Stadia can create a vibrant image for their host towns. At their best they can even be used as part of the tourism infrastructure and appeal.

The actual events in the stadium attract visitors, but these landmark buildings also act as magnets, drawing people to them. For example, visitor attractions, sport museums and halls of fame can increase a stadium's market appeal. The success of the Populous-designed Galpharm Stadium, in the UK town of Huddersfield, with its blue roof and exciting shapes, had a major impact on the city itself, as did the Toronto Skydome in a much larger way in Canada. Images of these venues appear in tourist brochures. TV coverage of major events such as the FIFA World Cup and the Olympic Games have brought images of dramatic and often aesthetically memorable stadia into the living rooms of millions of people. In fact, many people who will never visit a city might form an impression of the place based on the stadium. Beijing's Olympic Stadium, the Bird's Nest, is a good example.

Research has been carried out on stadia tourism in North America, reviewing the relationships between stadia and the cities they occupy. It has been suggested that many cities are interested in new stadia and arena developments as catalysts for urban regeneration and the development of entertainment districts. The mass popularity of sports, and the close relationship between civic identity and local teams, makes the construction of sports facilities an important tool for promoting public and private spending.

3.6.2 STADIA AND TOURISM

Stadia developments have been proven to stimulate economic regeneration in cities such as the Lobo area of Denver when Coors Field was built, and in the docklands area of Melbourne when the Telstra Dome (see Case studies) was constructed. Sports stadia are now accepted as a key component of the leisure industry in general. Local, regional and national governments are increasingly realising that stadia can play a vital role in the economic and social wealth of the community in which they are located.

An essential feature of a city's ability to host a major league sports team, or indeed a primary sporting event or festival, is the provision of modern stadia. There has been considerable development in such facilities throughout the USA, with the public sector recognising the economic value of stadia.

A good example of a new stadium being integrated into the wider urban planning of a city was in Baltimore, USA, where Oriole Park, designed by Populous, was used to anchor the south side of the city's waterfront regeneration scheme. This turned the derelict Camden Yards docklands into an extension of a thriving entertainment and tourist district, creating a landmark in destination marketing. The high-rise buildings of downtown Baltimore can be seen towering over the stadium, giving spectators a view of the city's commercial and economic centre. Around 1.6 million fans (nearly half of all fans) hail from out of town, often staying overnight in the Baltimore area. Nearly a quarter of them come from outside of the Washington DC area altogether.

This ability to generate secondary spending in and around the stadium is a critical factor. Spending on merchandise inside the facility, together with spending in hotels, restaurants, petrol stations and local shops outside the facility, has a marked effect on operating profits, but also boosts the local economy, typically multiplying the original level of spending by five or six times. In the case of Baltimore, more than 40 per cent of all fans going to games combine their trip with business or other leisure pursuits. As a result, spending exceeded predictions by as much as 300 per cent, with increases in hotel, restaurant and other trades. Moreover, when compared with the previous Memorial Stadium, 80 per cent of fans indicated that they were more likely to spend time in the stadium area before and after games. Stadia are important features in the overall image of a city. Their locations need to be carefully considered.

3.6.3   THE STADIUM AS AN ATTRACTION

The commercial and cultural potential of a successful stadium has been likened to a sleeping giant, capable of making a significant contribution to its neighbourhood, city or region as an all-year-round attraction.

The Welsh capital, Cardiff, has the 72,000-capacity Millennium Stadium. Since its opening in 1999 to host the Rugby World Cup, it has become a recognised driver of visits to the city. The stadium hosts international team sports, world championship speedway, rock concerts, and was even the venue for a major rally racing competition in 2005. In addition, following the closure of London's Wembley Stadium for its rebuild, Millennium Stadium hosted FA Cup Finals, as well as soccer league play-offs. These matches earned more than £25 million for the city's economy and attracted over half a million visitors a year.

The stadium as a venue for non-sporting events is a logical step, making use of the extensive infrastructure in their masterplanning. The site needs to be in an appropriate setting and, over the years, it will become steeped in the history of the events that have played there. The potential of a stadium as an attractive venue for other events will depend on its location, its catchment area and the nature of the sport played there. For stadium owners who wish to generate additional revenue from corporate entertaining, product launches, meetings and conferences, it is important they involve the local community and business groups in events as much as possible. This type of external communication should be considered at the masterplanning stage to ensure the venue is easily accessible and welcoming.

3.6.4   THE WIDER POTENTIAL
OF THE SPORTS MASTERPLAN

In the USA, there is great earning potential for stadia because Americans have a narrow range of sporting interests compared to Europeans, with a large cross-section of people following and participating in fewer sports. Consequently, the economic rewards of major sporting activities have stimulated considerable development of new facilities over the past 20 years. The public sector has recognised that investment in stadia helps the local community, and it accepts that stadia can rarely be expected to make a profit. There is also an increasing recognition in municipal and state governments that new facility development – or refurbishment of existing facilities – is essential in attracting and retaining major league sport, and that the political risk involved in not investing in facilities is outweighed by economic gains to the community.

However, if contemporary stadia are to realise their potential, their management becomes as critical as their planning. Their economic survival relies on stadia designers and operators understanding user demands, and optimising revenue. This is reflected in a shift towards the privatisation of the management of facilities. Management interests are now involved in the conceptual and masterplanning process – essential if the stadium's capital and real estate assets are to be realised. Stadia are regarded as a microcosm of the hospitality industry, reflecting trends in the social and cultural leisure environment.

Whether they are locations for great sporting events, host venues for other attractions, or simply cathedrals with architectural appeal, stadia are an important part of our towns and cities. Just like great heritage buildings, stadia are becoming defining images of a place or a moment in time.

35

04

EXTERNAL PLANNING

4.1	LOCATION
4.2	TRANSPORTATION
4.3	PROVISION OF PARKING
4.4	STADIUM LANDSCAPING

4.1 LOCATION

4.1.1 PAST AND CURRENT TRENDS

Traditionally the sports stadium was a modest facility with a capacity of perhaps a few hundred, serving a small local community and forming part of the social fabric along with the churches, town halls and drinking houses.

As communities grew larger and more mobile, with ordinary people able and willing to travel great distances to follow their favourite sports, stadia became larger. Much of the new capacity was needed specifically for visiting spectators. The multitudes of away team supporters created problems in crowd control for which local communities, their police forces and stadium managers were not adequately prepared. We tend to think of this as a recent problem, but it goes back many decades. Evidence can be found in any book of social history, or in an account such as this which describes events at an aircraft show in France, in 1933, and was written by the famous architectural visionary Le Corbusier:

> along the track . . . were returning coaches. We conscientiously demolished them with stones. We had broken everything breakable in our own train. The trains that followed, hastily pressed into service and waiting behind us in a straggling queue, were inspired by our methods. We also demolished the signals. Towards four o'clock the massed officials of the suburbs mobilised the firemen to intimidate us . . . the mob, one knows, generally becomes inspired when it is necessary to take action. As our train did not leave and other trains arrived in the night, filled with would-be spectators . . . we set to work to demolish the station. The station at Juvisy was a big one. The waiting rooms went first, then the station-master's office . . .

Even allowing for the habitual hyperbole of the author, it shows that the destructive impulse which may arise in crowds of otherwise civilised sporting fans is, alas, nothing new.

The ANZ Stadium Sydney from the boulevard of the Olympic Park during the 2000 games.
Architects: Populous with Bligh Voller Nield.

Crowd control proceeded on a trial-and-error basis, and many mistakes were made. But nowadays we have a more systematic understanding which can be applied to both the design of stadia and their management. The lessons for stadium design are incorporated in the various chapters of this book; but an additional response has been a locational one – to move major stadia away from town centres to open land on town peripheries.

LARGE OUT-OF-TOWN STADIA

A major trend of the 1960s and 1970s was the building of large stadia on out-of-town locations where crowds – whether well or badly behaved – would create less disturbance to the everyday lives of people not attending events. Such locations would also reduce land costs and increase ease of access by private car. The largest developments of this kind are to be seen in Germany, where advantage was taken of post-war reconstruction opportunities, and in the USA, where high personal mobility and the availability of open land made it easier to locate stadia away from the communities they were meant to serve and provide the amount of car parking required. Leading examples of a cross-section of types include:

- The Astrodome at Houston (1964), a dome stadium designed for both American football and baseball.
- The Arrowhead and Royals Stadia at Kansas City (see Case studies) (1973), a complex which provides separate dedicated facilities for the two sports – the Arrowhead Stadium for baseball, and the Royals Stadium for American football.
- The Allianz Arena in Munich, Germany (2005), a later example, but also used by two local teams – both soccer (see Case studies).

These stadia tended to cater for a variety of activities to make them financially viable. They had huge spectator capacities, and were surrounded by acres of car parking. They were built in a period when spectator sports were attracting markedly increased followings, probably owing to the influence of television. Even so, they found it difficult to show a profit. Recovering their vast development costs would have been problematical anyway, but there were two aggravating factors. First, TV coverage had improved to the point where people could stay at home and follow the action very satisfactorily in their living rooms; and second, the stadia of the late 1970s and early 1980s were all too often barren places with little by way of spectator comforts.

There was also a growing number of violent incidents in various parts of the world (resulting from crowd misbehaviour, fire or structural collapse) which probably reinforced people's growing preference to watch from the comfort and safety of their living rooms.

LARGE IN-TOWN STADIA

The next significant step in the development of the stadium occurred in 1989 with the opening of the Toronto Skydome in Ontario, Canada. The public authorities in Toronto had recognised the problems of out-of-town sites and decided to take a brave step by building their new stadium in the very centre of their lake-side city.

The stadium is within walking distance of most of the city centre and uses much of the transport and social infrastructure of Toronto. Managers had learned the lesson of poorly serviced facilities so they incorporated many spectator services designed to enhance comfort and security.

But in spite of all these efforts, and an ingenious funding arrangement, Skydome's financial viability has unfortunately proved no better than previous attempts. (See Section 1.1.2.)

CURRENT TRENDS

In Britain, following an inquiry by Lord Justice Taylor into the disaster at the Hillsborough Stadium, in Sheffield (where 95 people died in a crowd surge), there was a formal report recommending major changes to sports stadia to improve their safety. This document has caused many British clubs to question whether it is better to redevelop their existing, mostly in-town grounds rather than relocating to new sites out of town with all the transport and planning problems entailed. Existing in-town sites have the advantages of being steeped in tradition and being situated in the communities on

38

whose support they depend, but the disadvantage of being so physically hemmed in that it may be difficult or impossible to provide the necessary safety, comfort and facilities. There are proving to be numerous town-planning difficulties in finding new sites.

The situation elsewhere in the world is equally ambiguous. Everywhere there is a preoccupation with financial viability. Everywhere there is pressure for greater comfort and safety. And everywhere the refurbishment of old stadia is gaining ground. But these vague generalisations are the few trends that can currently be identified.

4.1.2 LOCATIONAL FACTORS

Today it is technically feasible to build a safe, comfortable and functionally efficient stadium in any location (town centre, open countryside, or anywhere in between) provided there is sufficient land and the stadium's use is compatible with the surrounding environment. The deciding factors are itemised in the following paragraphs.

CLIENT BASE

Any stadium must be easily accessible to its client base – the people whose attendance will generate the projected revenues. This is usually the primary motive for looking at a particular site. To test feasibility, a careful analysis must be made of who the projected customers are, how many there are, where they live, and how they are to get to the stadium. All these criteria must be satisfied by the proposed stadium location.

LAND AVAILABILITY

A new stadium can require around 15 acres of reasonably flat land just for the stadium and ancillary facilities, plus car parking space at 25 square metres per car (see Section 4.3.1). It may be difficult to find this amount of space.

LAND COST

Land costs must be kept to a minimum and this is why sports facilities are frequently built on low-grade land such as refuse tips or reclaimed land that is too poor for residential or industrial use (but which may then lead to additional structural costs as noted in Section 5.5.1).

LAND USE REGULATIONS

Local or regional planning legislation must be checked to ensure that the proposed development will be allowed in that area.

4.1.3 THE FUTURE

Given these factors, wholly independent, stand-alone stadia may increasingly have to share their sites with commercial and retail complexes. Examples of such developments include:

- In the USA, the Hoosier Dome, in Indianapolis (1972).
- In Canada, the Skydome, in Toronto (1989).
- In the Netherlands, the Galgenwaard Stadium, in Utrecht.
- In Norway, the Ulleval Stadium (1991).
- In the UK, the Galpharm (formerly the Sir Alfred McAlpine) Stadium, in Huddersfield. This state-of-the-art 24,500-seat stadium caters for both soccer and rugby and shares its site with a hotel, a banqueting hall, a golf driving range and dry ski slope, and numerous shopping and eating facilities.

4.2 TRANSPORTATION
4.2.1 SPECTATOR REQUIREMENTS

If the journeys involved in getting to a sporting event seem excessively difficult or time-consuming, the potential spectator may well decide not to bother – particularly if alternative attractions are available. There may be a sequence of journeys involved, not necessarily just the journey from home on the morning of the match. Sometimes the following details need to be planned for:

- Will I be travelling with a friend, family or on my own?
- Will I be travelling by car, bus or train?
- Where will the transport leave from, and when?
- How do I get to and from the transport?
- What are the things which can go wrong with the above arrangements, and what alternatives do I have?

The transport infrastructure of a major stadium should offer ways of getting to (and away from) an event which are relatively quick, simple and trouble-free, otherwise attendance and revenues will undoubtedly suffer.

Pages 72 and 73 of *Accessible Stadia* (see Bibliography) give a useful checklist of matters that should be considered at this stage to ensure that all prospective spectators – able-bodied and disabled alike – can properly plan their visit to a sporting event.

4.2.2   PUBLIC TRANSPORT

Any large stadium should be close to a well-served railway or metro station or both, preferably with paved and clearly defined access all the way to the stadium gate. If the stadium cannot be located near an existing station, it may be possible to come to a financial arrangement with the transportation authorities whereby they open a dedicated station for the stadium. In the UK, this is the case with the existing Watford and Arsenal soccer stadia. In Australia, a new railway station was constructed to serve the Olympic site at Homebush, in Sydney.

The entire route, from the alighting point on the station platform to the seat in the stadium, should be easily usable by disabled people, including those in wheelchairs. It should be kept free of kerbs or steps that obstruct wheelchair users.

4.2.3   THE ROAD SYSTEM

The road system must allow easy access into, around and out of a major stadium complex. There must also be adequate electronic monitoring and control systems to ensure that any build-up of traffic congestion in the approach roads can be identified well in advance and dealt with by police and traffic authorities.

4.2.4   INFORMATION SYSTEMS

Before major events, advice can be mailed to spectators with their tickets and car parking passes; some information can be printed on the tickets themselves. In the run-up to the event, information giving the choice of routes and the most convenient methods of transport should be thoroughly publicised via local, regional or national media.

In the UK, the Disability Discrimination Act places a legal obligation upon event managers to supply disabled persons – which includes people with impaired vision,

impaired hearing, or impaired understanding – with information in formats that they can easily understand. This obligation applies to all types of information including print, online and telephone messages, both before and during the match.

On the day of a major event every effort should be made to ensure an orderly traffic flow. Local radio and newspapers can be used to illustrate preferred routes and potential problem areas. Dedicated road signs, whether permanent or temporary, should start some distance away from the stadium and become increasingly frequent and detailed as the visitor approaches the venue. Near to the stadium, information and directions should be particularly plentiful and clear, indicating whether car parks are full, and identifying meeting points, and train and bus stations. The same amount of effort should be made to ensure a smooth flow of people and cars away from the stadium after the event. It cannot be assumed that people will find their own way out.

4.3   PROVISION OF PARKING
4.3.1   TYPES OF PROVISION

Parking is most convenient in the area immediately surrounding the stadium, and at the same level as the exits and entrances. But this tends to be an inefficient use of land which is both scarce and expensive in urban areas. The vast expanses of tarmac have a deadening effect on the surrounding environment unless extremely skilfully handled. Four alternative solutions follow.

MULTI-LEVEL CAR PARKING

Building the stadium over a covered car park, as in the Louis IV Stadium, in Monte-Carlo, reduces the amount of land required and avoids barren expanses of car parks. But such a solution is very expensive and its viability may depend on the next option.

SHARED PARKING WITH OTHER FACILITIES

A stadium may share parking space with adjacent offices or industrial buildings as at Utrecht, or even (as is the case with Aston Villa Football Club, in Birmingham, UK) with superstores or shopping complexes. But problems arise if both facilities need the parking space at the same time. This is quite likely in the case of shops and supermarkets which stay open in the evenings and at weekends. In the case of Aston Villa there is a condition in the agreement that the store cannot open during first team home matches. Therefore careful planning is required.

ON-STREET PARKING

This is not encouraged by the authorities. However, stadium sites in green parkland can allow parking to be distributed over a large area.

PARK AND RIDE

This term refers to car parking provided at a distance from the venue, with some kind of shuttle service ferrying spectators between the parking area and the stadium. It is mainly used on the European continent, especially in Germany. In the UK, Silverstone motor racing circuit and Cheltenham racecourse have helicopter park-and-ride services, both of which are usually fully booked.

PROVISION FOR DISABLED PEOPLE

In the UK, pages 26 to 28 of *Accessible Stadia* and Section 4 of *BS 8300* (see Bibliography) give authoritative guidance on car parking provision for disabled people.

For the USA, see Section 502 of *ADA and ABA Accessibility Guidelines for Buildings and Facilities* (see Bibliography).

4.3.2   ACCESS ROADS

It is essential to provide the right number of parking spaces and to ensure they are efficiently accessed, because nothing is more likely to deter visitors from returning than lengthy traffic jams before or after an event. There must be a clear system of routes all the way from the public highways via feeder roads into the parking area, and an equally clear way out. Arrivals will probably be fairly leisurely, possibly spread over a period of two hours or more before start time, whereas most spectators will try to get away as quickly as possible after the event. Such traffic patterns must be anticipated and planned for. It may also be possible to change these patterns

of use. For instance, visitors can be enticed to stay longer and leave more gradually – thus reducing traffic congestion – if restaurants and other social facilities are provided, and if entertainment programmes are shown on the video screens after the event (see Chapters 13 and 15 and Section 21.2.2).

Parking spaces, and the routes feeding them, must not encroach on areas required for emergency evacuation of the stadium, or for fire engines, ambulances, police vehicles etc.

4.3.3   SPECTATOR PARKING

Vehicular parking can account for more than half the total site, and the quantity and quality of parking provided will depend on the types of spectators attending. Here is data on a variety of existing stadia. It is not intended as a strict guideline, but purely to give a feel of what may be required.

In the USA, where the shift from public transportation to travel by private car has gone furthest, the trend has been towards stadia located out of town, not served by any significant public transportation network but surrounded by huge expanses of parking spaces.

In Europe, by contrast, most stadia are well served by public transport. Land is not easily available for large parking lots, and it is quite common in European cities, where the majority of stadia are still located, for only a handful of parking spaces to be provided for officials and for there to be no on-site parking for fans. A rural facility, such as the UK's Silverstone Circuit for motor racing, which caters for 98,000 spectators and provides parking for 50,000 cars, is definitely the exception.

When designing a new stadium, parking requirements for spectators should be estimated from an analysis of the following considerations.

STADIUM SEATING CAPACITY

It would be wasteful to provide car parking for every seat in the stadium, as the maximum seating capacity is only rarely achieved. A design capacity should be calculated by assessing a typical programme of events over a season, and estimating a typical attendance for each event.

41

05

FORM AND STRUCTURE

5.1	**THE STADIUM AS ARCHITECTURE**
5.2	**STRUCTURE AND FORM**
5.3	**MATERIALS**
5.4	**THE PLAYING SURFACE**
5.5	**FOUNDATIONS**
5.6	**SEATING TIERS**
5.7	**CONCOURSES, STAIRS AND RAMPS**
5.8	**ROOF**

5.1   **THE STADIUM AS ARCHITECTURE**

5.1.1   **THE IDEAL**

As suggested in the introduction, sports stadia are essentially large theatres of entertainment which ought to be as pleasant to visit as a cinema, opera house or theatre, whilst also being social and architectural landmarks in their towns and cities.

The designers of pre-modern stadia rose to this challenge with admirable skill. The Colosseum and the circuses of Rome, the amphitheatre in Verona, and similar buildings throughout the Roman Empire played central roles in the civic lives of their communities. Based on the circle and the oval, they were also wonderfully successful in translating functional requirements and the known building technologies of the time into noble architectural forms. The profile of the Colosseum (Figure 1.2) solves at a stroke the challenges of clear viewing, structural stability and efficient circulation, the latter allowing the building to be cleared of thousands of spectators in a matter of minutes. Meanwhile the outer façade is related to the human scale by its colonnaded arcades. So powerful and inventive was this unprecedented façade that, 14 centuries later, it became a primary source of inspiration for the architects of the Renaissance.

Whilst the basic form of the modern stadium remains very similar to that of antiquity (stepped tiers of seats facing a central arena), brick and stone have largely been replaced by concrete and steel. It must also be said that architectural standards have fallen: all too many current stadia are banal at best, anti-human at worst.

Design excellence is achieved in stadia when structure, enclosure and finishes express a single concept which functions well, is rich and expressive, and avoids jarring conflicts. This must happen at all scales – from overall form right down to the smallest detail. There are current examples of excellence, such as the Bari Stadium, in Italy, by the architect Renzo Piano, but complete success is rare. The first step towards higher architectural standards must be to identify particular problems which nowadays make it so difficult to achieve functional and beautiful stadium design.

The Olympistadion Munich built for the 1972 Olympics. The innovative design of a cable-supported transparent roof above landscaped venues has never been repeated. Architect: Gunter Behnisch Engineer: Frei Otto

5.1.2   THE PROBLEMS

Because sports stadia are so closely geared to onerous functional requirements (clear sightlines, efficient high-volume circulation etc.), this is a building type where form follows fairly directly from function; unfortunately, delight is more elusive – for the reasons which follow.

INWARD-LOOKING FORM

Stadia naturally look inward towards the action, turning their backs on their surroundings. The elevation facing the street or surrounding landscape must avoid becoming unwelcoming, often made even more forbidding by security fences and other crowd-control measures.

CAR PARKING

Stadia must often be surrounded by acres of car and bus parking which are not only unattractive in themselves but tend to cut them off from their surroundings.

GIGANTIC SCALE

Whilst the huge physical scale of a major stadium may not create problems in an out-of-town environment, it is more difficult to fit happily into a town setting. Reconciling the scales of stadia with those of their surroundings is a difficult challenge.

INFLEXIBLE ELEMENTS

A stadium is composed of elements (seating tiers, stairs and ramps, entrances and roof forms) which are inflexible and sometimes difficult to assimilate into a traditional façade or compositional scheme. And even if traditional rules of composition are abandoned and innovatory architectural forms sought, these stiff elements resist being bent or smoothed or tucked away to achieve the grace, harmony and apparent effortlessness that makes good architecture. They tend to obstinately assert themselves, and the resultant form often simply does not look right.

TOUGH FINISHES

Stadia must have tough and highly resilient surfaces able to stand up, without much maintenance effort, to the worst

that weather, uncaring crowds and deliberate vandalism can do to them. All too easily, the requirement of resilience tends to translate into finishes which are tough, brutal and anti-human.

PERIODS OF DISUSE

Stadia tend to stand empty and unoccupied for weeks at a time, casting a spell of bleakness and lifelessness on their surroundings. Then, for short periods, they are so intensively used as to overwhelm their environment. This pattern of use, almost unique among building types, inflicts upon the stadium and its surroundings the worst effects of both under-use and over-use.

5.2   STRUCTURE AND FORM

5.2.1   INTRODUCTION

It is impossible to lay down a neat set of design rules which will guarantee good stadium architecture, but three suggestions may be helpful regarding architectural form:

- First, designers should think very hard about each of the matters identified above, which are the key architectural problems.
- Second, they should look at existing stadia in which these (or other) problems have been solved with conspicuous success, and try to identify precedents relevant to their own case. There are very few entirely original building concepts in the history of architecture: much good design is an intelligent modification of an existing model that has been shown to work, and there is no shame in learning from the past.
- Third, the approaches outlined below may prove helpful. They are not intended as prescriptive rules, rather suggestions, prompting designers to clarify their own thoughts.

5.2.2   PERMANENT OR TEMPORARY

Although this book is primarily about permanent stadia, the designer should consider whether constructing the building from temporary construction might be a better option. There are two types of temporary construction – impermanent temporary and event temporary. By impermanent temporary we mean permanent-type construction that is intended to have a short life. By event temporary we mean rented seating or buildings brought in for a single event. An example of impermanent temporary are the north and south upper tiers of the ANZ Stadium, in Sydney (see Case studies), which were constructed for the 2000 Olympic Games, then removed afterwards to reduce the capacity of the stadium from 110,000 to 80,000. These tiers were constructed of steel and concrete, with a short design life. An example of event temporary is the 16,000-seat stadium for beach volleyball, constructed on Horse Guards Parade, in London, for the 2012 Games, which was only in place for the few weeks of the event.

Temporary installations are often considered for one-off events larger than the regular programme of the stadium, where building them on a permanent basis would not be justified economically or for other reasons. If the requirements of the event are not known at the time of initial construction, it is important to allow plenty of space for the short-term installation. The design of temporary accommodation and seating has rules somewhat different from permanent construction that should be reviewed before the start of the design phase.

5.2.3   LOW PROFILE
Many stadia would look best with a profile kept as low as possible. Two techniques which help achieve this are dropping the pitch below ground level and raising the surrounding landscape by means of planted mounds.

There are, in fact, great financial benefits in lowering the pitch below existing ground level, so that a proportion of the terracing can be constructed as ground-bearing. This results not only in less steelwork, but also in a reduced and less costly vertical circulation element. (See Chapter 23.)

5.2.4   ROOF AND FAÇADE
In roofed stadia, which are becoming more common (particularly in Europe), the most important step towards a satisfying and harmonious architectural solution is to avoid having an assertive façade competing with an equally assertive roof. If one of these elements is dominant, with the other subdued or completely invisible, the composition may immediately become easier to handle.

DOMINANT ROOF
A successful example of a dominant-roof design is Gunter Behnisch's complex of sports buildings in the Olympiapark, in Munich, designed by Behnisch and Frei Otto. In these buildings, the wall has been virtually eliminated and the stadia reduced visually to a series of graceful roof forms hovering over green landscape (see frontispiece to this chapter). The playing surfaces are recessed below ground level.

Where the walls cannot be eliminated altogether, it helps to reduce them to submissive, horizontal elements of built landscape over which floats a separate graceful roof.

DOMINANT FAÇADE
A successful example of the dominant façade approach is the Mound Stand at Lord's Cricket Ground, in London, by Michael Hopkins & Partners. This stadium façade can genuinely be called successful. It maintains an urban scale, follows the street line, and contains variety and grace. There is a satisfying progression from the heavy, earthbound base course to the light pavilion-like tent roof at the top.

DOMINANT STRUCTURE
In large stadia there could be a third approach: to make the structure dominant. For instance, both façade and roof could be visually contained behind a dominant cage of vertical structural ribs. Examples include the Chamsil Olympic Main Stadium, in Seoul, and the Parc des Princes, in Paris. This may work best on large, open sites where the building is mostly seen from a distance.

Kenzo Tange's twin gymnasia for the 1964 Tokyo Olympics provide supreme examples of structural expressionism of a different kind. Both have organically-shaped roofs suspended from cables which, in turn, are anchored to massive concrete buttresses. The horizontal sweep of the seating tiers and the upward-curving spirals of the suspended roofs obey few of the traditional canons of architectural composition. Yet they look magnificent.

51

But it has to be said that few designers could handle such unorthodox forms so successfully.

An excellent recent example is provided by Santiago Calatrava's 2004 Olympic Stadium roof, in Athens.

APPROPRIATE CHOICE: OPEN SITES

Stadia situated in open parkland can make a positive contribution to the environment if the form rising above the landscape is genuinely attractive and well-composed. If these qualities cannot be achieved, for whatever reason, then there is no shame in hiding the stadium completely behind landscaping.

Achieving a form that blends with the surroundings is usually not too difficult in the case of an open stadium. Roofed stadia present a greater challenge. Sinking the playing field below ground level and/or surrounding the stadium with planted mounds to reduce the apparent height are useful devices, and could enable the stadium almost to melt away into the landscape.

APPROPRIATE CHOICE: URBAN SITES

If a stadium is situated in a town or city, the façades will probably be dominant, partly to allow the site to be exploited right up to its perimeter at all levels, and partly to maintain rather than disrupt the rows of façades which form the streetscape on either side of the stadium. It may then be desirable to subdue the huge stair ramps, and the backs of the seating tiers with their horizontal or sloping geometry, to blend with a surrounding streetscape of closely-spaced, vertically-accented building façades.

One approach, exemplified by the Mound Stand, in London, is to adopt a structural pattern for the stadium that enables the rhythm, scale, materials and details to harmonise with the surroundings, and to ensure also that the façade smoothly follows the street line.

The other, exemplified by the Louis IV stadium, in Monte Carlo, is to place a row of shops, restaurants, a hotel or some other orthodox building type between stadium and street as part of a multi-purpose development. In addition to its architectural merits, such a solution would help bring life to the street and could have economic benefits for the stadium, as explained in Section 23.4.

5.2.5　　TURNING THE CORNER

When stands are placed on three or four sides of a pitch, the problem of gracefully turning the corner where they join has defeated many designers, particularly with roofed stadia. Each individual seating terrace may be elegant in itself and be fitted with an equally elegant roof – but how to bend these stiff forms round the corners?

Some stadia, such as the one at Dortmund, in Germany, or Ibrox Park, in the UK, simply dodge the problem: four rectangular sheds are placed on the four sides of the pitch, and the corners are left as gaps. This saves money and helps avoid awkward structural and planning problems; and in the case of natural grass pitches, the ventilation provided by the open corners is very helpful. Nevertheless, the effect is visually unhappy and the geometry sacrifices potentially revenue-earning corner seating, as pointed out in Section 11.3.4. One solution is to infill the corners with towers, with the side and end stands spanning between them. The stadium in Genoa (architect: Vittorio Gregotti), which is in tight urban surroundings, is an example of this approach. Such towers could accommodate offices or other functions.

Satisfying results have also been obtained by designs in which both the stands and roofs are swept round the pitch in some form. Examples include the Stadium of the Alps, in Turin. This approach may be difficult on tight urban plots, partly because of insufficient space, partly because it may be desirable for the stadium façades to follow the street line, and partly because swept forms may look wrong in some contexts. But there is Philip Cox's elegant Sydney Football Stadium to prove it can be done. As in so many successful designs, the playing area is submerged below ground (about 5m in this case), usefully lowering the stadium profile. The original design had the fluidly-shaped roof floating free above the seating structure. It soared high along the sides of the pitch, where most people want to sit and where the depth of seating extends back furthest and highest; it swooped down close to ground level at the pitch ends, where there are fewer and shallower seating tiers. This dip towards ground level also reduced the apparent scale where the stadium approached a residential area. But the gap between the roof and the rear of the spectator tiers proved too great and offered insufficient weather protection, a problem which had later to be rectified by a multi-million dollar contract to fill in the gaps.

The Manchester Commonwealth Games Stadium (now the Manchester City FC ground), designed by Arup Associates, with Populous, is a further example of the same design theme.

5.2.6   ASSIMILATING CIRCULATION RAMPS

Ramps are sometimes more effective than stairs as the preferred means of escape for the valid reasons given in Section 14.7.3. But their enormous scale (a circular ramp will probably have an internal diameter of around 12m) makes them difficult to handle with elegance. Relatively successful examples include the San Siro stadium, in Milan, and the Sun Life stadium, formerly the Joe Robbie stadium, in Miami, USA.

5.2.7   ASSIMILATING THE STRUCTURE

LATTICE-LIKE STRUCTURES

Massive columns, beams and cantilevers are often difficult to assimilate into a coherent design concept. A very useful trend in recent years has been the increasing use of more delicate lattice or tension structures to replace (wholly or in part) these assertive structural elements.

These concepts do not automatically solve all problems or guarantee aesthetic success, but they do help achieve shapely and graceful structures which are related to the human scale. Good examples include:

- The roof of the Prater Stadium, in Vienna.
- The ANZ (Sydney Olympic) Stadium, by Populous and Bligh Voller Nield (see Case studies).

MASSIVE STRUCTURES

The alternative brutalist approach of powerfully expressed large-scale structural elements fascinates architects but, alas, for every masterpiece of sculptural concrete there are a dozen cruder examples, deeply disliked by the public. The sheer scale of a modern stadium is part of the problem. As an indication, the 110m-long girder spanning the North Stand at Ibrox Park stadium is large enough to hold four double-decker buses.

If massive concrete forms are to be used, they ought possibly to be softened by heavy planting, consisting of trees, shrubs or smaller plants positioned around or on the building.

5.3   MATERIALS
5.3.1   VISUAL ASPECTS

FINISHES

Unfinished concrete has many functional virtues and is widely used in stadium design. But it is disliked by the general public, tends to weather unattractively, and when used for façades should be specified with caution.

The following suggestions may be helpful.

- Exposed concrete finishes are best avoided in rainy climates, particularly in urban or industrial locations where the rainwater becomes contaminated by pollutants which then stain the concrete as the water runs down the surface. In theory, the staining can be avoided by surface treatment, by well-designed drip mouldings and the like. But, in practice, these measures are seldom completely effective. Also, in theory, the staining of concrete can be positively exploited by carefully planning and guiding the patterns of water-flow to produce a pre-designed effect. But it is difficult to think of any examples where attractive results have been achieved.

- If exposed concrete must be used in these situations, then expert advice should be sought and the greatest care taken (in both design and workmanship) to avoid surface staining. Aggregates, sand and cement should all be very carefully specified and be of high quality. The increasing use of pre-cast concrete, which can be manufactured under more controlled conditions than in situ, helps achieve higher-quality finishes.

- Painting the concrete can also help, and several existing stadia (including the Seoul Olympic stadium) have been treated in this way. But it requires enormous maintenance.

The above problems are reduced in locations with unpolluted air (where the rainwater is therefore cleaner and less liable to soil the concrete), and in dry climates with low or very intermittent rainfalls. An example of success is Renzo Piano's Bari Stadium, in Italy.

Finally, concrete surfaces that are close to people should, if possible, be clad with brickwork, timber or some other friendly material. This will be expensive, but will make stadia more popular with spectators.

COLOURS

Designers sometimes fall into the trap of producing gaudily coloured stadia. They are tempted by the enormous range of colours now available for stadium seats, claddings and synthetic pitch surfaces, and they are trying to overcome the bleakness of the average stadium, particularly when it is half-empty, without crowds of people to give colour variety to the terraces. Imagination controlled by the strictest discipline may give the best results.

5.3.2   TECHNICAL ASPECTS

Stadia have been built of every conceivable material. The ancient Romans built theirs in brick and stone, and modern Romans refurbished their existing Olympic stadium in concrete, steel, aluminium and plastic fabric roofing for the 1990 FIFA World Cup.

Cost is a major factor because structure, as discussed in Chapter 23, is a larger proportion of total cost in the case of stadia than in most other building types. Cost comparisons between all the alternative structural materials are therefore vital, with particular attention to the roof (as discussed in Section 5.8, below).

Other performance characteristics such as durability and fire resistance must be just as thoroughly investigated. They must then be balanced against user-friendliness, grace and beauty. Stadia can prosper only if they attract spectators, and increasingly people will stay away if the facility is rough or sordid-looking – no matter how technically correct the specifications.

5.3.3   CONCRETE

Reinforced concrete competes with steel as the most commonly-used structural material for stadia. It has the great advantage of being naturally fireproof and cheaper than steel in some countries, but it has the disadvantage of being unpopular if left unfinished (which is usually the case). By and large, it is the only practical material for constructing the seating profiles of the stadium. Concrete may be either cast in situ or applied as pre-cast units. Both types are frequently used together.

IN SITU CONCRETE

The plastic properties of in situ concrete have been exploited to produce some very dramatic stadia, for instance the shell canopies of the Grandstand at Zarzuela racetrack, near Madrid (Eduardo Torroja, 1935); in Rome, the Palazzetto dello Sport (Annibale Vitellozzi and Pier Luigi Nervi, 1957) and the Palazzo dello Sport (Pier Luigi Nervi and Marcello Piacentini, 1960); and in the composite structures of the Hockey Rink at Yale University, Connecticut (Eero Saarinen, 1958), and the National Olympic Gymnasia, in Tokyo. Recently, such use has diminished in favour of more lightweight structures.

PRE-CAST CONCRETE

Pre-cast concrete, like steel, has the advantage over in situ concrete that structural members can be prefabricated away from the site well in advance of site possession, thus greatly reducing construction time. This is important when construction must be planned to minimise disruptions to the season's fixtures. Such is often the case with sports stadia in the UK, which must be constructed in phases during the few months between one season and the next. This practice is not yet common in the USA where stadia tend to be constructed in one operation, but even here, stadia owners are beginning to experience the difficulties Europe has had for decades. Clubs do not want to move from the stadium while necessary redevelopment or upgrading work takes place.

PRE-STRESSED AND POST-TENSIONED CONCRETE

Pre-cast concrete is widely used for the tread and riser units which form the seating platform. These step units are often pre-stressed so that they can be thin and light, but their jointing can cause problems. Choice of materials and detailing of junctions is as important here as in roof

54

construction, particularly if the spaces below are to be usable rooms. Waterproofing, especially, will be very important.

When using pre-cast framing, thought should also be given to the future uses of the stadium. If stadia are used for pop music concerts, the spectators can set up rhythms in time to the music which may affect the structure. It should be specifically designed to cater for this.

Both pre-stressing and post-tensioning are useful techniques in stadium construction – pre-stressing for reasons of lightness, and post-tensioning so as to reduce the number of movement joints throughout the structure. This is an important advantage because many stadia are 100m or more in extent, and normally such a length of concrete structure should be built as two independent units with a clear expansion gap between. In a post-tensioned structure the thermal movement still occurs but is greatly reduced by the enormous tension placed on the reinforcing rods. The entire structure is held together like a string of beads pulled together by a thread – the threads in this case being steel rods stressed to a hundred tonnes or more.

5.3.4   STEEL

Steel is cheaper in some parts of the world than concrete and it allows prefabrication off-site, which can be a great advantage for the reasons given above.

It is, of course, lighter than concrete, both physically and aesthetically. This offers functional advantages, such as cheaper footings on bad soil, and the possibility of slender, graceful structures. Steel is an obvious choice for roof structures, two excellent examples being the Olympic Stadium, in Rome, and the Prater Stadium, in Vienna, both of which were given new steel roofs over the existing stadia.

Fire regulations will probably require steel members below the roof to be fireproofed with encasing, with mineral-fibre or vermiculite-cement spray, or with thin-film intumescent coating. The latter detracts least from the appearance of steel profiles. This could cause steel to lose its cost advantage over concrete. But fire-safety regulations are changing as the emphasis shifts towards fire-engineered solutions. Unprotected steel seems likely to become more widely acceptable provided certain additional measures are taken. These include:

- Ensuring that people can escape from the stadium within a defined time, as discussed in Section 14.6.2, and reach safety well before structural failure commences. This should not be a major problem because the main danger with fire in stadia is not that of structural collapse but of smoke suffocation. The Valley Parade Stadium, in Bradford, where 56 people died and many were badly injured in a fire in 1985, had an old pitched roof which effectively contained the smoke and flames.
- Installing a sprinkler system. New UK fire regulations do allow unprotected steelwork if sprinklers are installed, a concession that may in some cases tip the economic balance from concrete to steel. On the other hand, the effects of a sprinkler downpour on an already panicking crowd have yet to be seen.

5.3.5   BRICKWORK

In a large stadium, brickwork is more likely to be used as cladding rather than as a structural material in itself. Its use is particularly apt at human height level throughout the stadium so as to humanise otherwise brutal surfaces, or at street level to help the stadium blend in with the surrounding townscape.

5.4   THE PLAYING SURFACE
5.4.1   LEVEL

The level of the playing surface is often sunk below the ground line so that part of the front seating tier can be rested directly on the natural ground (Figure 5.1). This can save in construction costs and has the aesthetic benefit of reducing the apparent height of the building. But constructing viewing terraces directly on the ground is not always as straightforward as it may sound: poor soil conditions (see Section 5.5.1 below) could create problems which cancel out the envisaged savings.

5.4.2   SURFACE

Chapter 7 deals in detail with playing surfaces: here we merely wish to point out that certain stadium forms will rule out (or at least have an adverse effect upon) certain playing surfaces.

55

- A cantilever roof can rise to its highest point at the back of the stand – the street side, as it were – and may therefore appear taller and more intimidating to passers-by than alternative forms of structure enclosing a similar seating capacity. The East Stand at Stamford Bridge football stadium, in London, while being an admirably heroic and exciting design, also demonstrates the colossal visual impact that a large cantilevered structure may have. Not every site can absorb such a dramatic intrusion, particularly on the street side, where the stadium must relate to the scale of much more ordinary buildings.
- A cantilevered roof thrusting boldly out into space without any visible means of support provides not only an aesthetic opportunity but also a risk. Great care and some self-restraint is required if an obtrusive, out-of-scale result is to be avoided.

EXAMPLES

The East Stand at Stamford Bridge football stadium, in London, is not without problems. Its construction costs were high; the upper seats seem a long way from the pitch; the lower seats are uncomfortably exposed to wind and rain; there are difficulties with cleaning. Nevertheless, its design has presence and architectural power. Other examples include the Bari Stadium, in Italy, Twickenham Rugby Football Ground, in London, and Seoul Olympic Stadium, in South Korea.

IV   CONCRETE SHELL STRUCTURES

Shells are thin surface structures which are curved in one or two directions, deriving their strength from the geometric shape rather than the thickness or firmness of the material. (Just as a flimsy sheet of paper may become capable of carrying a load if correctly curved.) They include cylindrical, domed, conoid and hyperbolic shapes, and allow for very elegant roof forms. A shell as thin as 75mm or 100mm may easily span 100m.

ADVANTAGES

- Shell structures have the potential of great visual elegance. This does not, however, come automatically.

Such innovative forms require very thorough testing of architectural character, using both computer modelling and physical scale models.
- If carefully detailed, shells can be self-finished both underneath and on the upper surface. The latter requires sufficiently steep drainage falls to ensure rapid and complete disposal of rainwater.

DISADVANTAGES

- Specialist designers must be used, as the mathematics involved are advanced.
- If in situ concrete is used, the formwork costs will be very high since a birdcage or similar type of scaffold will be required. A pre-cast concrete solution should be considered, or a combination of pre-cast and in situ concrete.

EXAMPLES

The grandstand at Zarzuela racecourse, near Madrid (1935), by Eduardo Torroja; the Palazzetto dello Sport, in Rome (1957), by Annibale Vitellozzi and Pier Luigi Nervi; the Palazzo dello Sport, in Rome (1960), by Marcello Piacentini and Pier Luigi Nervi.

V   COMPRESSION/TENSION RING

These roofs consist of an inner tension ring and an outer compression ring, the two being connected by radial members which maintain the geometry of the overall doughnut-shaped structure and carry the roof covering.

ADVANTAGES

- Very deep stands can be spanned with comparative ease. The new roof to the Vienna Prater Stadium spans a distance of 48m between the inner and outer rings. The recently added roof on the Olympic Stadium, in Rome, spans a distance of 52m.
- As can be seen from the above examples, this roof type lends itself both technically and aesthetically to the problem of retro-fitting a new roof to an existing bowl stadium.
- The inner perimeter is completely column-free, so there are no obstructions whatever between spectators and pitch.

- The roof has a light, weightless appearance, as seen from the stadium interior, and is unobtrusive or even invisible when seen from the outside. The latter can be a particular advantage in many situations, as discussed in Section 5.2.3.
- Both the overall roof form and the structural details have inherent qualities of harmony and grace, and do not resist the designer's attempts to produce beautiful architecture. This contrasts with some other structural types which are technically efficient but aesthetically difficult to handle.
- Transparent or translucent roof coverings are possible, as in the Olympic Stadium, in Rome.
- Some types permit the addition of a permanent or temporary roof cover over the playing field.

DISADVANTAGES

- This structural system can be used only with bowl stadia.

EXAMPLES

The Prater Stadium, in Vienna, was built between 1928 and 1931, and extended in 1956. The new roof was retro-fitted in 1986 with no need for any additional reinforcement to the existing concrete structures. The pitch itself has been left open, while the surrounding 63,000-capacity stands are entirely covered by a continuous oval roof, the outer perimeter forming an ellipse of 270m by 215m. The roof covering consists of galvanised and plastic-coated corrugated steel sheets, while the structure comprises an inner tension ring and an external compression ring (both of these being box girders) with a connecting framework of steel tubes. The latter have a structural function and also support the steel covering plates. Special ties hold down the lightweight structure against wind uplift. Roof depth, front to back, is 48m, and the overall roof area over 32,000m^2. Floodlights are mounted on the inner ring and TV camera stands, while public address systems and other services are integrated into the roof.

　　　A more recent and even larger example is the open stadium in Rome which was used for the 1960 Olympic Games and then retro-fitted with a roof for the 1990 FIFA World Cup. In this case, roof depth is 52m from front to back, and the roof covering consists of translucent Teflon, allowing some light to penetrate to the seats below.

VI   TENSION STRUCTURES

These are roofs in which all the primary forces are taken by members acting in tension alone, such as cables. They are always more economical in material (though not necessarily in costs) than other forms of structure, but must be very carefully stabilised and restrained against any deformation which could cause parts of the system to go into compression. There are three principal forms – catenary cable, cable net and membrane.

CATENARY CABLE STRUCTURES

These consist of a compression arch (or arches) supporting one or more cables hanging in catenary shape, which in turn support a roof structure.

　　　The beautifully shaped roof of Eero Saarinen's hockey rink at Yale University, in New Haven (1958), is formed by cables suspended from a rigid arched keel. In Tokyo, seven years later, Kenzo Tange roofed the twin gymnasia for the 1964 Olympic Games with concrete slabs hung from massive steel cables to create two of the most dramatic architectural forms of the century.

　　　These are very heavy forms of tension structure compared with the types below.

CABLE NET STRUCTURES

As above, the supporting structure is separated from the roof covering. The structure consists of a three-dimensional net of steel cables, and the covering normally of plastics (acrylic, PVC or polycarbonate). Glass-reinforced plastic has been used but it tends to become brittle and less translucent with age. Suitable plastics for coverings are listed in Table 5.1, published by kind permission of the Football Stadia Advisory Design Council and the Sports Council.

　　　An excellent example of a cable net roof is the Olympic Stadium complex, in Munich (see frontispiece to this chapter), where a covering of transparent acrylic panels is supported by a web of steel cables. Because the covering in this case was designed to be relatively rigid, deformation in the cable system had to be minimised by very powerful pre-tensioning, leading to high costs for the masts and other anchoring members.

| | Profiled metal sheeting | | Concrete | PVC | | Acrylic | GRP | Polycarbonate | | Fabric | PTFE- | ETFE inflated |
	Steel	Aluminium		Single glazed	Double glazed			Single glazed	Double glazed	PVC-s coated	coated	pillows
Relative cost factor (supply and fix) as at 2012 in the UK		1.2	4 to 8	2.5 to 4	3 to 5	2.5 to 4	1 to 2.5	3 to 7	6 to 8	3 to 5	5 to 8	10 to 15
Durability	Good	Good	Good	Medium	Medium	Medium	Medium	Good	Good	Medium	Good	Medium
Flame retardancy	Incombustible		Incombustible	Self-extinguishing		Class 1 (when edges are protected)	Class 1	Self-extinguishing		Approx. class 1 equivalent	Class 0	Low flammability
Transparency	Opaque		Opaque	Transparent: 70% to 80% light transmission, which lessens markedly with time		Translucent or transparent: 50% to 70% possible light transmission which lessens moderately with time	Opaque or translucent	Transparent: 80% to 90% visible light transmission, which lessens slightly with time		Translucent.		Transparent: 95% of visible light transmission

The above relative cost factor compares the cost of the roof covering only. It should be noted that some of the listed materials have differing structural properties which can impact upon the weight of the primary and secondary structure, and may lead to cost differentials for this element. This is, however, a complex equation linked to type of structure and complexity of roof erection methodology.

Table 5.1   Comparative properties of roof covering materials

MEMBRANE STRUCTURES

Unlike the preceding two types, the roof covering material forms both the structure and the enclosure. Suitable fabrics include:

- PVC-coated polyester fabric. This is cheaper initially than the next type (below), and easy to handle. But it has a life of only about 15 years. Also, the fabric tends to sag with time, and the surface becomes sticky with age and requires frequent cleaning.
- Teflon-coated glass fibre fabric (also known as PTFE-coated glass fibre fabric). This is an expensive roof, by any standards, but it has a longer life than the type listed above and, being Teflon, it is to some degree self-cleaning. Use of this material is limited or banned by some authorities because of a tendency to produce toxic fumes in a fire.

But as fire is not normally a hazard in a stadium roof, the material ought to be acceptable in this context. Use of an expert designer is essential, together with a fire engineering approach.

The Faro Stadium, in Portugal, and Oita Stadium, in Japan, (see Case studies) provide elegant examples. Examples in the UK include the Mound Stand at Lord's Cricket Ground, in London (1987), with a translucent PVC-coated woven polyester fabric with PVDF top coat; the Sussex Stand, at Goodwood Racecourse (1990); and the Don Valley Stadium, in Sheffield (1991). The Riyadh Stadium, in Saudi Arabia, is an example of a complete stadium roofed in fabric.

ADVANTAGES

- Cable net or fabric roofs can be designed to lend an airy, festive appearance to a stadium, especially when seen from a distance. Given the aesthetic difficulties discussed in Sections 5.1 and 5.2, this can be a valuable attribute.
- If a translucent membrane is used, the spectator spaces underneath may have a lighter, more open feel than with opaque roofs. It may also reduce the shading of the pitch which causes problems for grass growth, as discussed in Section 5.4.2, and for television coverage, as discussed in Section 18.1.3.
- Tension structures can be adapted to many stadium layouts, and do not dictate a particular plan form.

DISADVANTAGES

- Very sophisticated design is needed for all tension structures, and it is best to use structural engineers with a track record of successful designs.
- More systematic and intensive maintenance is required than with other structural forms.
- Fabric roofs require very careful detailing of rainwater guttering.

VII　　　AIR-SUPPORTED ROOFS

An air-supported roof consists of a plastic membrane which forms an enclosure – either on its own or in combination with a wall structure – and is supported by positive internal pressure provided by electric fans. These membranes are commonly formed in PVC polyester, sometimes with cable reinforcement in the case of larger roofs.

ADVANTAGES

Air-supported roofs are relatively low in capital cost.

DISADVANTAGES

- Full enclosures are vulnerable to damage.
- Design life is relatively short.
- The system needs to be continually pumped to keep the interior adequately pressurised.
- They are not regarded as being environmentally friendly nor sustainable.

EXAMPLES

The leading air-supported roofs are mostly in North America. Those in the USA are the RCA Dome, formerly the Hoosier Dome, in Indianapolis (1972), with a seating capacity of 61,000 and the Silverdome, in Pontiac (1973), with a seating capacity of 80,000. The leading Canadian example is BC Place, in Vancouver (1983), with a seating capacity of 60,000. All these roofs are of fibreglass. The best-known Japanese example is the so-called 'Big Egg' in Tokyo.

VIII　　　SPACE FRAMES

A space frame is a grid of structural members which is three-dimensional in shape and also stable in three dimensions, unlike, for instance, a roof truss, which is stable only in its own plane. Such frames can be constructed of any material but are commonly of steel.

ADVANTAGES

- Capable of spanning large distances.
- Suitable for all-over roofs with only perimeter support.

DISADVANTAGES

- A space frame is efficient and sensible only if spanning in two directions. Plan proportions should therefore be roughly square, and preferably not have a length-to-width ratio greater than 1.5 to 1. This structural form will therefore not be appropriate for normal stand roofs unless the sections of roof between structural supports can be of these proportions.
- Space frames tend to be expensive.

EXAMPLES

The San Siro Stadium, in Milan, is roofed over by an aluminium deck supported from steel lattice beams. The roof covering is translucent polycarbonate sheeting. It must be said that this was a very expensive solution which has not functioned as well as expected. The main failure is that the grass on the pitch is struggling to survive, probably as a result of excessive shading. However, this is not indicative of space frame roofs in general.

65

IX   OPENING ROOFS

Increasing numbers of stadia are being designed with roofs that can open and close, giving protection from the weather and thus enabling indoor events of all kinds to take place. See Chapter 8.

The geometry and mechanism of a moving roof can take many forms. An early ambitious example was the design for the Montreal Olympic Stadium (1976) which proposed a gigantic fabric roof over the central area, supported by cables from a high reinforced concrete tower. This would be pulled up and lowered, rather like an umbrella. Unfortunately, the proposal proved to be too ambitious and the roof was fixed in a permanent form.

Since then the technology of retractable roofs has greatly improved.

A highly elegant example is the Oita Stadium, in Japan (see Case studies), designed by the KT Group, Takenaka Corporation. The venue has a maximum capacity of 43,000 spectators and was completed in 2001 for the 2002 FIFA World Cup. The stationary part of the roof is clad in titanium, while the movable panels are lightweight Teflon membranes. These panels are retracted by a wire traction system and slide over the main beam arch, meeting exactly above the centre of the field. The action resembles an eyelid closing, hence the stadium's popular name 'the Big Eye'.

The Millennium Stadium, in Cardiff, designed by Populous and WS Atkins, provides a particularly large-scale example. The venue seats up to 74,500 spectators and opened in 1999 to host the Rugby World Cup. The roof has a total fixed area of approximately 27,000m^2 around the perimeter, and a moving area in the centre of 9,500m^2. The latter comprises two panels above the playing field which slide apart to create an opening of 105m by 80m. It takes 20 minutes to winch the closing sections into place along rails which rest on the massive 220m-long primary trusses. Its form and operation are simple and uncomplicated – a factor to be taken into account when looking at lifelong maintenance.

Further selected examples of moving roofs include the following:

- The Amsterdam Arena (see Case studies) which opened in 1996 and seats up to 51,000 spectators. It is primarily a soccer stadium but is also extensively used for pop concerts and other entertainments.
- The 63,000-seat Arizona Cardinals football stadium – (see Case studies).
- The Miller Park (Brewer) baseball stadium, in Milwaukee, which has a seven-panel roof that opens and closes like a fan, and is claimed to close in about 10 minutes.
- The Reliant football stadium, in Houston (see Case studies).
- The Rod Laver Arena, in Melbourne.
- The 47,000-seat Safeco Field baseball stadium, in Seattle.
- The Telstra Dome, in Melbourne (see Case studies).
- The Toronto Skydome.
- The Centre Court at the All England Lawn Tennis and Croquet Club, Wimbledon, now fitted with a new sliding roof (see Case studies). The closing has to be accompanied by sophisticated air conditioning to ensure that the atmosphere of the interior and the natural grass surface perform.

5.8.5   ROOF COVERINGS

Materials used for roof covering need to be lightweight, tough, water-tight, incombustible, aesthetically acceptable, cost-effective and durable enough to withstand the effects of outdoor weathering, including ultraviolet light. They should also be strong and stiff enough to span between primary and secondary elements, supporting snow and other superimposed loads, including wind forces. Over the facility areas such as private boxes, kitchens, restaurants and toilets, the roof construction may require additional thermal and/or acoustic insulation.

OPAQUE COVERINGS

Profiled metal sheeting is cheap, easy to fix, and very commonly used. Steel sheets generally come in galvanised, plastic-coated or painted form. Aluminium sheets are lighter and inherently resistant to atmospheric attack, but have less impact resistance and will suffer electrolytic corrosion when in contact with other metals or with concrete, and chemical attack when in contact with wood that may get wet.

In both cases, separating membranes must be used at all contact points.

Concrete is so heavy that it will seldom be used as a roof covering. But where the roof structure is also the covering (for example, a shell or slab) the chosen material may well be concrete. The problems are then likely to be excessive weight (which may be reduced by using lightweight aggregates) and the unattractive weathering that is associated with concrete surfaces. Silicone treatments may help reduce the latter, but if the stadium is built in a climate that is both rainy and polluted, the concrete should preferably be given a finish such as tiling.

Figure 5.3
The Centre Court at Wimbledon, now fitted with a sliding roof.

06

SECURITY AND ANTI-TERRORISM MEASURES

6.1	INTRODUCTION
6.2	THE THREATS FROM TERRORISM
6.3	AUTHORITIES
6.4	IMPLICATIONS FOR MANAGEMENT AND OPERATION
6.5	RESPONSES BY THE DESIGN TEAM
6.6	CONCLUSION

6.1   INTRODUCTION

In this context, security means the protection of a building or its occupants from external threats that might cause danger to the people in the building, or interfere with its normal operation. These threats could, for example, be crime, terrorism, natural disasters or human error. The actions to counter them will range from design elements of the building to operational procedures by the management or outside agencies. In recent years, the threat from terrorism has become a factor that must be taken into account when staging major sporting competitions. This chapter concentrates on that threat.

There can be no absolute answers in countering such threats, and this chapter only gives an outline of some of the major issues. It should be read in conjunction with the guidance on emergency exit in the event of fire in Section 14.6.2. The authors stress that anti-terrorist measures are a highly specialised subject, and expert advice is essential. The level of threat is judged by the police, who should be consulted on this aspect throughout the design process.

6.2   THE THREATS FROM TERRORISM

The following is a summary of some of the methods that terrorists might use to attack high-profile events, extrapolated from the experience of past terrorist incidents. The aim of terrorists might be to harm people, to take them hostage or to cause alarm.

EXPLOSIVE DEVICES

These may be delivered by a number of means including parked vehicles, large vehicles driven by a suicide bomber, devices carried by an individual, or explosives delivered by a missile. They could include devices with radioactive ingredients. In the past, they have been delivered to the building on the day of the attack, or set up in advance and detonated at a significant moment.

- Applying transparent safety film to ordinary annealed glass. Though they are paper-thin, such films will hold the glass together if broken, and counteract the formation of flying shards. The typical cost is a third or a quarter of the cost of laminated safety glass.
- More sophisticated blast-absorbing and wire-catch systems are also available.
- New developments in plastic should be considered.

Frames and blast-resistant glazing should be designed to resist blast loads together. The frames may need to be reinforced to take the strain, and the glass securely seated in deep rebates.

Resisting blast loads does not mean that the outside of the building should be strengthened to the point that blast loads cannot escape. Some façades are now designed to resist the effect of an *external* blast on the structure without proper consideration of the likely effect of an *internal* blast on this blast-resistant envelope. In these cases, designers must consider where the pressure wave of the blast is going to go.

6.6   CONCLUSION

No conceivable range of security measures can provide 100 per cent security to a building or its occupants. The aim is to mitigate threats. Venue managers must find the right balance between the perceived security threat, and the range of counter-terror measures in the design and management of the stadium. At the same time they do not want to unduly disturb the operation of the building or inconvenience the spectators. All the systems must be integrated to work smoothly together: the building structure and materials, the information technology, and the management strategies. Consultation with the agencies mentioned in this   section will be essential.

07

ACTIVITY AREA

7.1	**PLAYING SURFACES**
7.2	**PITCH DIMENSIONS, LAYOUT AND BOUNDARIES**

7.1   PLAYING SURFACES

7.1.1   HISTORY

Informal sport has been played on grass fields, city squares or open ground for hundreds of years but it was not until the middle of the 19th century that sports became organised with conditions under which they could be played fairly. These early, rather loose conditions later became codified rules, and eventually the laws of sport were born. A notable exception is tennis which had its origins as an indoor sport and only later took to the outdoors. The surface to be played upon was often specified in these rules, as it was recognised that the nature of a game differed when surfaces changed.

The established rule of ball sports being played on natural surfaces was unchallenged until 1966 when the Houston Astrodome opened. This was the world's first completely covered stadium and was designed, using the best technology at the time, with a transparent roof and natural turf playing surface. Unfortunately, the grass did not grow below the transparent roof for a number of reasons, one of which was that the steel structure holding up the solid roof prevented natural light from reaching the playing surface.

To avoid this showcase stadium turning into a disaster, a manufactured synthetic grass was woven using green plastic, and then laid over the existing ground. The product was called Astroturf, after its host venue, the Astrodome. Variants of this original synthetic grass have covered many other sports surfaces around the world.

Synthetic sports surfaces have since been used in more sophisticated constructions, all with the enormous advantage that stadia can host different events on the same playing surface, one after another. Although players and team coaches tended to prefer a natural grass surface for its playability, artificial surfaces were approved for American football and spread quickly through the USA. They are now officially accepted by FIFA for soccer matches and are beginning to be installed by soccer clubs around the world, though they have not yet been accepted by national federations for major matches.

Wembley Stadium London designed for football, rugby, concerts and other events. Architects: Populous with Foster + Partners

7.1.2   CURRENT REQUIREMENTS

Table 7.1 shows the playing characteristics of tennis court surfaces, reproduced with the permission of the Lawn Tennis Association.

7.1.3   NATURAL GRASS SURFACES

ADVANTAGES

Natural grass remains the most user-friendly of surfaces, and the only permissible choice for some sports. The advantages of natural grass are:

- It is aesthetically attractive.
- It gives a speed of rebound and a degree of rolling resistance that is just about right for most ball sports.
- It provides reasonable – though variable – purchase for players' feet when dry or wet.
- It gives a surface that is neither excessively hard nor excessively soft for comfortable running.
- It is less injurious to players who fall than most alternative finishes.

- If irrigated, it is a relatively cool surface in hot climates.
- It will continually self-repair and regenerate.

DISADVANTAGES

The major limitation of grass surfaces is that they cannot be used in roofed stadia, and are difficult to keep healthy even under partial cover. The reason is that grass needs ample light for really healthy growth; air movement, humidity and temperature levels also need to be kept within fairly strict parameters. Only recently have roof materials and stadium design advanced so that a natural grass pitch can be grown under cover.

Even in a partly roofed stadium, the size of the roof aperture, the shadow effects of the surrounding structure and other such factors may lead to disappointing results. One example of failure is the San Siro Stadium, in Milan, which was redeveloped to accommodate 80,000 spectators for the FIFA World Cup in 1990. Only the spectator seating areas are roofed, with a central opening over the playing area; but even though this aperture is approximately the size of the football

Surfaces	Ball-surface interaction			Spin		Player-surface interaction		
	Speed of court	Height of bounce	Trueness of bounce	Topspin	Slice	Sliding/ firm footing	Traction (slip or non-slip)	Resilience (hardness)
Grass	Fast	Low	Variable	Little	Yes	Firm footing with partial slide	Slip	Soft
Synthetic turf	Fast to slow	Medium	Variable	Little	Yes	Firm footing but partial slide on sand filled	Mainly non-slip	Medium to soft
Impervious acrylic	Medium	Medium	Uniform	Yes	Yes	Firm footing	Non-slip	Hard to medium
Porous macadam	Slow	High	Almost uniform	Yes	Little	Firm footing	Non-slip	Hard
Shale	Medium	Medium	Variable	Yes	Yes	Sliding	Slip	Medium to soft
Continental clay	Slow	Medium	Almost uniform	Yes	Yes	Sliding	Non-slip	Medium to soft

Source: Tennis Courts, published by the LTA Court Advisory Service. Reproduced by kind permission of Christopher Trickey.

Table 7.1   Playing characteristics of tennis court surfaces.

pitch below, the grass is struggling to survive. The lesson to designers must be one of caution.

Supplementary artificial lighting is increasingly used to improve the growth of the grass, though this system has an operational energy cost. When combined with vents to encourage air movement across the grass surface, a good-quality pitch can be grown without much natural light. Careful management of the pitch is needed in these circumstances.

A second limitation is that grass cannot survive the same intensity and frequency of use as most artificial surfaces. This relative fragility conflicts with the stadium's need to maximise the number of event days per annum for profitability.

THE PITCH REPLACEMENT CONCEPT

One response to the problems outlined above is the concept of pitch replacement on a systematic basis. The principle is to remove the grass when it is not needed, and to allow other events to take place on an artificial surface underneath. There are many removal techniques: (i) a Canadian method of growing the turf in large boxes which can then be moved out of the stadium on rails; (ii) a German method of growing the turf on pallets of 4m² which are then moved on the hovercraft principle; and (iii) a Dutch concept of leaving

the natural grass in place and constructing above it a new platform supported on remote-controlled hydraulic legs. In the UK, Odsal Stadium, in Bradford, has used a simple system of restoring the corners of a soccer pitch which had been cut off by a speedway track around the pitch: grass was grown on wooden pallets with a reinforced plastic mesh sub-base, and these were moved away to storage by forklift truck before speedway events. Further notes on this topic are provided in Section 5.4.2.

INSTALLATION

Planting and maintaining a grass pitch is a task for specialists. All the advice given below is for general background understanding only. A specialist consultant should be retained from the outset to give advice, draw up a detailed specification, invite tenders and supervise the work.

Figure 7.1 shows the elements of a typical grass-turfed surface, and should be studied in conjunction with the following notes.

For bowling greens and croquet, the upper grass surface must be smooth, true and absolutely level, with very good subsoil drainage. For other sports the grass surface can be less exacting but should be smooth and free

79

Figure 7.1
Elements of a typical natural grass playing surface.

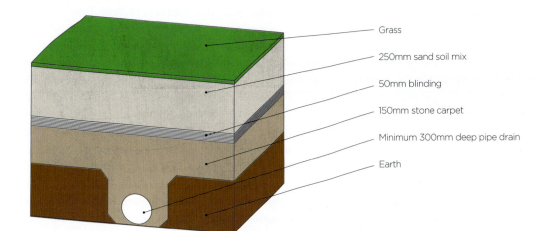

Grass

250mm sand soil mix

50mm blinding

150mm stone carpet

Minimum 300mm deep pipe drain

Earth

08

SPORTS AND MULTI-PURPOSE USE

8.1   **INTRODUCTION**

8.2   **NATIONAL SPORTS TRADITIONS**

8.3   **FINANCIAL VIABILITY**

8.4   **CATERING FOR DIFFERENT SPORTS**

8.5   **CATERING FOR NON-SPORTS PERFORMANCES**

8.1   INTRODUCTION   99

As stated at the beginning of this book, stadium economics make it difficult – though not impossible – for a stadium to earn a profit for its owners. One of the key ways of closing the gap between costs and revenues is by reducing to an absolute minimum the number of days per year when the stadium is unused and earning no money – i.e. maximising the number of event days. For covered stadia the aim should be 200 or even 250 event days per annum.

To make this feasible, the physical design of the venue should allow a wide range of different activities to be accommodated, both sporting and non-sporting.

Unfortunately not all activities are readily compatible. In the case of sports, compatibility depends on factors such as:

- The size and shape of the playing field.
- The playing field surface.
- The preferred relationship between spectators and performers.
- Whether the stadium is roofed or open to the weather.
- National sporting traditions.

This book deals only with stadia (i.e. buildings that accommodate the larger format sports, whether in the open or under cover) and not with arenas (indoor venues, usually smaller than stadia). But it is worth noting that the latter are often multi-purpose buildings for sports plus concerts, exhibitions and the like. If a stadium is designed for concerts and has a roof that covers the pitch, either permanently or by shutting for a particular occasion, it could perhaps be defined as a large arena. The above factors are discussed in more detail below.

U2 playing at Croke Park
Stadium in Dublin.

09

CROWD CONTROL

9.1	GENERAL
9.2	PERIMETER FENCES
9.3	MOATS
9.4	CHANGES OF LEVEL

9.1 GENERAL

Controlling crowds and separating spectators from participants has been a problem for stadium authorities since Roman times. A group of people coming together to enjoy a stadium event must be carefully managed from the moment they enter the stadium's zone of influence. Sometimes very little encouragement is needed for that crowd to become a mob, and that mob to become a riot (a list of disasters is given in Section 1.3.4). To minimise this, crowd management must be considered from the very beginning of a stadium project. The majority of people place great importance on the way they are treated by staff at a venue. In a US survey, 92 per cent indicated that customer service should be the top priority of management. It is this customer service, together with the architecture of the venue, which maintains the goodwill of the spectators.

If members of the public misbehave, the management of the venue needs to intervene quickly to ensure a small incident does not get out of control. It helps if the building itself does not provide opportunities for misbehaviour, and perhaps even encourages people to behave well. Closed-circuit television is crucial, too, so that stewards have enough space to see problems arising, and enough time to get there and deal with the situation.

It is the authors' experience that in some instances where stadia have been designed to a good quality, fans have respected the building. Whereas when spaces have been constructed with the expectation they will be vandalised, there is more likelihood they will be.

One of the primary problems in the past has been spectators entering the field of play when not wanted. The design of the barrier at the front of the seating tiers can have an influence on this.

The Colosseum and similar Roman amphitheatres developed their own type of separation in the form of a surrounding wall – possibly designed more to protect the spectators from the activities taking place in the arena than the other way round. Bullrings in Spain and southern France developed along similar lines, with a change in height between the first row of seating and the bullring – essential to ensure the safety of the audience. In the latter part of the 20th century the roles have been reversed, with the boundary serving to protect the activity area from the spectators.

There are three commonly used design techniques for separating the activity area from the spectators: perimeter fences, moats and changes of level.

9.2   PERIMETER FENCES
9.2.1   ADVANTAGES

There are two good reasons for having a robust fence (Figure 9.1) between spectators and pitch. The first is to protect players and officials from hostile spectators. The second is to protect a natural grass pitch surface from compaction of the subsoil by spectators' feet.

9.2.2   DISADVANTAGES

Most fences are an obstruction to proper viewing of the game, and are usually unsightly.

There is also the question of safety. In cases of mass panic on the stands or escape from fire, the playing field is an obvious zone of safety (see Section 3.3.6). An intervening fence which prevents people from reaching it can create a death trap. Two recent experiences in Britain demonstrate this. The first, more fully described in Section 3.3.1, was at Valley Parade Stadium, in Bradford, where an even greater disaster was prevented when some spectators were able to escape on to the playing field. The second was at Hillsborough Stadium, in Sheffield, where the perimeter fence between the standing terrace and the pitch was a contributing factor to the death of 95 people in a crowd surge.

Figure 9.1
Perimeter fences protect the pitch from crowd invasion but they obstruct viewing, are often unsightly and may hinder emergency escape.

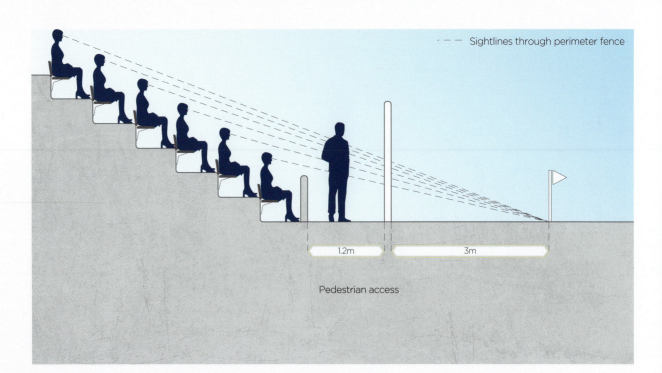

- – – Sightlines through perimeter fence

1.2m   3m

Pedestrian access

9.2.3 CHOICE

In each case, the pros and cons of a fence must be carefully balanced, and the case discussed with the sports governing body, local police and safety authorities, whose views will carry great weight. The following factors should be taken into consideration:

- The need for a fence is most likely in the case of soccer, particularly in countries or individual grounds with a history of violent crowd behaviour.
- The most problematical cases are those where highly valued traditional customs conflict with the latest safety trends – for instance, sports grounds with a tradition of allowing crowds on to the pitch at certain matches. Croke Park, in Dublin, is the home of the Gaelic Athletic

Association, where Gaelic football and hurling have their roots. It has a custom of allowing the crowd on to the pitch to carry off the winning captain on their shoulders. It also allows parents to lift small children over the turnstiles to sit on their laps in the stands. These practices are under threat from the new wave of safety consciousness but are not inherently dangerous if properly controlled. Twickenham, in London, had a tradition of spectators coming on to the pitch after rugby matches, but this is no longer allowed. Customs such as these contribute to the special character of individual stadia and should not be thoughtlessly destroyed by blanket insistence on universally applied safety rules. There should be some modification to take account of individual circumstances. For instance, Wembley Stadium, in London (see Case studies), and

111

Figure 9.2
The cat's cradle fence at Wembley Stadium, in London.

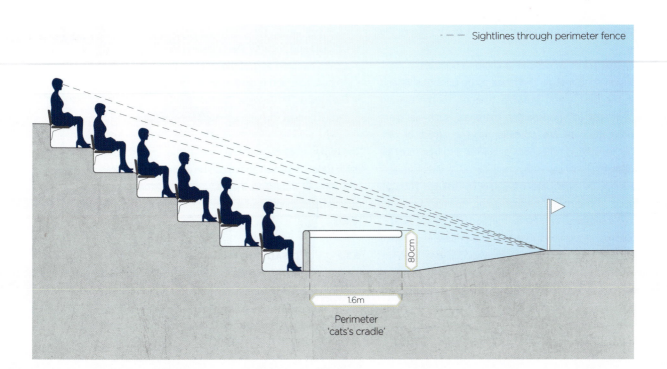

- – – Sightlines through perimeter fence

80cm

1.6m

Perimeter
'cats's cradle'

10

PROVIDING FOR DISABLED PEOPLE

10.1   **EQUAL TREATMENT**

10.2   **SOURCES OF INFORMATION**

10.3   **DESIGN PROCESS**

10.1   EQUAL TREATMENT

10.1.1   BASIC PRINCIPLES

It is now accepted in most developed countries that disabled people should be able to participate in sports events, have reasonable opportunities to be employed as officials or referees, and be able to attend as spectators without being disadvantaged.

In planning for spectators this means that disabled people should be able to find out about forthcoming events; plan their visit; make the journey; and buy their tickets just as easily as everyone else. They should have a good choice of seating positions; enjoy the same sightlines from their seats as other spectators; have equal access to refreshment and retail facilities; and have equal access to suitable toilets.

The reasons for greater inclusiveness are, to some degree, social and commercial, but increasingly equal treatment is being demanded by law. As examples:

- The USA led the way with the Americans with Disabilities Act 1990. For an overview visit www.usdoj.gov/crt/ada/adahom1.htm
- Australia followed soon after with its Disability Discrimination Act 1992. For an overview visit www.hreoc.gov.au/disability_rights/
- The UK passed its own Disability Discrimination Act in 1995, and has since enacted several amendments. For an overview visit www.disability.gov.uk/

Except where otherwise stated, all guidance in this chapter is based on UK legislation.

To state the position in the UK briefly: the Disability Discrimination Act prohibits service providers (a term that includes the organisers of sporting events) from providing a worse service to disabled persons than to the rest of the population. This legal requirement affects both the physical design of the stadium, which must be as easily usable by disabled people as by able-bodied people, and the organisational aspects of the event.

Wembley Stadium London includes wheelchair viewing spaces in all seating areas. Architects: Populous with Foster + Partners

Examples include: if the lettering on a booking form is too small to be read by a person with impaired vision; if a person who is hard of hearing cannot hear the assistant at the ticket office; if a wheelchair user does not have a reasonable choice of good seats in various parts of the stadium, cannot readily reach such a seat, or has worse sightlines than able-bodied spectators once in that seat; or if a disabled person does not have ready access to a suitable toilet. In all these cases, the event organisers may be in breach of the law and liable to legal action on the basis of discrimination.

10.1.2   THE MEANING OF DISABILITY

The legal meaning of the term 'disabled' is now very wide and goes far beyond wheelchair users. However, people in wheelchairs are, in terms of physical building design, perhaps the most difficult category to cater for and therefore a crucially important user group.

Pages 14 to 19 of *Accessible Stadia* (see Bibliography) summarise the physical and mental conditions that are recognised as disabilities under the UK's Disability Discrimination Act. They include the following:

Figure 10.1
Width of a sporting wheelchair. Standard wheelchair width, for comparison, is normally taken as 700mm.

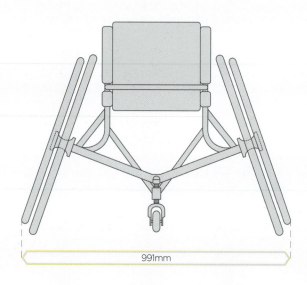

991mm

- Impaired mobility. People with impaired mobility include wheelchair users who cannot leave their wheelchairs; wheelchair users who arrive at the ground in a wheelchair and then transfer to a seat; and ambulant disabled people who do not need a wheelchair but move with difficulty and may use a stick or walking frame.
- Impaired vision. These are people with eyesight problems which cannot be corrected simply by wearing spectacles. They may have difficulty in reading booking forms, tickets, programmes or wayfinding and other signs.
- Impaired hearing. These are people who are hard of hearing or deaf. They may find it difficult or impossible to communicate with assistants in ticket offices, to hear stadium announcements, or to follow spoken commentaries.
- Impaired understanding. These are people with learning difficulties or mental disabilities. They are even more reliant on simple, clear building layouts, clear signposting, and helpful and kindly staff than the rest of the population. In fact, these features are helpful to virtually all stadium users, and should be a high priority for event organisers.

It is officially estimated that, in 2006, a fifth or more of the whole British population may be covered by the Disability Discrimination Act. There are proposals to widen the definition even further. In the UK, full and equal provision must be made for all such people whether they are present at the stadium as spectators, players, athletes (at events such as the Paralympics), officials, or venue employees. Similar trends are at work in the USA, Australia and other developed countries.

10.2   SOURCES OF INFORMATION
10.2.1   GUIDANCE ON SATISFYING UK REGULATIONS

Accessible Stadia, produced and published by the Football Stadia Improvement Fund and the Football Licensing Authority, is the most authoritative guide to the design of accessible stadia in the UK.

Designing for Accessibility, published by the Centre for Accessible Environments, is an equally authoritative guide to the design of public buildings in general. It is much simpler than the official documents listed below, and will greatly help designers in getting the basic design decisions right.

Approved Document M of the Building Regulations has the force of law. Its provisions must be heeded in England and Wales. Northern Ireland and Scotland have their own regulations, but these are fundamentally quite similar to *AD M*.

British Standard BS 8300 is considerably more detailed than *AD M*, and is the leading UK standard on the inclusive design of buildings in general. It is advisory and does not have the force of law, but conformity with its recommendations will help demonstrate that the requirements of the Disability Discrimination Act have been met.

Inclusive Mobility: a Guide to Best Practice on Access to Pedestrian and Transport Infrastructure is the most authoritative UK reference on the design of footways and other pedestrian areas; car parking, bus stops and taxi ranks; the correct use of tactile paving surfaces; and the correct use of signage and other information systems in public buildings.

The Bibliography gives more detail on all the above publications.

10.2.2 GUIDANCE ON SATISFYING USA REGULATIONS

ADA and ABA: Accessibility Guidelines for Buildings and Facilities is the official USA guide on designing for disabled people. The whole document should be consulted, but Section 802 is particularly relevant to stadium design. The Bibliography gives more detail.

10.3 DESIGN PROCESS
10.3.1 SIMPLIFYING STRATEGIES

Accessibility regulations can be dauntingly complex, as a glance at some of the above documents will demonstrate, but the following suggestions may help designers get a grip on the overall process:

• Do not start by planning a stadium for general users, and then check references such as *Accessible Stadia* at a later point to add special features for disabled users. Instead, set out from the very outset to design a venue that has maximally clear routes for both entrance and

emergency exit; excellent signposting; generous spaces; good acoustics and excellent sightlines so that everyone – including those who move with difficulty, don't see well, don't hear well, or are slow in understanding – will find it a safe and easy environment.

• Then use the journey-sequence approach to imagine the entire sequence of events for each type of spectator (or player, or official) as he or she looks up information about a forthcoming event; plans the visit; makes the journey to the venue; moves from the bus, coach, or car to the main entrance; buys the ticket; gets to the seat; views the match; visits the toilets; has a drink or a meal; and leaves the venue. Within reason, no one, regardless of physical or mental fitness, should encounter any difficulty at any point along such a journey sequence.

For the UK, pages 25 to 66 of *Accessible Stadia* give authoritative guidance, starting with disabled spectators' arrival at the stadium entrance, continuing through most of the stages noted above, and ending with the provisions that must be made for emergency exit. The sections below follow a similar sequence.

10.3.2 ADVANCE INFORMATION

Disabled people are even more reliant than able-bodied spectators on good information about a forthcoming event – good in the sense of both (a) what information is provided, and (b) the form in which it is made available.

As an example of (a): people with impaired mobility (most importantly, but not only, wheelchair users) must be confident that their journey to the venue, and the venue itself, will be obstacle-free, and that they will have ready access to a toilet when necessary. If they cannot be sure of these things, then they dare not risk setting out on the journey.

As an example of (b): people whose eyesight is so poor that they cannot read small or normal-sized print may need their information in large print or in audio form.

For stadia in the UK, the checklist on pages 72 and 73 of *Accessible Stadia* (see Bibliography) will help event organisers deal with the above matters.

121

For stadia in the USA, there is no readily available nationally recognised guidance on these particular matters.

10.3.3   ARRIVING AT THE STADIUM

The routes from rail stations, bus stops, and coach drop-off points to the stadium entrance should have firm and smooth (but anti-slip) surfaces such as asphalt, concrete, evenly laid pavings, or resin-bound gravel. Loose gravel or earth is not acceptable. Kerbs at road crossings should be flush with the carriageway so that wheelchair users are not obstructed.

For stadia in the UK, modified coaches carrying disabled spectators should be able to drop off their passengers less than 50m from the stadium entrance. The route from drop-off point to entrance should preferably be under cover.

For stadia in the USA, Chapter 4 of *ADA and ABA: Accessibility Guidelines for Buildings and Facilities* (see Bibliography) provides guidelines on accessible routes, and Chapter 5 deals with parking spaces and related matters.

CAR PARKING

For stadia in the UK, paragraph 4.1.2.3 of British Standard *BS 8300* (see Bibliography) states that, in addition to a designated space for each employee who is a disabled car driver, six per cent of total car parking capacity at recreation and leisure facilities should be allocated to disabled people. But it adds that this number may need to be increased in sports stadia that 'specialise in accommodating groups of disabled people'. At all stadia, the parking bays designated for disabled people should be provided as close as is feasible to the principal entrance, and the routes from car park to stadium entrance should conform with the criteria for safe and easy usage noted above.

For stadia in the USA, Chapter 5 of *ADA and ABA: Accessibility Guidelines for Buildings and Facilities* (see Bibliography) deals with parking spaces, passenger loading zones, and related matters.

ACCESS ROUTES

In Britain, access routes to and around stadia should have a clear width of at least 1.8m if there is intensive use by spectators in both directions, and 1.5m (with 1.8m-wide passing places at intervals) if routes are less busy. Surfaces should be as noted above.

Walkway gradients steeper than 1:20 should be designed as ramps, with handrails, kerbs and level landings at regular intervals as resting places. If the overall rise of the ramp is greater than 300mm then steps should be provided in addition.

There should be excellent signage all the way from the stadium gate to each individual seat – see Section 10.3.11 below.

For stadia in the UK, paragraphs 2.1–2.3 and the checklist on page 73 of *Accessible Stadia* should be consulted on all the above matters.

For stadia in the USA, Chapter 4 of *ADA and ABA: Accessibility Guidelines for Buildings and Facilities* (see Bibliography) provides guidelines on accessible routes; and Chapter 7 deals with signs.

10.3.4   BUYING A TICKET

The ticket office should have an induction loop for people who are hard of hearing, and a section of the counter should be lowered to 760mm for wheelchair users. This section should have a knee space beneath that is at least 500mm deep and 1,500mm wide, with a clear height of at least 700mm to the underside of the counter.

For stadia in the UK, Section 11.1 of British Standard *BS 8300* gives detailed design recommendations on the design of counters and reception desks in general.

For stadia in the USA, Chapter 9 of *ADA and ABA: Accessibility Guidelines for Buildings and Facilities* (see Bibliography) provides guidelines on the design of counters, and Chapter 7 deals with assistive listening systems.

10.3.5   PASSING THROUGH THE TURNSTILES

Disabled spectators should not enter the stadium via the main turnstiles, but should have separate entry gates specially designed and managed for their use. Preferably, these should be manned by a specially trained steward. One reason for providing special entrances for disabled people, apart from the fact that they themselves appear to prefer such an arrangement, is that this enables managers to accurately count in the wheelchair users. In the UK, this is a safety requirement, as explained in more detail in paragraphs 7.1–7.3 of *Guide to Safety at Sports Grounds* (see Bibliography).

In England and Wales, Table 2 of *Approved Document M* of the Building Regulations gives the minimum clear width of entrance doors to buildings used by the general public as 1,000mm.

For stadia in the UK, paragraphs 2.4–2.7 and the checklist on page 73 of *Accessible Stadia* should be consulted. See also Section 6 of *Guide to Safety at Sports Grounds*.

For stadia in the USA, Chapter 4 of *ADA and ABA: Accessibility Guidelines for Buildings and Facilities* (see Bibliography) provides guidelines on doors, doorways, and gates.

10.3.6   CIRCULATING WITHIN THE STADIUM

For stadia in the UK, horizontal routes for wheelchair users, such as concourses and corridors, should have a clear width of at least 1.8m. If intrusions by columns or ducts are unavoidable, these should always leave a clear corridor width of at least 1.0m. In England and Wales, Section 3 of *Approved Document M* of the Building Regulations governs all aspects of horizontal movement, and Section 8 of *Guide to Safety at Sports Grounds* makes specific recommendations for sports facilities.

Where there are stairway entrances, these should always have accompanying passenger lifts and/or ramps for spectators who cannot negotiate stairs. Design criteria for all of these will be set by national codes and building regulations. In England and Wales, Section 3 of *Approved Document M* of the Building Regulations governs all aspects of vertical movement, and Chapter 8 of *Guide to Safety at Sports Grounds* makes specific recommendations for stairs and ramps in sports facilities.

For stadia in the USA, Chapter 4 of *ADA and ABA: Accessibility Guidelines for Buildings and Facilities* provides guidelines on accessible routes, including ramps and lifts; and Chapter 5 deals with stairways and handrails.

10.3.7   VIEWING THE EVENT

All spectators, disabled and able-bodied alike, should have a good choice of viewing locations in various parts of the stadium. They should have comfortable seats (as explained in Section 12.7) and enjoy good sightlines (as explained in Section 11.4). Gone are the days when disabled spectators could be herded into ghetto-like enclosures, separated from their friends and the rest of the crowd, and unable to see over the heads of spectators who stood at exciting moments.

These matters are covered in greater detail in Chapter 11 and 12.

For stadia in the UK, paragraphs 2.13–2.25 and the checklist on pages 73–74 of *Accessible Stadia* should be consulted. See also Sections 12–14 of *Guide to Safety at Sports Grounds*.

For stadia in the USA, Chapter 8 of *ADA and ABA: Accessibility Guidelines for Buildings and Facilities* (see Bibliography) provides guidelines on wheelchair spaces, and gives detailed advice on sightlines for spectators in wheelchairs.

10.3.8   USING THE REFRESHMENT FACILITIES

Disabled people should find it just as easy as other spectators to enjoy the use of bars and restaurants, either alone or with their friends. Suitable facilities should be located as close as possible to viewing areas. Because disabled spectators may not be able to get to both toilets and refreshment facilities in the short breaks during matches, when circulation areas tend to be very crowded, it may be wise for clubs to provide them with a dedicated refreshment order service, performed by trained stewards or volunteers.

Bars and service counters (including self-service counters) should have one section lowered to a level of not more than 850mm above the floor for the use of wheelchair users. Such sections should have a knee space beneath with a clear height of at least 700mm to the underside of the counter.

For stadia in the UK, paragraphs 2.30–2.31 of *Accessible Stadia* should be consulted.

For stadia in the USA, Chapter 9 of *ADA and ABA: Accessibility Guidelines for Buildings and Facilities* (see Bibliography) provides guidelines on dining surfaces and counters.

123

10.3.9   USING THE TOILETS

Disabled people should be able to access toilets as easily as the able-bodied. Suitable toilets should be dispersed around the stadium, and no wheelchair user should need to travel a horizontal distance of more than 40m from his or her seat to the nearest suitable toilet.

Scales of provision and design details vary, and must be ascertained for the particular country in question. For details of toilet provision for disabled people in the UK and USA, see Chapter 16.

10.3.10   LEAVING THE STADIUM

Because spectators tend to arrive at sports venues in small groups over a period of time, but leave simultaneously, designing and managing for safe exit requires much greater care than designing for safe entry. This applies particularly to emergency exit, when tens of thousands of panic-stricken people may be rushing for the exits in disorderly fashion.

Disabled spectators, particularly those in wheelchairs, should be able to enter and leave as easily as others, and they are particularly vulnerable in the above conditions. This topic is too specialised to treat in depth here. However, seating areas designated for disabled spectators might have their own entry and exit routes in order to minimise conflict between disabled and able-bodied people during an emergency.

For stadia in the UK, paragraphs 2.35–2.44 of *Accessible Stadia* should be consulted. See also Sections 9 and 15 of the *Guide to Safety at Sports Grounds*.

For stadia in the USA, Chapter 4 of *ADA and ABA: Accessibility Guidelines for Buildings and Facilities* (see Bibliography) provides guidelines on accessible routes.

10.3.11   SIGNS

Disabled people are even more dependent than others upon good signage. A well-coordinated, consistent signage system should be used throughout the stadium, accompanied by audio information and tactile signs (such as raised lettering, numerals and symbols) to help those with poor eyesight.

THE UK

Section 10 of *Inclusive Mobility* (see Bibliography) gives comprehensive and detailed guidance on the size of letters and symbols, typefaces, colour contrast and positioning of visual signs. It also gives brief guidance on tactile signs and on audible information in public places.

THE USA

Chapter 7 of *ADA and ABA: Accessibility Guidelines for Buildings and Facilities* (see Bibliography) provides guidelines on signs and other information systems.

11

SPECTATOR VIEWING

11.1	**INTRODUCTION**
11.2	**GROUND CAPACITY**
11.3	**VIEWING DISTANCES**
11.4	**VIEWING ANGLES AND SIGHTLINES**
11.5	**OBSTRUCTIONS TO VIEWING**

11.1 INTRODUCTION

11.1.1 DESIGN AIMS

The design team's task is to provide seats or standing places for the number of spectators required by the brief, and to do so in such a way that the spectators (including wheelchair users and other disabled people) have a clear view of the event, and are comfortable and safe. This chapter outlines all the viewing design factors.

11.1.2 SEQUENCE OF DECISIONS

The starting point for design is the size and orientation of the playing field. Both of these are dictated by the sports played there. See Chapter 3 for pitch orientation and Chapter 7 for pitch dimensions.

Next, a notional envelope can be drawn for the spectator areas surrounding the pitch. The inner edge will be as close to the pitch as possible, allowing for a safety barrier as described in Chapter 9, while the outer edges will be determined by:

- The required spectator capacity (Section 11.2).
- The maximum acceptable distance from the pitch to the furthest seats (Section 11.3.1), and the preferred viewing locations for that particular sport (Section 11.3.3).

Finally, this schematic plan must be converted to a fully developed three-dimensional stadium design which provides good viewing angles and sightlines (Section 11.4.2), has safety limits on the steepness of rake (Section 11.4.3), and features no unacceptable barriers such as roof supports that interfere with the view (Section 11.5).

11.2 GROUND CAPACITY

11.2.1 THE NEED FOR REALISM

The most important decision in planning a new stadium, or expanding an existing one, is the number of spectators to be accommodated.

ANZ Stadium Sydney (formerly Stadium Australia) during the 2000 Olympic Games. Architects Populous with Bligh Voller Nield

When developing a building brief, the design team and client organisation often over-estimate this figure. Natural optimism plays a part in this. Sporting clubs always believe their attendance is about to increase dramatically, even though statistical evidence may show that it has been stable for years or is even dropping. Stadium owners like to believe that if only they had a bigger venue, then more people would attend, even though many seats in their existing smaller stadium remain unfilled. And consultants may find it more exciting to get involved in big plans than small ones, which tends to encourage expansive thinking.

There are circumstances in which an attractive, well-planned new facility may attract more spectators. For instance, the club may be able to increase its gate through an organised recruitment campaign or, in the case of European soccer, if it gains promotion in the league system. Also, the fact that a new stadium is comfortable, safe and well designed may in itself attract more spectators. But experience shows that, after the novelty of a new stadium has worn off, attendance tends to revert to earlier figures, unless the new crowd can be enticed to stay through marketing or the team's improved performance.

It is therefore a golden rule never to increase stadium capacity beyond that which is known to be necessary, and which is affordable in both capital cost and running cost. The factors in a preliminary estimation of ground capacity are the following:

- The sport(s) and other activities to be accommodated.
- The size of the catchment area surrounding the development.
- The aspirations of sponsors, public institutions and owners.
- The past history of the site or sports club.
- Practical site limitations.

This decision on capacity can only be provisional. It may not be possible to provide the desired number of seats while maintaining view quality, sheltering spectators, or fitting the stadium successfully onto its site and into its surroundings. The implications of seating numbers must be carefully checked against considerations such as:

- The quality of view and distance from the action.
- The type of roof possible, and therefore the extent of shelter.
- The internal and external aesthetics of the stadium.
- The cost of the structure and support facilities, and the running costs.
- Safety management and staffing on event and non-event days.
- The extent and range of viable support facilities.

11.2.2   OFFICIAL REQUIREMENTS

A minimum seating capacity, including a more detailed breakdown into the following categories, may be set by the types of events to be held at the venue.

- A minimum overall capacity.
- The proportion of viewing spaces allocated to officials, VIPs and directors.
- The proportion of viewing spaces allocated to (a) wheelchair users and (b) ambulant disabled spectators.
- The proportion of standing places to seats.

In some cases the governing bodies will lay down standards in one or more of the above categories. These must be met if certain types of matches are to be played there.

PROVISION FOR GENERAL SPECTATORS, OFFICIALS, VIPS AND DIRECTORS

The recommended seating capacities for various types of sports are constantly being revised, and designers should contact the relevant governing bodies for latest information. The allowable proportion of standing places should particularly be checked since most of these are being phased out.

PROVISION FOR WHEELCHAIR USERS

In the UK, Table 4 of the *Guide to Safety at Sports Grounds* and paragraph 2.13 of *Accessible Stadia* (see Bibliography) recommend that spaces should be provided for the numbers of wheelchair users shown below; and Table 3 of *Approved Document M* of the Building Regulations (see Bibliography) recommends a small number of additional removable seats.

These very general figures should be tested by consultation with local disabled groups.

Total seated capacity	Number of wheelchair spaces
Under 10,000	At least 6, or 1 in 100 of seated capacity, whichever is greater.
10,000 to 20,000	100 plus 5 per 1,000 above 10,000
20,000 to 40,000	150 plus 3 per 1,000 above 20,000
40,000 or more	210 plus 2 per 1,000 above 40,000

As regards location, the reference *Accessible Stadia* (see Bibliography) makes several recommendations which include the following.

- Areas for disabled spectators should, where possible, be dispersed throughout the stadium to provide a range of locations at various levels and various prices. We would, however, emphasise that for practical and safety management reasons it will normally be necessary to retain some grouping of wheelchair-using spectators.
- Viewing areas should be accessible to disabled spectators with the minimum of assistance.
- Designated viewing areas should be provided for both home and away supporters. Many supporters with disabilities are isolated and intimidated when situated among, or close to, able-bodied supporters of the opposing team.
- Spectators who use wheelchairs should not feel cut off from spectators in the main body of the stand.
- Access should be available to different areas of a seating deck for semi-ambulant and ambulant disabled people.
- Smaller groups of disabled spectators dispersed throughout a stand are a more manageable proposition for safe evacuation than larger groups.

Paragraph 2.15 of *Accessible Stadia* recommends that each designated wheelchair space should measure at least 1.4m x 1.4m, so as to allow a helper to sit alongside the wheelchair user.

PROVISION FOR AMBULANT DISABLED SPECTATORS

There will normally be many more ambulant disabled spectators than ones in wheelchairs but, as of 2006, there are in the UK no specific recommendations on the number of spaces to be provided. Paragraph 2.16 of *Accessible Stadia* states vaguely that the above table of recommendations for wheelchair users 'should be used to determine the minimum proportion of seated accommodation for ambulant disabled spectators in the whole stadium' but gives no indication of the ratio that might be applied. Again, the scale of provision should be tested by consulting with local disabled groups.

As regards location, paragraph 2.16 makes the following recommendations:

- Seats intended for ambulant disabled people should be dispersed throughout the stadium, and should be specifically identified by management.
- Because ambulant disabled people move with difficulty, such identified seats might best be located at the ends of rows, and close to exits.
- Some of these seats should be situated where there are few steps to negotiate, and where the seating rake is not more than 20 degrees.
- In some cases, an entire row of seats, appropriately located, could be designed to a higher standard of comfort for disabled spectators, as suggested in Section 12.7.
- In all of the above, bear in mind that ambulant disabled spectators may prefer not to sit in areas primarily intended for wheelchair users and their helpers.

STANDING ACCOMMODATION VERSUS SEATS

The question of seating versus standing accommodation has been so hotly debated, particularly for soccer matches in the UK, that a few comments are needed.

In theory, it is possible to accommodate around two spectators per square metre seated compared to around four per square metre standing. Or, if the minimum dimensions for seating given in the *Guide to Safety at Sports Grounds* (see Bibliography) is followed, about 3.1 spectators per square metre seated, versus a maximum of 4.7 standing, giving a ratio of approximately 2:3.

129

These figures make standing room seem economically attractive. In fact, this advantage is diminishing, because many amenities must be substantially increased for standing spectators. Once the additional numbers of toilets and catering outlets, and the increased circulation, escape and safety barrier space are taken into account, the cost per person may actually be greater for standing accommodation than for seated.

Leaving economics aside, the decision will be influenced by two main factors: customer expectation and legal requirements. In some sports, spectators prefer to stand. Many sports fans are convinced that standing together on the terraces is essential to the spirit of watching the game. In horse racing, it is traditional for over two-thirds of spectators to stand, and wander around, rather than sit on tiered seats. Establishing what kind of spectator will patronise a given stadium (in terms of socio-economic group and other relevant characteristics) is crucial to getting the whole philosophy of comfort, shelter and seat price right for that stadium. No design should go forward until these matters have been fully clarified.

As regards the law, most authorities believe that the greater the proportion of seated spectators, the less likely there will be crowd problems, hence the trend for more seated stadia. British soccer authorities decreed that existing soccer stadia in the Premier League and the Championship should be converted to all-seater stadia over a specified period during the 1990s, and that no standing terraces should be provided in new stadia for these senior divisions. FIFA and UEFA regulations allow for no standing places in new stadia for national or international matches.

If standing accommodation is designed for, there's a risk that it may later need to be converted to seating, should a soccer team secure promotion to a higher division, for instance, or when governing bodies demand all-seating stadia. In Britain, the Football Licensing Authority believes seating accommodation is an inherently safer option than standing, and recommends that new standing accommodation should always be constructed so that it's easily converted to seating.

One way out of this dilemma is to have a certain proportion of convertible areas. In Germany, for instance, it is quite common for stadia to be temporarily converted to all-seating for certain matches. While it is technically feasible to design convertible stands, it increases the capital cost.

One event where standing spectators are still being tolerated on a large scale is at concerts given in stadia, where the actual playing area is often used for spectators to sit or stand. Fans find their own way and decide where to stand, many believing that this spontaneity is essential to the atmosphere of such events. This system is called festival seating in the USA, but it is regarded by the authorities as unacceptable and dangerous because of the lack of control the organisers have over the positioning of the crowd. European practice is beginning to change and several countries now require the playing area to have securely fixed seats in place for a pop concert. The covering of the pitch in these circumstances is discussed in Chapter 7.

In conclusion, the authors believe that instances remain where well-designed standing terraces are acceptable – especially in horse racing and British soccer – but they accept that trends worldwide are undeniably towards all-seater stadia, mainly because spectators expect greater comfort.

If standing areas are provided, then equality laws such as the UK's Disability Discrimination Act 1995 may well insist that disabled spectators are entitled to gain access to those areas. In the UK, this principle is accepted, but as of 2006 there are no specific recommendations on the provision that should be made. For such guidance as does exist, refer to paragraph 2.23 of *Accessible Stadia* (see Bibliography).

11.2.3 CATCHMENT AREA AND PAST HISTORY OF THE SITE

In addition to the theoretical numbers laid down by regulation, as in Table 11.1, it is essential to look at the reality of the site itself. While FIFA might require a capacity of, say, 30,000 for certain soccer matches, an analysis of the potential catchment area and past attendances may show this is highly unlikely. Realism must prevail.

Cost Category	Stadium Capacity	Typical Seating configuration	Typical forms of structure, modes of access, etc.
Low	Up to 10,000	10 to 15 rows in a single tier	Structure possibly ground bearing. Access direct from front of seating tier or from short stairs/ramp at rear. Support facilities beneath. Roof cantilever only about 10m, using light steel or concrete sections.
Medium	10,000 to 20,000	15 to 20 rows in a single tier	
High	20,000 to 50,000	Up to 50 rows total, disposed in 2 tiers	
Very High	30,000 to 50,000	Over 50 rows in total, in 3 or 4 tiers. 3rd or 4th tiers are usually introduced to overcome site restrictions, or to accommodate a plethora of VIP boxes and similar facilities, and not for increased capacity.	

Table 11.1   Typical cost categories in stadium construction

131

11.2.4 COST CATEGORIES OF STADIUM CONSTRUCTION

Stadium capacity may be limited by the required cost of construction. The relationship between construction costs and seating capacities tends to fall into definite categories. If capacity can be kept below the next threshold, and an additional tier and/or structural complication avoided, it may be possible to avoid a disproportionate leap in costs. Table 11.1 notionally summarises four major categories of this kind (see also Chapter 23).

There are exceptions to this classification of seating capacities and costs. For instance, the Aztec stadium, in Mexico, accommodates over 100,000 spectators on a single tier of seats surrounding the pitch; and the McMahon stadium at the University of Calgary, in Alberta, in Canada, accommodates over 38,000 people in two single-tier stands situated only on the sides of the pitch. Because they avoid second or third tiers, both of these stadia undoubtedly have lower relative costs than one would expect, but at the expense of long viewing distances.

11.2.5 STAGED EXPANSION

Once a minimum and a maximum number of seats for a particular stadium have been established, the client may opt for a modest initial facility which can grow with the club.

In the case of an open stadium, staged expansion is relatively simple. It becomes very difficult if the final stadium is to be entirely roofed (or domed, in American terminology). The problem is not the design or construction of the final phase, but the fact that if the initial stages are too modest, the cost of future additions may be prohibitive.

British roofed stadia which have been constructed in a phased manner include Twickenham Rugby Football Ground, in west London, Murrayfield rugby stadium, in Edinburgh, and the Galpharm stadium, in Huddersfield.

11.2.6 EXTENT OF ROOF

Roofing is expensive and has a significant impact on the aesthetic impact of a stadium, but a percentage of roofed area is essential for spectator comfort in most climates. In some localities the roof must provide shelter against the sun, in others against rain, snow and perhaps wind.

For each stadium, a careful investigation must be made into the sports to be played, the seasons and time of day they may be staged, and the local climate. See Sections 3.2 and 5.8. There may also be official regulations requiring a certain proportion of seats under cover. The latest rules should be checked with the relevant governing bodies.

In practice, the seating sections of all new stadia currently being built in Britain and northern Europe are roofed, while the standing terraces are occasionally left open. It is only in mild climates, such as parts of Australia and the USA, that new stadia are being built with uncovered seats.

11.3   VIEWING DISTANCES

11.3.1   OPTIMUM VIEWING DISTANCE

Calculation of maximum viewing distance is based on the fact that the human eye finds it difficult to perceive anything clearly that subtends an angle of less than about 0.4 degrees – particularly if the object is moving rapidly. In the case of a rugby ball, which is approximately 250mm in diameter, or a soccer ball, the calculation sets the preferred viewing distance at no more than 150m between the extreme corner of the field and spectator's eye, with an absolute maximum of 190m. In the case of a tennis ball, which is only 75mm in diameter, the preferred maximum distance reduces to around 30m. Some guidance on viewing distances for various sports is given in *BS EN 13200 2003 Spectator facilities – Part 1: Layout criteria for spectator viewing area – specification* (see the Bibliography).

Setting out these distances from the extreme viewing positions, such as the diagonally opposed corners of a playing field, gives a preferred viewing zone. Their average configuration suggests a circle struck from the centre spot on the field, generally referred to as the optimum viewing circle. This circle, in the case of soccer and rugby, would have a radius of 90m. See Figure 11.1 for other sports.

11.3.2   PRACTICAL LIMITATIONS

The simple circular plan areas developed above are only a starting point for laying out the viewing terraces and must be modified in several ways.

Firstly, it must be admitted that some sports (such as field hockey and cricket) are played with a small-diameter ball on a field so large that the size of the field makes it impossible to locate spectators within the theoretical viewing distance. In these cases one must face the fact that viewers will have to watch the players rather than the ball.

Secondly, in a large stadium the spectators are not sitting at ground level but are raised above the ground by as much as 20m or 30m. In big stadia the effect of this elevation must be taken into account by calculating the direct distances from the elevated spectators to the centre of the field.

Thirdly, spectators have preferred viewing locations for each particular sport, so that seats in some areas of the optimum viewing circle would be less satisfactory than others at the same distance from the game. This is discussed in the next section.

11.3.3   PREFERRED VIEWING LOCATIONS

It is not always self-evident where viewers like to sit for particular sports. In the case of soccer, conventional wisdom holds that the best seats are on the long sides of the field which give a good view of the ebb and flow of the game between the two opposing goalposts. But there is also a tradition for highly motivated team supporters to view the game from the short ends, behind the goal posts, where they get a good view of the side movements and line openings which present themselves to the opposing teams. To designers who do not understand these traditions it may seem ludicrous that a soccer supporter insists on watching from behind the netting of the goalposts in crowded conditions when there is ample space available on the long sides. But such preferences exist, and the design team must identify them for the stadium under consideration, and suitably modify the optimum viewing circle to locate the maximum density of spectators in their preferred positions.

Figure 11.2 shows preferred viewing positions for various sports; and Figures 11.3 to 11.9 analyse some well-known existing stadia.

Figure 11.1

Relationship between playing field, optimum and maximum viewing distances and a deduced optimum viewing circle. (a) For soccer and rugby, the optimum viewing circle would have a radius of 90m from the centre spot. (b) Dimensions for lawn tennis viewing. (c) Separate stands – leaving the potential seating space at the corners unexploited – have traditionally been common. (d) This arrangement brings more spectators within the optimum viewing circle and offers the possibility of a more attractive stadium design (see Section 5.2.5 of this book). (e) A variation of (c) with the seating areas extending to the limit of the optimum viewing circle, but not beyond it. This type of layout gives an excellent spectator/player relationship. (f) A variation of (d) with only the seating area to the west of the playing field extended back to the limit of the optimum viewing circle. With this layout, the majority of spectators have their backs to the sun during an afternoon game.

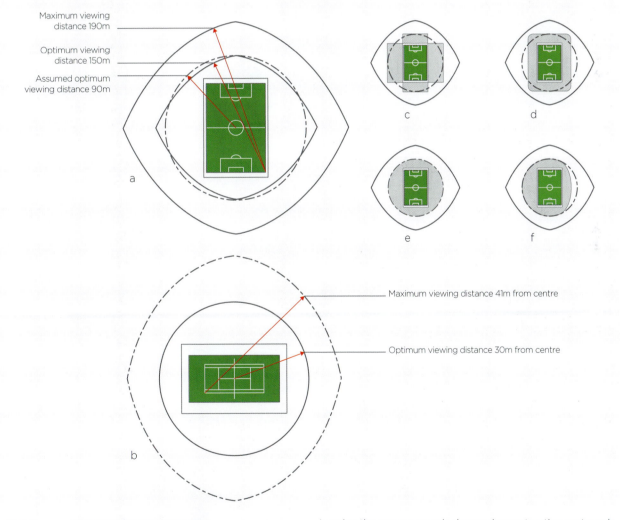

11.3.4   EXPLOITING THE CORNERS

A decision must be made whether to place four rectangular stands on the four sides of the field with open corners (Figure 11.1c) or whether to surround the pitch with a continuous bowl stadium (Figure 11.1d).

Leaving the corners open is cheaper in construction costs and may in some cases benefit a natural grass pitch by promoting better circulation of air and quicker drying of the grass. But it also sacrifices valuable viewing space, and the trend is towards fully exploiting the area within the maximum viewing

Figure 11.2
Preferred viewing positions for some major sports. (a) Soccer; (b) American football; (c) rugby league; (d) lawn tennis; (e) baseball; (f) Australian Rules football.

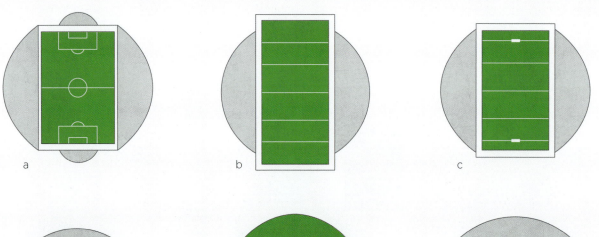

a   b   c

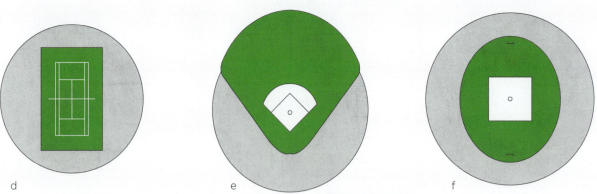

d   e   f

Figure 11.3
Wembley Stadium, London (see Case studies). The new stadium with 90,000 capacity for soccer or rugby, and the ability to include an athletics track, has a few seats outside the maximum viewing distance line.

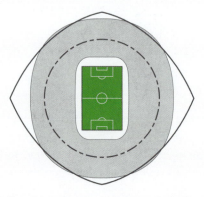

Figure 11.4

Aztec Stadium, Mexico City, built in 1966 exclusively for soccer. The layout is of the type shown in Figure 11.1d but far too large for satisfactory viewing since most of the 105,000 seats on the single-tier terrace are outside the optimum viewing circle and very many are beyond the maximum viewing distance.

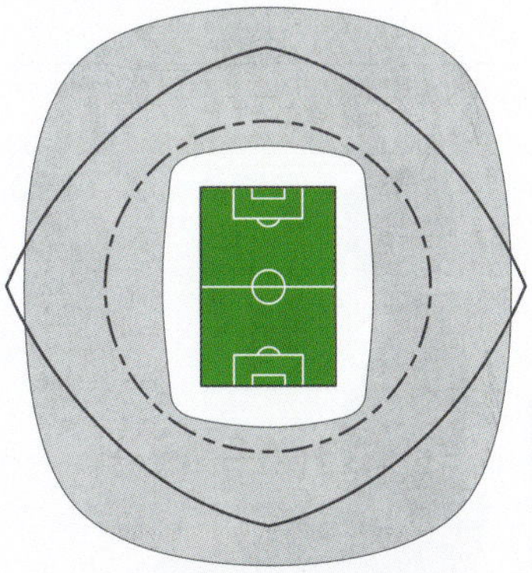

Figure 11.6

The Olympic Stadium built for the 1972 Olympics, in Munich, and designed primarily for athletic events. The seating geometry is closer to a circle than those above, and is asymmetrical to accommodate most of the 80,000 spectators to the south of the playing field. The arena is so large that virtually all spectators are pushed beyond the optimum viewing circle, but the outer perimeter of the seating areas is kept mostly within the maximum viewing distance. The depth of seating is at a maximum along the sprint lines and finish line.

135

Figure 11.5

The Millennium Stadium, Cardiff. With three tiers and a capacity for rugby of approximately 72,000, all spectators are inside the maximum viewing distance line.

Figure 11.7

A completely circular stadium in the District of Columbia, USA, for American football and baseball. Spectator distances for football are acceptable but those for baseball too great, demonstrating the difficulty of providing for both sports in the same facility.

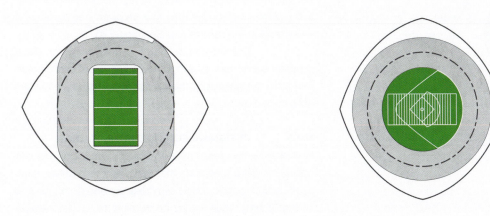

12

SPECTATOR SEATING

12.1   **BASIC DECISIONS**

12.2   **SEAT TYPES**

12.3   **SEAT MATERIALS, FINISHES AND COLOURS**

12.4   **CHOICE**

12.5   **DIMENSIONS**

12.6   **SEAT FIXINGS**

12.7   **SEATING FOR SPECTATORS WITH DISABILITIES**

12.1   BASIC DECISIONS

The next design task is the seats themselves. Seating design is a matter of reconciling four major factors: comfort, safety, robustness and economy.

12.1.1   COMFORT

The degree of comfort required depends partly on the seating time for that particular sport, as shown in Table 12.1. The longer the spectator must sit in one position, the more comfortable the seats must be. Comfort costs money, but it also helps attract the customers without whose support the stadium cannot succeed. No easy rules can be given for the trade-off between comfort and cost, except to say that the worldwide trend is towards higher comfort rather than lower cost.

12.1.2   SAFETY

From the viewpoint of crowd behaviour, there are opposing arguments concerning the safety of seating types.

The common view is that tip-up seats make for greatest safety because they provide a wider passage (Figure 12.3) than other types, thus making it easier for the public, police, stewards or first-aid personnel to pass along the rows during an emergency. Against this, some critics argue that bench (i.e. backless) seats are safer because spectators can step over them during an emergency, but this argument seems lost.

Seats with backs provide greater comfort and are generally the norm in modern stadia. But in view of the preceding comments, design teams should investigate carefully the kinds of events and the types of crowds involved before finally deciding on seat types.

For fire safety (i.e. the combustibility of the seat material), see Section 12.3.3 overleaf.

Aviva Stadium Dublin designed for rugby, football and concerts.
Architects: Populous and Scott Tallon Walker

Event	Seating time
American football	3 to 4 hours
Athletics	3 to 5 hours; sometimes all day (e.g. Olympic events)
Australian Rules football	1.5 to 2 hours
Baseball	3 to 4 hours
Cricket	8 hours a day, perhaps for several days in a row
Football	1.5 to 2 hours
Gaelic football	2 hours
Lawn tennis	2 to 3 hours
Pop concerts	3 hours or more
Rugby	1.5 to 2 hours
Rugby 7-a-side	8 hours

Table 12.1   Seating times for various types of events

12.1.3   ROBUSTNESS

Two principal questions will help decide how robust seats need to be:

- Are the spectators in the particular stadium likely to behave destructively? For example, will they stand on seats, climb on them, or rest their feet against them?
- Will the seats be under cover and protected from sun and rain? Will they be regularly maintained and cleaned?

A careful evaluation of these factors will influence choice of seat, frame and fixings, as described later in this chapter.

12.1.4   ECONOMY

The very cheapest seating type, usually wood or aluminium slats on a concrete plinth, will seldom be acceptable in major new stadia (Figure 12.1). Apart from the fact that spectators are unwilling to sit on such an uncomfortable surface for any

length of time, this primitive arrangement will probably be unacceptable to regulators.

So the cheapest realistic option will be moulded metal or plastic multiple seats fixed directly onto the concrete terraces. The most expensive will be upholstered tip-up seats with arm-rests.

12.2   SEAT TYPES

The following examination starts at the cheapest end of the market and describes the various types of seat in rising order of cost and comfort.

12.2.1   BENCH SEATS

Modern bench seats consist of lengths of moulded metal or plastic with individual seat indents, and are usually fixed to the concrete terrace by means of a metal under-frame to give the correct height. They are cheap and robust and take up less space than any other kind. (The minimum seating row depth recommended by the British Association of Spectator Equipment Suppliers (BASES) is 700mm, but see also Table 12.2.) However, these seats are not comfortable and should be used only in the cheapest admission areas, if at all. If they are used, corrosion and decay prevention must be very carefully considered.

BS EN 13200-2003 Spectator facilities – Part 1: Layout criteria for spectator viewing area – specification (see Bibliography) suggests a minimum seating row depth of 700mm and a recommended seating row depth of 800mm.

12.2.2   ONE-PIECE SEATS WITHOUT BACKS

These are much like the type above, but supplied as individual seats. They are also known as tractor seats.

12.2.3   BUCKET SEATS WITH BACKS

These are generally similar to tractor seats, sharing the advantages of low cost and easy cleaning, but they are more comfortable. However, they have the disadvantage of requiring much more space than any other seat type except for fixed seats with backs. Minimum seating row depth is recommended by BASES at 900mm, compared with 700mm for bench or backless seats, and 760mm for tip-

Figure 12.1
There are many seating variations but the plastic tip-up type, either riser-fixed or tread-fixed, is the most common.

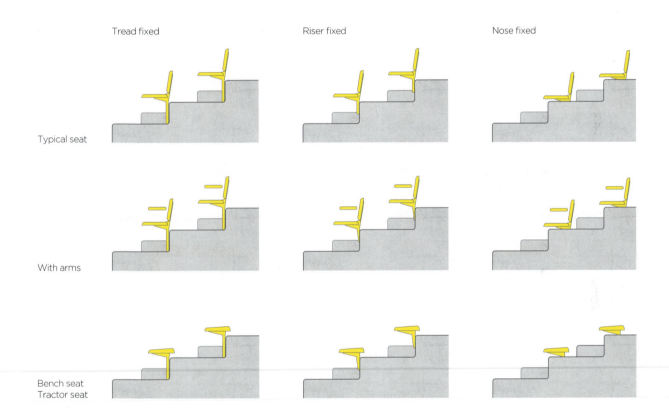

Tread fixed   Riser fixed   Nose fixed

Typical seat

With arms

Bench seat
Tractor seat

up seats. (These figures should be read in conjunction with Table 12.2.)

12.2.4   TIP-UP SEATS

These cost more than any of the above types, and are less robust, but they are rapidly becoming the most widely-used seating type in stadia. They are comfortable, and even if non-upholstered when first installed, they can be upgraded later. Tipping up the seat allows easy passage for spectators, police, stewards or first-aid assistants, making for greater safety. It is also easier to clean around and beneath the seat.

It is recommended that the seat should be counterweighted (or perhaps sprung) to tip up automatically when not in use; and that moving parts should not have metal-to-metal contact, so that the pivoting action is not degraded by corrosion.

Minimum seat width in paragraph 11.11 of the *Guide to Safety at Sports Grounds* (see Bibliography), also known as the *Green Guide*, is 460mm without arms, or 500mm with arms. However, for comfort and accessibility, the guide recommends a minimum width of 500mm for all seats. The present authors believe that 465mm is a

PRIVATE VIEWING FACILITIES

13.1   **INTRODUCTION**

13.2   **TRENDS**

13.3   **DESIGN**

13.4   **MULTI-USE**

13.1   INTRODUCTION

Whether private viewing facilities are required, and on what scale, is an aspect of the brief that must be carefully thought out for each stadium. These areas often subsidise the seat prices elsewhere in the stadium. The underlying principle is to offer different facilities and prices in order to cater for as many market segments as possible, as explained below.

13.1.1   RANGE OF SEATING STANDARDS

Demand for superior standards of comfort and refreshment facilities, and the willingness or ability to pay for these benefits, varies from person to person. A successful stadium will positively exploit these differences by providing the widest feasible range of seating quality (in terms of viewing position and seat comfort), an equally wide range of catering and other support facilities, and a choice of prices geared to what individual customers are prepared to pay.

Table 13.1 lists ten basic categories of seating and standing accommodation in descending order of luxury and price. These are not the only possibilities; other variations such as upper and lower tier, or front and rear positioning, are also possible. The third column of the table indicates the approximate percentage of spectators who may be expected to fall into each category, the basis on which tickets are likely to be sold, and the probable space standards. All of this data is indicative only.

13.1.2   PRIVATE FACILITIES

If Andy Warhol was right in suggesting that everyone nowadays is famous for 15 minutes, then it follows that we will all require VIP facilities at some stage in our lives. However, for an increasing number of people, these high standards of facilities will become a normal expectation. Whatever the validity of this theory, private viewing accommodation will be needed in virtually all future stadium developments which need to be financially self-supporting. As sporting events must compete more intensively

The club level at the Emirates stadium London. The dining rooms offer high-quality dining for club spectators on match days and are used for conferences, dinners and other events on non-match days. Architects: Populous

158

1	Private boxes	Self-contained private dining and bar facilities	10 to 20 person boxes 1–2% spectators 3 year contract Tread 850mm padded and arms
2	Executive suites	Group private dining and shared bar	4–20 person suites 1–2% spectators 1–3 year contract Tread 850mm padded and arms
3	Club seating and dining	Group seating and group with shared bar and lounge	Tables of 2–6 in restaurant dining 1–2% spectators 1–3 year contract Tread 800mm padded and arms
4	Club seating	Group seating with shared bar and lounge facilities	Lounge self-contained 2–4% spectators 1–3 year contract Tread 800mm padded and arms
5	Members' seating and dining	Group seating with shared dining bar facilities	Dining and bar self-contained 1–2% spectators season ticket plus dining Tread 760mm with arm rests
6	Members' seating	Group seating with shared bar facilities	Bar part of 5 above 2–5% spectators season ticket plus Tread 760mm with arm rests
7	Public seating (several standards)	Seating with public bars and concession areas	Wide range of concessions 50% spectators match or season ticket Tread 760mm with backs
8	General seating	Bench seating with public bars and concession areas	Range of concessions 5–15% spectators match or season ticket Tread 700mm no backs
9	Tennis boxes	Groups of seats (say 8–12) in self-contained areas	Used in the Telstra Stadium Equipped with cool box and refreshments delivered
10	Standing terrace (some stadia)	Standing areas with public facilities (more stewarding might be needed)	Range of facilities 5–15% spectators match or season ticket Tread 380mm

Table 13.1   Range of viewing standards that might be provided in a stadium

PRIVATE VIEWING AND FACILITIES

with the many alternative leisure pursuits available, the provision of comfort instead of spartan simplicity becomes essential for a growing sector of the market, although it must also be said that stadium facilities and corporate standards are being enjoyed by a wider section of those attending. Also, these exclusive seats make a large contribution to stadium profitability. Individuals attending private boxes may pay many times the price of an average seat. They, or their hosts, are usually committed to spending handsomely on food and drink bought on stadium premises.

The income generated from such services is normally quite disproportionate to the cost of provision. Many new developments could not viably proceed without these more exclusive facilities. For some clubs they are essential to financial success. Many of the older stadia are therefore being retro-fitted to capture new markets and maximise revenues in this way.

Because private and club facilities can be exploited for a variety of social and other functions, a stadium containing such facilities is generally better suited to multi-purpose uses than a stadium without. To allow for this, these facilities should always be designed for flexible use and adaptation.

In these areas, quality and the appearance of quality will be important. Dimmable lighting and well-designed furniture are good examples. Branding by corporate clients may be needed. Allowing guests to roam between various boxes, suites and club enclosures can be desirable, but this is a management decision. Security and control must be taken into account.

13.2   TRENDS

13.2.1   NORTH AMERICA

In the USA, stadium managers work hard at maximising the number of VIP seats. They try equally hard to maximise the number of revenue-generating facilities added to these areas, thus enticing customers to spend as much time as possible on the premises before, during and after sporting events. In this way, managers hope to extract the maximum amount of money from their captive patrons.

Patrons with exclusive accommodation rights are encouraged to arrive well before the event and to use the stadium facilities for meals before or after matches, for entertaining business colleagues, and for doing business transactions by means of telephones, internet and computer facilities provided in a business centre in the VIP area. In the more advanced stadia, customers may spend most of the day enjoying themselves (and possibly doing some business) in the VIP area on match days, instead of merely attending for a few hours. The Cowboys Stadium near Dallas, Texas, is a good example of this (see Case studies).

13.2.2   THE UK

Stadium management in the UK is generally not as commercialised as in the USA, but all the trends outlined above are at work. The new Wembley Stadium, in London (see Case studies), is a leading example, as is Arsenal Football Club's Emirates Stadium (also in London) and the Galpharm soccer and rugby stadium in Huddersfield, in Yorkshire (designed by Populous). Here are some key features:

Galpharm Stadium, Huddersfield
- 25,000 spectator seats in total.
- 50 executive boxes.
- 400-seat banqueting hall.
- Bars, restaurants, shops and offices.
- 30-bay floodlit golf driving-range, and a dry ski-slope.
- Pop concert venue.
- 800 car parking spaces.
- Soccer and rugby museums.
- Crèche.
- Concessions.
- Indoor swimming pool, dance studio and gymnasium.

Wembley Stadium, London
- 90,000 spectator seats in total.
- Mid-tier seating for 14,400 club spectators.
- 160 boxes accommodating 1,918 people.
- Two pitch-view restaurants seating 154 people each.
- Hall that can seat 2,000 for dinners or conferences.
- Bobby Moore Club in the lower tier, with its own restaurant, seating 1,900.

14

CIRCULATION

14.1   BASIC PRINCIPLES
14.2   STADIUM LAYOUT
14.3   ACCESS BETWEEN ZONE 5 AND ZONE 4
14.4   ACCESS BETWEEN ZONE 4 AND ZONE 3
14.5   OVERALL DESIGN FOR INWARD MOVEMENT
14.6   OVERALL DESIGN FOR OUTWARD MOVEMENT
14.7   ELEMENTS
14.8   FACILITIES FOR PEOPLE WITH DISABILITIES

14.1   BASIC PRINCIPLES   167

When it comes to circulation planning in stadium design, the two main objectives are the comfort and safety of occupants.

COMFORT

Spectators should be able to find their way easily to their seats (or to toilets, refreshments or exits), without getting lost or confused. They should be able to move about leisurely. They shouldn't get jostled in overcrowded spaces, or have to climb excessively steep stairs, or risk losing their footing as they negotiate the inevitable changes of level in large stadia.

SAFETY

All the above are particularly important in panic conditions. For example, when hundreds (perhaps thousands) of spectators flee a fire, an outbreak of violence in the crowd, or some other real or imagined danger. Preventive measures should minimise the risk of such situations arising in the first place. Skilful stadium design will encourage people to go where they ought to go instead of forcing them to go there.

In the following sections we show how these requirements can be catered for in practical terms.

- Firstly, in Section 14.2, we examine the implications of circulation requirements upon stadium layout as a whole.
- Then, in Sections 14.3 and 14.4, we give planning guidelines for the circulation routes themselves.
- Finally, in Sections 14.5 to 14.7, we augment the above planning principles with detailed design data: dimensions, types of equipment etc.

Wembley Stadium London has escalators for general admission spectators to reach the upper tier.
Architects: Populous with Foster + Partners

14.2   STADIUM LAYOUT

Circulation planning has two major influences on the overall stadium layout: zoning the stadium for safe escape from fire, and subdividing the stadium for crowd management.

14.2.1   ZONING

As already described in Section 3.3, the modern stadium is designed as five concentric zones:

• Zone 1 is the playing field or activity area, and central area of the stadium.
• Zone 2 comprises the spectator viewing areas consisting of standing terraces, seating tiers, hospitality boxes and associated gangways and exits.
• Zone 3 is the internal circulation area: the concourses with food and drink kiosks, toilets and other facilities, all leading via gates or stairs to...
• Zone 4, which is the external circulation area surrounding the stadium building but within the perimeter fence.
• Zone 5 is the area outside the perimeter fence. It will contain the car parks and the bus and coach off-loading areas.

The purpose of the zones is to enable spectators to escape in case of emergency – first from Zone 2 to either Zones 1, 3 or 4 (the temporary safety zones); and from there to the permanent safety zones (Zone 4 or 5) and off the stadium property altogether. Such escape must be possible in specified times. These determine the distances and widths of the relevant escape routes. See Section 14.6.2.

In stadia accommodating more than 15,000 or 20,000 spectators, all five of the zones can be present. In smaller stadia, where spectators exit directly to the exterior from the spectator viewing and internal circulation areas, Zones 3 and 4 can be combined. Small stadia will not justify a perimeter fence but, to compensate for that, they will require particularly diligent stewarding at the exits.

14.2.2   SUBDIVISION

Subdividing the total ground capacity into smaller units or sectors of about 2,500 to 3,000 spectators allows for easier crowd control and for a more even distribution of

toilets, bars and restaurants. Each of these sectors should have independent circulation routes as well as a share of ancillary facilities. Spectators should be divided into different categories. For example:

• Seated and standing areas should be separate.
• Fans from opposing clubs should be segregated.

The division between areas can sometimes be achieved simply through barriers or level changes.

In the case of separating rival fans, each sector should be completely independent. This may require protected routes leading all the way from the transport services to the turnstiles (secured by police), and from the turnstiles to the seating areas.

Segregation will have an effect on circulation route plans, therefore management must be consulted at an early stage on how the seating areas in the stadium are to be split up.

In single-tier stands the division lines may run from top to bottom, with policed sterile zones separating the two blocks of home and away fans. This pattern is more flexible since the sterile zone can easily be shifted from side to side to allow for a greater or smaller number of fans in a particular area. However, the sterile zones mean a loss of revenue, and the problem of ensuring access to exits, toilets and catering facilities needs careful planning.

In two-tier stands the top-to-bottom division is again a possibility. Alternatively, one group of fans can be put in the upper tier and the other in the lower tier. If the away fans are in the upper tier there is no risk of pitch invasion, but there is a real possibility of missiles being hurled on to the home fans below; and any kind of trouble is difficult to deal with because of the relative inaccessibility of the upper levels. If the away fans are put in the lower tier, trouble is easier to deal with, but there is a risk of pitch invasion. More intensive policing and stewarding will be needed.

14.3   ACCESS BETWEEN ZONE 5 AND ZONE 4

Ideally, and if space allows, a modern stadium should be surrounded by an outer circulation zone 20m or more in width to allow spectators to walk around the outside to reach their seating area. The security control line where tickets are checked can be either at the face of the building, between Zones 3 and 4, or at the outside of the external circulation, between Zones 4 and 5. Where the control line is at the outside of the external circulation area (Zone 4), a perimeter wall or fence some distance from the stadium will be required.

Such a perimeter barrier should be at least 20m from the stadium, ideally strong enough to withstand crowd pressures, and high enough to prevent people climbing over. It should include several types of entrance and exit gates:

- Public entrances leading to the main seating terraces.
- Private entrances giving players, concession holders and VIP ticket holders separate access to their particular areas.
- Emergency service access for ambulances etc.
- Flood exits for emergency emptying of the grounds.

14.3.1   PUBLIC ENTRANCES

In some stadia, checking of tickets on entry is made at this perimeter point. In others it is made at the stadium entrances between Zones 4 and 3. Some stadia combine the two.

CIRCUMNAVIGATION BETWEEN GATES

If ticket control is exercised at the perimeter of the building, and if each entrance gives access only to some parts of the stadium (either by physical design, or by subsequent management policy), then circulation routes should be provided in Zone 4, outside the perimeter barrier. People who have come to the wrong entrance gate should be able to circumnavigate to the correct one while still remaining in the same zone. Conversely, if there is no control on seating positions at the perimeter then there is no need for such circulation routes since spectators can enter the stadium via any turnstile. These matters should be clarified with management at briefing stage if faulty design is to be avoided.

CONGREGATION SPACE OUTSIDE GATES

Outside all perimeter access points in Zone 5 or 4 there should be sufficient space for spectators to congregate before entering through gates or turnstiles. This congregation space

should be sized and positioned so as to avoid congestion and allow a free flow of spectators when the gates or turnstiles are opened. See also the notes on crowd control barriers under Section 14.7.1.

OTHER SAFETY MEASURES

In all cases, public entry doors should be used only for the purposes of entry, and all public exit doors only for the purposes of exit. The simultaneous use of any gateway for both entry and exit can create risk. If two-directional gates are used, they must be *additional* to the exit gates required for emergency outflow as calculated in Section 14.6.2 (timed exit analysis).

Amenities such as ticket offices, toilets, bars or restaurants should always be located a safe distance away from the nearest entrance or exit so there is no risk of a spectator crush.

NUMBER OF GATES

There are several ways to allow spectators into the stadium, but most fall into the two broad categories of gates and turnstiles. Gates are cheap, and an open gate of a metre's width can allow approximately 4,000 spectators through every hour. Turnstiles are expensive and will permit only 500 to 750 spectators every hour. Detailed design notes are given in Section 14.7.1.

LOCATION OF GATES

The location of entrance gates in the perimeter barrier will depend on three factors which may conflict with each other:

- To avoid congestion, entrances should be spaced at regular intervals around the circumference.
- If mutually hostile fans need to be kept apart, it is again desirable for entrances to be widely separated.
- But management may want entrances to be grouped closely together for convenience of staffing and security.

Any conflicts between the above requirements must be resolved with stadium management before design commences.

15

FOOD AND BEVERAGE CATERING

15.1	INTRODUCTION
15.2	AUTOMATIC VENDING MACHINES
15.3	CONCESSIONS
15.4	BARS
15.5	SELF-SERVICE CAFETERIAS, FOOD COURTS AND RESTAURANTS
15.6	LUXURY RESTAURANTS

183

15.1   INTRODUCTION

Attractive and efficient catering facilities will increase customer satisfaction and can also make a vital contribution to stadium profitability and spectator safety.

Spectators now expect to buy a reasonable quality and range of food and drink on the premises. The challenge to stadium owners and managers is to provide the widest possible range of eating and drinking facilities, from quick-serve outlets at one extreme to luxurious private dining rooms at the other. If they can coordinate the scale of provision, the locations, the quality of service and the price levels for all their customer types, then they stand to earn valuable additional revenue.

In general, the spend per head on food and beverage at an event is higher in the USA than elsewhere, partly, no doubt, because US spectators have more money to spend, but also because American stadia catering is higher in scale, quality and attractiveness. Other countries, including the UK, are beginning to follow the North American example.

A balance must be struck between the capital and running costs of extensive kitchen and serving facilities, and the return they generate in terms of direct sales.

15.1.1   MAXIMISING REVENUES

An obvious way to improve the revenue-to-cost ratio is to use catering facilities to the maximum once they have been installed. Wherever possible, these should be designed to cater not only for regular stadium spectators but also for receptions, banquets, dinners and other functions throughout the year. Restaurants ought to be open not only on match days, but on as many other occasions as customers can be encouraged on to the premises. Private box-holders should be encouraged to use their facilities not only during matches, but also for general social relaxation or corporate entertainment on event days and at other times, as discussed in Chapter 13.

If spectators are encouraged to make full use of restaurants and catering concessions, other aspects of stadium design and management need to be addressed.

A bar at the O2 arena London.
This bar is sponsored by
the telecoms company O2.
Architects: Populous

Spectators should be encouraged to arrive at the stadium early and stay late – a use pattern which would also ease the problems of crowd circulation and traffic movement.

In the UK and Australia, part of the problem lies in changing spectator traditions. Before a sports event, particularly soccer and rugby, spectators often visit a local pub. This results in late arrival at the stadium and an unnecessary crush, creating crowd control problems. (Indeed, pre-match drinking was one of the suggested contributory factors in the 1989 Hillsborough disaster, in Sheffield, in the UK.) In addition, having fans spend their money off the premises does nothing for stadium profitability.

Marketing and management can increase customer time at the stadium. For example, it's possible to stage warm-up events before the match, or show match highlights on a video screen afterwards.

But design, too, must play its part. There must be adequate circulation routes to seats, and treads of sufficient width to make spectators feel comfortable about carrying food and drink back to their seats without disturbing others. Accessories such as drinks holders in the seats, and

carrier bags, trays and frames for carrying several drinks also help increase sales.

Long-established habits will change only if people learn to expect a good standard of product and service, with an enticing range of food and beverage available. There should, within reason, be something for everyone: the customer who wants to enjoy a leisurely sit-down meal in prestige surroundings; the customer with less to spend who will be satisfied with a self-service cafeteria; and the customer in a hurry who wants a variety of fast-food or take-away outlets to choose from in a nearby concourse. It is important to realise that these categories no longer reflect the stratifications of society. The take-away kiosk may be patronised by high-price ticket holders who happen to be in a hurry; the sit-down restaurant by a less affluent family giving themselves a treat. All facilities should be available to everyone (Figure 15.1).

15.1.2   SHARING CAPITAL COSTS

It is now common for the stadium owner to enlist the support of an established catering organisation, thus sharing the

Figure 15.1
The trend in stadium design is away from fixed relationships between customer class and service type, towards freedom of choice between a wide range of services. The diagram shows the rich network of potential cross-connections that is desirable.

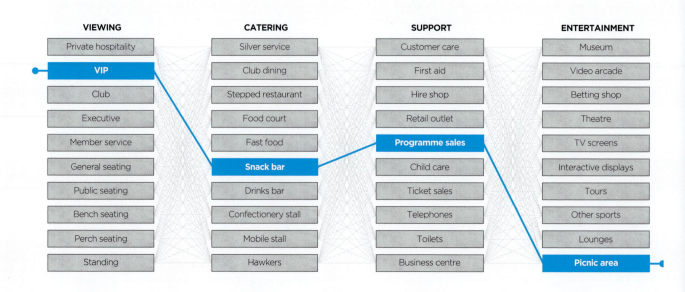

burden of capital costs, and bringing in extra marketing and managerial expertise. In turn, catering firms are starting to appreciate the opportunities at sporting venues where tens of thousands of people come to spend their day in an atmosphere of relaxed leisure. This is precisely the mood in which the public parts with its hard-earned money, and catering specialists know how to capitalise on this mood.

The viability of using a catering firm is directly related to the number of events held per annum. The fewer the events, the greater the attraction of using outside catering. (Once-a-year events, as described in Section 15.1.4 below, are an extreme example.) Conversely, the greater the number of events, the greater the opportunity for the stadium to set up its own internal catering operation using permanently employed staff.

LEASED CONCESSIONS

It is now common for a named franchise such as McDonald's or Burger King to take a concession space for the sale of its products. In larger stadia there may well be several independent franchise outlets in a single concourse.

Leased concessions can operate in several different ways. One arrangement is for the catering firm to finance the construction of certain catering outlets in a stadium in return for a period of exclusive sales at that venue. The stadium will usually take a percentage of the sales in this situation. Such a partnership needs careful control. From a design point of view, the caterer will understandably want to dictate much of the planning and layout of the stadium catering facilities as it affects their income. They will have essential knowledge on the provision of cabled and piped services to feed these areas. The stadium owners and management must heed these views, especially as the caterer might well invest millions as part of the arrangement. Yet it is essential the stadium owner remains in overall control of functional and aesthetic design matters, so as to keep the stadium looking consistent.

15.1.3 SELF-MANAGED OPERATIONS

Self-managed operations are owned and managed by the stadium administration, though usually operated by a

separate department to the one running the grounds. They can, in theory, include the same wide range of operations as specialist contractors but, in practice, are often limited to the large fixed catering facilities such as restaurants, bars and private boxes, leaving the fast-food sales to concession holders.

The advantage of a stadium operating its own catering organisation is that it may then have better control of revenue and customer service, with more power to vary the catering mix.

Rangers Football Club, in Glasgow, whose home is the Ibrox Stadium, is a British example of stadium owners managing all aspects of the catering operation themselves.

15.1.4 TEMPORARY CATERING FACILITIES

There are many examples of enormous catering operations undertaken with very little in the way of permanent infrastructure. Although this mobile method of catering is used throughout the world, the British seem to be particularly adept at it, probably because so few major sporting events in the UK possess adequate permanent facilities.

At the Silverstone Grand Prix, the total permanent catering facility consists of restaurants serving only 4,000 people, plus associated kitchens. On the day of the Grand Prix, however, thousands of hot meals are sold to the 185,000 spectators who attend over the three days. Around 95,000 people attend on the day of the final, with more than 12,000 hot sit-down meals served in the one and a half hours before the race. Around 95 per cent of these meals are served under canvas from temporary kitchens and dining areas set up inside tents and other temporary buildings.

Even more impressive are the figures for the Wimbledon Championships. Because of its two-week duration, it is the largest sporting catering organisation in the world. In addition to snacks and drinks, 1,500 catering staff serve 100,000 lunches in private marquees erected on the grounds. The amount of food and drink consumed during this brief period each year includes 12 tons of smoked salmon, 23 tons of strawberries, 190,000 sandwiches, 110,000 ice creams, 285,000 teas and coffees, 150,000 scones and buns, 12,500 bottles of Champagne and 90,000 pints of beer.

185

16

TOILET PROVISION

16.1	TOILET PROVISION GENERALLY
16.2	TOILETS FOR SPECTATORS
16.3	SCALE OF PROVISION FOR SPECTATOR TOILETS
16.4	LOCATION OF SPECTATOR TOILETS
16.5	DETAILED DESIGN

16.1   TOILET PROVISION GENERALLY

Toilets and washing facilities may be needed for individual groups of stadium users as well as general spectators. These individual groups include:

- Private box-holders and other VIPs. See Chapter 13.
- Television crews, press reporters and radio commentators. See Sections 18.2.2 and 18.6.2.
- Management and staff. See Section 19.7.
- Match stewards and police. See Section 19.7.
- Players and referees. See Section 20.2.
- Medical examination teams. See Section 20.6.

These facilities should be considered in conjunction with spectator toilets so as to minimise the number of sanitary appliances and drainage stacks in the stadium.

In smaller stadia it would be uneconomical and quite unnecessary to provide separate toilets for all the groups listed above. Common facilities can serve several categories of user provided everyone is within easy reach of a usable and suitable toilet. In the largest stadia it may be necessary to provide completely separate facilities. For each particular case the design team must find the right balance between:

- The cost advantages of having only a few centralised drainage stacks in a stadium. (These are particularly costly in the upper levels of multi-tiered stands.)
- The convenience of having toilets dispersed throughout the stadium, with short distances (preferably no more than 60m) and few level changes between users and the nearest facility.

	Urinals	WCs	Wash basins
Male	Minimum of 2 for up to 50, plus 1 for every other 50 males or part thereof	Minimum of 2 for up to 250, plus 1 for every other 250 males or part thereof	1 per WC and 1 per 5 urinals or part thereof
Female	No recommendations	Minimum of 2 for up to 20, plus 1 for every 20 or part thereof up to 500 females, then 1 per 25 or part thereof	Minimum of 1, plus 1 per 2 WCs

Note: There are no official UK recommendations specifically for sports stadia, and the above figures for places of entertainment are the closest approximation. If applied to sports stadia, the balance of provision is unlikely to be right. But if the stadium is to be used also for non-sporting events, then toilet and washbasin provision should satisfy the above formula rather than the lower figures in Table 16.2.

Table 16.1　　BS6465, Part 1. Minimum provision of sanitary appliances for assembly buildings where most toilet use is during intervals

16.2　　TOILETS FOR SPECTATORS

The bulk of these will of course be inside the stadium but there should also be toilets outside the perimeter fence (Zone 5, as defined in Section 3.3) for those queuing.

16.3　　SCALES OF PROVISION FOR SPECTATOR TOILETS

Good toilet provision is intrinsic to a venue's image. Inadequate provision, uneven distribution and poor quality cause complaints from spectators. With large crowds, insufficient toilets or urinals can lead to the misuse of the facilities, offending and driving away potential visitors and club members, thus reducing stadium revenue.

There are three separate design problems to be addressed:

- Providing an appropriate ratio of male to female toilets.
- Providing for the intensive use of toilets in very short periods of time.
- Providing an appropriate proportion of toilets for disabled spectators.

RATIO OF MALE TO FEMALE TOILETS

For public buildings in general, the most recent UK recommendations are the following:

- The authoritative *Good Loo Design Guide*, published in 2004, quotes approvingly the British Toilet Association's recommendation that the required number of female cubicles should be double the number of male cubicles and male urinals. Thus, if there are three male cubicles and four male urinals, the BTA recommends 14 female cubicles.
- British Standard *BS6465, Part 1, 2006 Code of practice for the design of sanitary facilities and scales of provision of sanitary and associated appliances*, published in 2006, gives a set of minimum recommendations that are summarised here in Table 16.1.

For stadia in particular, there are no official UK recommendations, but the UK Sport Council published in 1993 a useful guidance on behalf of the Football Stadia Advisory Council. That guidance is discontinued but its principal recommendations are summarised here in Table 16.2. It is anticipated that a future edition of the SGSG Series of Sport Grounds and Stadia Guides will update this otherwise excellent guidance.

Within the framework set by the above documents, specific figures must be decided for each stadium after a thorough analysis. Every type of event, or club membership, will have its own ratio of male to female spectators. For instance:

	Urinals	WCs	Wash basins
Male	1 per 70 males	1 for every 600 males, but not fewer than 2 per toilet area, however small	1 for every 300 males, but not fewer than 2 per toilet area, however small
Female	No recommendations	1 for every 35 females, but not fewer than 2 per toilet area, however small	1 for every 70 females, but not fewer than 2 per toilet area, however small

Note: Slab or trough-type urinals should be calculated on the basis of not less than 600mm per person. All suitable wall areas not needed for other purposes should be exploited for additional urinal provision over and above the minimum recommendations.

Table 16.2   The UK Football Stadia Design Advisory Council's minimum recommendations for newly constructed or refurbished sports stadia and stands. These figures apply to each individual accessible area.

- If a stadium is designed for multi-purpose use, including concerts, then the male to female ratio will approach 1:1.
- Tennis or athletics events will have higher proportions of women attending than soccer or rugby events.
- Clubs with high family memberships will usually have above average proportions of females.
- Higher status clubs, and clubs in pleasant parts of town, will tend to have a higher proportion of women than those with a less sophisticated image or environment.

At a particular event there may also be different gender mixes in different parts of the stadium. For instance:

- There will be a higher proportion of women in the private or family enclosures of British soccer stadia than in the standing terraces.
- There will be a higher proportion of women among the home supporters at a European soccer match than among the away supporters.

On the basis of the above data, the gender mix should be reflected in the proportions of toilets provided for that event. Organised clubs keep a record of the male to female split for particular occasions, and such club records are the only reliable source of briefing information for a new stadium design. Figure 16.1a shows a female unit, and Figure 16.1b

a male unit, based on an 80:20 male to female ratio which would be suitable for many current stadia, and which could be distributed evenly throughout the building. The male unit incorporates a unisex cubicle for wheelchair users (see below), opening off the corridor so that both men and women have access to it. The diagram should not be taken to imply that this is the only suitable location for such a facility, though it should be near the main toilets.

In view of the variation of the male to female ratio from event to event, some flexibility should be built into toilet provision. It's possible to have movable partitions, or defined sections which can be labelled either 'male' or 'female' for a particular event. The problems of inadequate provision and customer dissatisfaction are so great in stadium design that all possible solutions must be considered in the interests of attracting more spectators.

NUMBERS OF APPLIANCES

Stadium toilet usage peaks during certain periods and can barely cope with the number of users. However, most of the time, the toilets are completely unused. This creates a serious problem for the design team. The cost of providing enough toilets and urinals to avoid all queuing would be extravagant, while the problems caused by saving money and not providing enough facilities affronts customers.

17

RETAIL SALES AND EXHIBITIONS

17.1   INTRODUCTION
17.2   ADVANCE TICKET SALES
17.3   PROGRAMME SALES
17.4   GIFT AND SOUVENIR SHOPS
17.5   MUSEUMS, VISITOR CENTRES AND STADIUM TOURS

17.1   INTRODUCTION

People attending a stadium event are a captive market. They have come to enjoy themselves, they are in a leisurely (sometimes euphoric) state of mind, and they may well want to take away some memento of the occasion.

As every unit of currency spent within the stadium perimeter will contribute to the financial viability of the stadium as a whole, it is in the interest of management to exploit this profit-making opportunity to the full. An enticing variety of retail outlets in and around the stadium should be a vital part of every design or management brief.

Some owners and managers have been very energetic in exploiting these opportunities. In the UK, for instance, Wembley Stadium has aggressively pursued several different uses of its facilities (sport, entertainment, exhibitions and conferences), and has, in each case, exploited the merchandising opportunities offered by the huge captive markets. The results are impressive, with retail sales at its pop concerts measured in hundreds of thousands of pounds per annum. To take a very different example, at the Cheltenham Gold Cup, in the UK, a whole village of shops is set up around the racecourse for two or three days every year, successfully selling everything from key-rings to Rolls-Royce cars.

17.2   ADVANCE TICKET SALES

Spectators who have enjoyed their day are in an ideal frame of mind to buy tickets for future events, and they must be given every opportunity to do so. Advance tickets should therefore be sold before, during and after each sporting event from booths strategically located for maximum sales.

17.2.1   LOCATIONS AND SCALES OF PROVISION

In addition to the main ticket offices in the central ticket sales area, at least four advance-ticket booths should be provided between Zone 4 and Zone 5 (see Section 3.3), with a number of windows accessible from Zone 5, and one window accessible from Zone

The sale of clothes and souvenirs by teams, clubs and venues has become, for some, an important source of revenue.

4 (i.e. inside the perimeter fence) or Zone 3 (on the stadium internal concourse), depending on stadium size.

The total number of windows should be one window per 1,000 spectators serving Zone 5, plus one window per 5,000 spectators serving Zone 4. On this basis, a 20,000-seat stadium would have four advance-ticket booths, each with five serving windows facing Zone 5 and one window facing Zone 4.

The booths should be evenly distributed around the grounds, but in such a way that the windows serving Zone 4 are clearly seen by the crowds leaving the stadium after a match. The windows should be at least 10m away from the turnstiles so that normal circulation is not obstructed by queues of ticket-buyers congregating around the ticket booths.

17.2.2 DESIGN

Each kiosk should be provided with the following fittings:

- Counters fitted with money trays.
- Lockable cash drawers.
- Signs with interchangeable panels for seat prices.
- Heating or cooling as required.
- General power outlets and lighting.
- Queuing rails for crowd control.

The booths should be designed to be eye-catching, in terms of both their form and their signage. The latter could include imaginative neon signs – as used, for instance, in the Toronto Skydome, in Canada.

17.3 PROGRAMME SALES

The sale of programmes is vital to any stadium, and there should be plentiful selling points in all spectator areas.

17.3.1 LOCATIONS AND SCALES OF PROVISION

Programme kiosks must be provided in all subdivisions of the spectator area, both inside the perimeter (Zone 3 and Zone 4) and outside (Zone 5). Serving positions should be provided at a ratio of one position for every 2,000 to 3,000 spectators in the surrounding zone. Additionally, mobile

vendor or hawker sales should be considered in the ratio of one per 500 spectators.

17.3.2 DESIGN

Each kiosk should have between two and eight serving positions, depending on the type of sales and the number of spectators served. It should be fitted with a roller shutter, pinboards for a display of current events, and light and power points. Each kiosk should have direct access to a secure storeroom of about 6m², and a storage area for restocking of about 15m² to 20m², both fitted with shelves.

17.4 GIFT AND SOUVENIR SHOPS

An enterprising stadium may have the following range of gift shops and related facilities:

PERMANENT SOUVENIR SHOP

This is a gift shop selling stadium or club-related sports equipment, books, compact discs and other souvenirs. It may be combined with the following facility.

STADIUM MUSEUM OR EXHIBITION SPACE

This is a showcase for the history of the grounds (and the sports played there), displaying equipment, trophies and films. The latest ideas in interactive video displays are ideal for this location and have been used extensively at theme parks around the world. A good example is the Noucamp Stadium, in Barcelona.

DETACHED SHOP

This could be located away from the stadium; in the town centre, for example, if the sports facility is on the outskirts.

17.4.1 LOCATIONS AND SCALES OF PROVISION

The souvenir shop should be located so that it can be approached from both inside the grounds (Zone 3 and Zone 4) and outside (Zone 5). Accessibility from Zone 5 is important, allowing the shop to operate even when the stadium is not in use. Since parking would assist such off-period sales, a nearby short-stay parking area should be provided.

An ideal location for the souvenir shop would be adjoining the administration offices and central ticket sales office. This allows for ease of operation and staffing, plus dual use of a small parking area by both administrative staff and shop customers. The same applies to the stadium museum and the exhibition space.

17.4.2   DESIGN

Retail sales outlets in stadia are usually provided to concessionaires as serviced shells, possibly fitted out by the stadium management. There must be adequate storage space, either a room of about 10m² near each individual concession, or a centralised area of perhaps 200m². These must be securely lockable. Each shell should be provided with the following services:

- Heating or cooling as required.
- General power outlets and lighting.
- Security grille.
- Pinboards for posters.
- Audio and video system.
- Display cases and shelving. Clothes are the biggest-selling items, so suitable racks must be provided.

17.5   MUSEUMS, VISITOR CENTRES AND STADIUM TOURS

Museums and visitor centres can be very important additions, ensuring a large number of visitors to the stadium. The Barcelona Noucamp Stadium, for example, repeatedly has more visitors per annum to the museum than spectators to see matches in the stadium itself. It is possibly the most attractive museum in the city, rivalled only by the Picasso Museum, and is obviously a major source of income. The museum is fitted with extensive photographic displays, trophy cases, models of the stadium and moving-image displays. Outside, there is a popular shop selling clothing, souvenirs and memorabilia, together with parking for a large number of coaches, and refreshment facilities.

Similar successes include Wembley Stadium, in London, which runs visitor tours of the stadium with crowd sound effects, and Manchester United's stadium which also has an impressive museum. England's national 82,000-seat rugby stadium at Twickenham, in London, has a very large shop and a rugby museum with interactive displays and memorabilia, as well as an audio-visual theatre showing footage and matches from over the years. Visitors are invited to explore behind the scenes, the changing areas and the players' tunnel.

17.5.1   LOCATION AND SCALE OF PROVISION

The museum and visitor centre are primarily for use on non-match days. Therefore they should be entered from outside the stadium. If they are also to be used on match days, consideration must be given as to whether they should be accessible to ticket-holders inside the security line. A visitor centre is only likely to attract the public if it is of sufficient size to keep them interested. A stadium tour will only operate on non-match days and should be combined with other visitor areas.

17.5.2   DESIGN

The design of successful attractions is an area where knowledge of the latest ideas and technology are important, so specialist designers should be consulted. A typical stadium tour might visit the pitch, changing rooms, VIP areas and control room, and should finish in the stadium shop. If the stadium is expecting to be a tourist attraction, it will need to provide toilets and an attractive café for visitors.

205

18

THE MEDIA

18.1   **BASIC PLANNING**

18.2   **OUTSIDE FACILITIES**

18.3   **PRESS FACILITIES**

18.4   **RADIO BROADCAST FACILITIES**

18.5   **TELEVISION BROADCAST FACILITIES**

18.6   **RECEPTION, CONFERENCE AND INTERVIEW ROOMS**

18.7   **PROVISION FOR DISABLED PEOPLE**

18.1   **BASIC PLANNING**   207

18.1.1   **GENERAL**

Facilities for the media are an integral part of stadium design, not least because of the large sums of money that are nowadays earned from the media rights for sporting events. These facilities involve the three main categories of public information and entertainment services: the press (including newspapers and magazines), radio and television. Clubs may also have their own media requirements for club TV stations and websites.

In the case of major new stadia, the support facilities described below will be needed in full. In smaller venues, some may be scaled down or omitted, subject to advice from the client or from the media themselves. Because of the importance of these services, we recommend consultation with press and broadcast media at the earliest design stages.

18.1.2   **LOCATING MEDIA FACILITIES IN THE STADIUM LAYOUT**

Detailed advice for specific facilities is given in the sections below, but we start with four basic planning considerations which will influence the stadium layout as a whole.

- Firstly, all media facilities should be grouped together on the same side of the stand as the team dressing rooms. It is extremely inconvenient for media representatives to have to cross to the other side of the stadium to attend interviews.
- Secondly, this cluster of facilities should be close to, and easily accessible from, the parking zone for television and radio broadcast vehicles (and perhaps for outside catering and toilet vehicles, as described in Sections 18.2.1 and 18.2.2 below).
- Thirdly, these facilities should also be relatively close to the media parking area.
- One section of ordinary spectator seating should be adjacent to the press area, and accessible from it, so that it may be converted to press usage when demand requires, as will happen when major sports events take place. Provision for such dual use, while

The televising of sport and other events are central to stadia.

19

ADMINISTRATIVE OPERATIONS

19.1   BASIC PLANNING
19.2   FACILITIES FOR PERMANENT MANAGEMENT
19.3   FACILITIES FOR TEMPORARY EVENTS MANAGEMENT
19.4   FACILITIES FOR VISITORS
19.5   PROVISION FOR STEWARDS
19.6   FACILITIES FOR POLICE AND SECURITY OFFICIALS
19.7   TOILETS
19.8   FIRST AID FACILITIES FOR STAFF AND SPECTATORS
19.9   PROVISION FOR DISABLED PEOPLE

19.1   BASIC PLANNING   215

19.1.1   USER TYPES

The majority of administrative personnel to be accommodated are those employees responsible for the day-to-day running of the stadium, and for administration of the resident sports club (if there is one).

Their numbers will increase from time to time due to temporary staff working on a one-off basis. A suite of offices and associated accommodation must be provided for both these groups, as described in Sections 19.2 and 19.3, below. All of these officials will need hospitality facilities to entertain players and distinguished visitors. These are described in Section 19.4.

A third group of people to be catered for are the stewards brought in on match days for crowd control. Their requirements are set out in Section 19.5.

Finally, provision must be made for the police and security staff. Their needs are described in Section 19.6. All user groups need good access (Figure 19.1).

19.1.2   LOCATIONS

Administrative facilities (except for police and security offices) should generally be close to the following areas, with reasonably easy access to them:

• VIP facilities, especially the directors' and VIP hospitality rooms and viewing boxes (see Chapter 13).
• Media facilities, especially the press working area and the stadium press officer's room (see Section 18.6).
• Team managers', officials' and referees' facilities (see Chapter 20).

The administration entrance will normally be in the centre of the main side of the stadium. Car parking for officials and their guests must be provided nearby.

Figure 19.1
Access to the stadium by the seven main user groups.

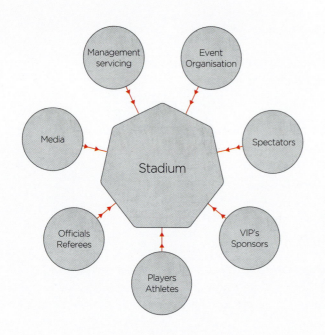

19.1.3   SCALES OF PROVISION

General guidance is given in the sections below, but specific accommodation requirements can only be determined after discussion with the client and police authorities. Figures given here must be carefully checked as the brief is compiled.

19.2   FACILITIES FOR PERMANENT MANAGEMENT

Offices and ancillary accommodation should be provided for:

• Staff responsible for marketing, promotion, advertising and ticketing of events.
• Staff responsible for administration and finance. Their needs will include secure facilities for cash receipts and credit card checking.
• Staff responsible for building services, energy control, lighting, mechanical and electrical equipment and sound equipment.

• Staff responsible for maintenance and security, and for emergency operations.
• Staff responsible for catering.

Subject to detailed discussion with the client, the rooms discussed in the following seven sections will be needed in most cases.

19.2.1   OFFICES

In a large stadium there should be offices for the director ($20m^2$), secretariat ($12m^2$), other staff members ($12m^2$ per person), public relations and marketing ($12m^2$ per person) and event organisation ($12m^2$ per person). In smaller stadia some of the above could be combined for economy. These rooms should be designed with finishes, equipment and lighting to good office standards.

19.2.2   BOARDROOM

Fittings and furnishings should be of a standard befitting this VIP space. They should include a suitable boardroom table and comfortable chairs, drinks and refreshment cupboard, refrigerator, and perhaps a small bar if the room is to be used for hospitality. A display of photographs and a secure cupboard for trophies and mementoes should be considered, the latter to be extremely secure in view of the value of the contents.

The area of this room would typically be between $30m^2$ and $50m^2$. Depending on the size of the stadium and its operation, the boardroom may be used for hospitality or other purposes.

19.2.3   APPEALS ROOM

A room should be available for hearing appeals, but this is usually not a dedicated room.

19.2.4   STADIUM CONTROL ROOM

This is the nerve centre from which the entire venue is controlled, both in normal times and in emergencies. Its location, design and fitting out are of great importance. Comprehensive advice for soccer stadia is given in *Control Rooms* (see Bibliography), and the following brief notes are no substitute for the full data given in this essential reference.

According to paragraph 2.5 of *Control Rooms*, any police officers who may need to be present during a match will work within the stadium control room. However, if a dedicated police control room is thought necessary, see Section 19.6 below.

For notes on the protection of the control room against attack by terrorists or others, see Section 6.5.6.

LOCATION

Firstly, the location should give the clearest possible view over the playing field, unobstructed by spectators. It should also give a view over the circulation areas (see Chapter 14), and spectator accommodation (see Chapter 11) by means of closed circuit TV cameras. The cross sections shown in diagrams 4 and 5 in *Control Rooms* illustrate some of these points.

For soccer grounds in the UK, diagrams 2 and 3 in *Control Rooms* show a range of options. In order not to look into the sun, the ideal location will be on the north, northwest, south, south-west or west stand. For a clear view, a position at the very back (i.e. the highest point) of the chosen stand will in many cases be best. For other sports and other countries, the precise location may be different, but the basic principles outlined in *Control Rooms* will still be relevant.

Secondly, the control room ought ideally to be adjacent to the police control room, and possibly combined with it, so that an integrated response to an emergency is possible.

Thirdly, the control room should be easily accessible to everyone who needs it, and as near as possible to the pre-event briefing area.

Diagram 6 in *Control Rooms* shows the spatial relationships of the control room and surrounding facilities. This diagram applies specifically to soccer stadia, but it will be generally helpful for other situations.

DESIGN

No particular room size can be recommended as circumstances vary so much, but the plans of four worked examples, shown on pages 37 to 40 of *Control Rooms*, will help designers with room dimensions and layout.

The room must be equipped with the following: TV monitors; telephone links both inside and outside the stadium; microphones for internal sound broadcasting and public address purposes; control panels for stadium lighting; and other technical features. All room finishes must be acoustically absorbent, and the door must be soundproof.

Although the windows overlooking the pitch may be opened, they will usually be kept shut for noise exclusion. Therefore artificial ventilation is vital.

A bench-top placed against this window will be the main working surface. Personnel should be provided with comfortable chairs, and should be able to see the pitch, the central area and the electronic screens from a seated position at this bench.

19.2.5   VIDEO AND ELECTRONIC SCREEN CONTROL ROOM

This room must be linked with the stadium control room above, and similarly designed and furnished, with space for two or three seats. These must have excellent views of the screens described below and of the spectator area.

VIDEO AND ELECTRONIC SCREENS

Any major stadium today must be equipped with one or two electronic or video screens which may be used for announcements, advertisements, safety instructions etc. They may sometimes be used for replays, either to entertain the spectators or (more rarely) to assist officials and judges.

Screen size and characteristics will depend on the type of stadium, the kinds of events staged and the distance to spectators. Large screens are increasingly becoming available, and the technology is improving rapidly (see also Appendix 2).

Screens should be at the ends of the pitch where they can be seen by the maximum number of spectators. In some cases it may be desirable to have two screens, one at each end of the playing area. It is important the sun does not fall directly on the screen face, as this can severely detract from the quality of the image.

All these matters, especially the position of the screens, should be carefully checked with the sports bodies

217

concerned. Screens must on no account distract participants, particularly in the case of athletics.

19.2.6   COMPUTER EQUIPMENT ROOM

Computer equipment rooms should be designed in line with the best current practice. Lighting should be even and to a high standard, and ventilation excellent. The floor can be raised with under-floor services and easily cleaned finishes. Vibration and noise from other parts of the building must be minimised.

As computers become smaller and less dependent on special environments, the above requirements are becoming less stringent. Requirements should be checked at briefing stage.

19.2.7   BUILDING MAINTENANCE AND SERVICES ROOMS

Accommodation will be needed for building maintenance staff and equipment, the number of facilities depending on management policy.

Some stadia are operated by specialist contractors who bring in not only their own staff but much of their own equipment, too. In these cases, only basic accommodation need be provided, comprising at least the following:

• Groundsmen's rooms.
• An equipment room.

In other cases, stadia are operated by their own permanent staff and equipment, with additional accommodation needed.

All equipment rooms must be finished with hard-wearing, low-maintenance surfaces. Floors may be smooth concrete or some other impervious, hard finish. The maintenance of service connections and equipment should be easily carried out.

19.3   FACILITIES FOR TEMPORARY EVENTS MANAGEMENT

As stated in Section 19.1.1, additional personnel will be brought in from time to time to manage particular events

such as circuses, pop concerts or religious gatherings. These requirements will depend so much on the particular case that no advice can be given here except to stress that the matter must be discussed with the client.

19.4   FACILITIES FOR VISITORS

These should include:

• VIP hospitality rooms.
• Players' bar.
• Facilities for match-day stewards.

19.5   PROVISION FOR STEWARDS
19.5.1   THE FUNCTIONS OF STEWARDS

Accommodation is needed for the stewards and security staff employed on match days as part of customer service. Their roles include helping spectators find their seats, generally assisting with information, and keeping order in a low-key manner. (More difficult situations are the responsibility of security personnel or police.)

The duties performed by stewards vary from country to country, between sports and even within a single national sport.

In Britain, stewards often used to be voluntary and unpaid, with older men chosen because of their loyalty to the club, and their desire to watch matches. Frequently they were responsible not only for normal customer service duties but also for crowd control, a task for which they had usually not been properly trained. This pattern is changing, with younger men and women increasingly being recruited on a paid basis. This is partly due to stadium economics, since it reduces the very expensive police presence demanded at many matches by local authorities, and partly a move towards better customer care. Training in safety control is therefore essential, and in the UK is now being provided to nationally recognised standards.

A very different pattern is seen in the USA where stewards tend to be more professional and are supported by what is known as peer security (i.e. stewards drawn from the same socio-economic group as those attending the event). Such stewards are sometimes also referred to as tee-shirt security because of the brightly coloured shirts they wear.

In the future, stewarding is likely to be more interactive, with stewards going out of their way to chat to spectators and make them feel welcome.

19.5.2　NUMBERS OF STEWARDS

Because patterns of stewarding vary so much, it is impossible to give simple accommodation advice. Every management will have its own methods, and these should be clarified at briefing stage. The following notes offer a starting point.

Based on normal British practice, a stadium with an attendance of 10,000 to 20,000 spectators may require 20 to 60 stewards, while one with an attendance of 20,000 to 40,000 spectators may require 60 to 100 stewards. In situations where peer security is included, the acceptable ratios may range from roughly one steward to 75 spectators in small stadia, up to one steward per 200 spectators in larger stadia. This number will be made up of the following broad categories:

- Turnstile stewards.
- Door stewards.
- Security stewards (these include peer security) who may comprise about half of the total number.
- Sector supervisor stewards.
- Crowd assessors.
- Crowd safety stewards.
- Fire-fighting stewards.

Ideally, the following spaces should be provided to accommodate the above people, but it may be possible for some of these areas to be shared with other staff:

- Briefing room (based on 1.5m² per steward) for issuing instructions to stewards on the day.
- Stewards' cloakroom.
- Storage room provided by the stadium management for official clothing.
- Small kitchen facility for making hot drinks and refreshments.
- Stewards' refreshment area to encourage their early arrival at the grounds.

19.6　FACILITIES FOR POLICE AND SECURITY OFFICIALS

Police and related security systems are vital considerations in modern stadia, but it is not possible to generalise about the number of police who will attend an event. On any typical winter weekend in the UK, when soccer is being played, around 5,000 police will be on duty around the country. Individual events can have as few as 10 to 50 on site while major soccer matches can have as many as 300 to 400. This will be a decision taken by the police themselves in consultation with the stadium management and the club concerned. The decision will have to take into account the following factors:

- Expected attendance.
- Club's past record of crowd behaviour.
- Number and type of visiting supporters.
- Nature and location of the ground.
- Experience of stewards.

As a guide to the number of police inside a ground for soccer matches in the UK, we have listed the numbers suggested in the 1990 Home Office publication *Policing Football Hooliganism*.

Category 1: For smaller clubs (e.g. lower divisions), as few as 30 to 40 officers may be needed.

Category 2: For larger clubs (e.g. premier division), some 300 officers may be required on a normal match day.

Policing was once provided free of charge but now it is usually charged at a high rate to the stadium management. In Europe there is a tendency to try to reduce the police presence required, perhaps because the numbers used in the USA and Canada tend to be less. As an example, the number of police used at events in the Toronto Skydome are set out in Table 19.1.

In comparing this level of policing, it must be remembered that most stadia in the USA and Canada also employ their own security staff. They are generally well trained and, in the case of the Skydome, are taught at their

20

FACILITIES FOR PLAYERS AND OFFICIALS

20.1   BASIC PLANNING

20.2   PLAYERS' FACILITIES

20.3   TEAM MANAGEMENT FACILITIES

20.4   OFFICIALS' FACILITIES

20.5   MEDICAL EXAMINATION FACILITIES

20.6   ANCILLARY FACILITIES

20.7   PROVISION FOR DISABLED PEOPLE

20.1   BASIC PLANNING

20.1.1   GENERAL

Every stadium, however small, must provide facilities for those taking part in the events. However, the type of accommodation needed varies enormously. A soccer or rugby match may need facilities for only two teams plus officials, whereas a major international athletics event may attract hundreds of participants.

It is almost impossible to provide accommodation on this scale on a permanent basis, in which case temporary accommodation will be needed for large-scale events. The guidance below suggests a reasonable provision of facilities.

If there is a home team, most of the accommodation will concentrate on their requirements as they will be using the facilities on a regular basis for training. If the stadium is home to more than one team then it must be decided whether the teams can share facilities or whether separate facilities must be provided for each. The latter is usually the case where major sports clubs are involved, although some sharing of training equipment may be possible.

Team changing facilities for the resident team are a very special area. It is their home, a place to which few people can gain entry. The resident organisation should be closely consulted on design, layout and character. If the stadium is also used for concerts and other events, this must be taken into account.

20.1.2   LOCATION OF FACILITIES IN THE STADIUM LAYOUT

ACCESS TO OUTSIDE

There must be direct access between players' changing facilities and the service road outside. This road will be used by coaches conveying teams to and from the stadium, and also by ambulances.

The service road should give access to the team entrance, and also to the playing area so that injured players can be reached quickly and easily by ambulances.

ACCESS TO THE PITCH

There must also be direct, protected access between players' changing rooms and the pitch. At events where players and referees may be subject to attack (such as the hurling of missiles) by the crowd, safety requirements are stringent. Soccer matches in countries with strong traditions of team loyalty fall into this category. Recommendations are outlined below.

In the case of new stadia for World Cup and European Championship finals, FIFA and UEFA recommend:

Ideally, each of the teams' dressing rooms and the referees' dressing room should have its own corridor for access to the pitch. These corridors may join up near the exit to the playing area.

The point where the players and the referees enter the playing area, which ideally should be at the centreline and on the same side as the VIP box, press stand and administrative offices, must be protected by means of a fireproof telescopic tunnel extending into the playing area far enough to prevent the risk of injury to the match participants caused by missiles thrown by spectators.

Such telescopic tunnels should be capable of being extended or closed quickly so that they may be used during the match when a player is leaving or entering the field, without causing unduly lengthy viewing obstruction.

Alternatively, the entrance to the playing area may be by means of an underground tunnel, the mouth of which is situated a similarly safe distance away from spectators.

There should be no possibility of public or media interference at any point within these corridors or security tunnels.

In the case of European Club competitions, the UEFA recommendations simply state:

In order to guarantee the safety of players and match officials, participating clubs shall provide for an access to the field ensuring safe entry and exit.

LOCATION

Whenever possible, players' and officials' accommodation should be situated at pitch level to allow easy and direct access to the playing area.

20.1.3   SCALES OF PROVISION

Requirements must be determined by discussions with clients and the relevant governing bodies.

20.2   PLAYERS' FACILITIES

20.2.1   INTRODUCTION

The facilities described below should be directly linked with the media area (see Section 18.1), the team administrative offices (see Section 19.1) and, if possible, the team directors' suite or chairman's box (see Section 13.1). If these facilities cannot be at ground level, as recommended above, they should be served by an elevator.

Corridor and door widths should be generous, because these are busy areas on a match day: 1.2m is a minimum width, and 1.5m preferable. Good ventilation is essential to prevent condensation, as well as a heating and cooling system in the changing areas, depending on local climate and seasons of play.

The whole area should be secure against unauthorised entry. It should be inaccessible to the public and the media, and have direct, protected access to the pitch, as outlined in Section 20.1.2.

Finishes must be robust and easily cleanable. Recent forms of non-slip plastic matting and hard-wearing carpets are ideal for the changing rooms themselves.

20.2.2   CHANGING ROOMS FOR SPORTS

A changing room or locker room should be provided for each home team and at least one visiting team. Two such rooms should be provided for visiting teams if matches are held between two visiting teams; unless the home team allows use of its facilities (unlikely) or the visiting teams are willing to share (more likely). Some stadia start the day's events with a curtain-raiser, often a match between teams in a lower league or junior teams, or even an event from a different sport. These teams also require changing facilities.

Figure 20.1
Schematic relationship between facilities for players and officials, the pitch, and facilities for media.

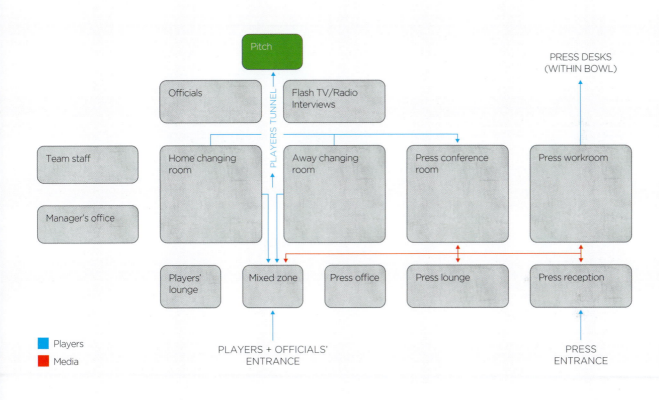

Each changing room should contain lockers, bench seats and hanging space for each individual player (including reserves). Space for each player should be between 600mm and 900mm wide, and at least 1200mm deep. In the case of soccer, FIFA requires 20 of these positions. The requirements for rugby are similar. The benches should be designed so that clothes can be kept dry and in good order. American football teams often prefer individual cabinets or open hanging units with side panels, rather than the open benching that is common for soccer and rugby.

In the case of new football stadia catering for major matches, FIFA and UEFA recommend four separate team dressing rooms.

20.2.3   MASSAGE ROOMS
At least one massage table or bench is required in each changing area. Two are needed for major stadia.

20.2.4   WASHING AND TOILET FACILITIES
Washing facilities should be directly accessible from the changing area, without going through the toilets. As a general guide, there should be one shower for every 1.5 to 2 players, allowing 1.5m² per player. However, specific requirements must be discussed with clients and the relevant governing bodies.

For male teams, toilet facilities fitted with both toilets and urinals should be provided at a ratio of one position per three players, or as required by clients and the

228

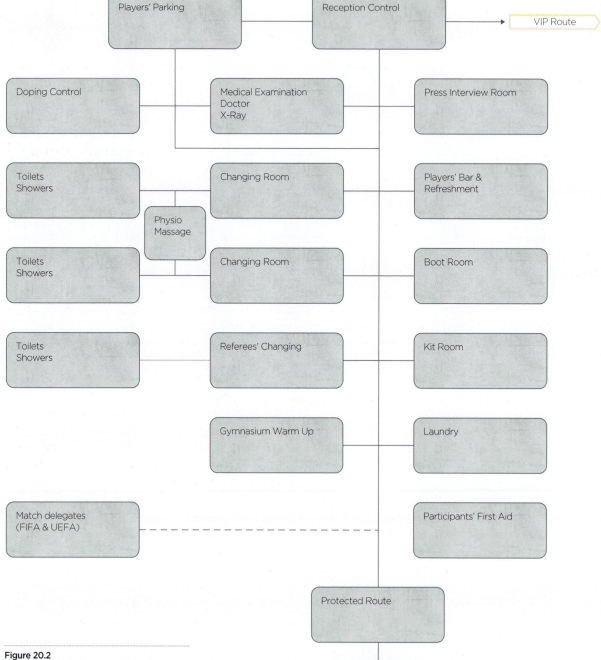

Figure 20.2
Schematic relation between various players'
and referees' facilities.

relevant governing bodies. Both washing and toilet areas should be well served by natural ventilation. All surfaces should be durable, impervious and designed so they can be thoroughly washed down.

Provision should be made for disabled people. For guidance, see Chapters 10 and 16.

20.2.5　ANCILLARY ACCOMMODATION

The following accommodation should be provided as part of the changing areas described above:

• A large training room used for preliminary warm-up exercises.
• A players' first-aid room near the pitch, en route to the changing areas.

Additional facilities which may be included or shared between teams (depending on the teams' importance):

• A general meeting room for the team with projector and screen. (This room could also be used for other purposes such as press interviews.)
• A players' bar and games area where players can relax after a game or training session. (It should be equipped with a light refreshment kitchen.)
• A gym, weights and exercise area.
• A sauna and hydrotherapy area.
• A waiting room with its own toilet for players' relatives.
• An equipment storage area with shelves and cupboards.
• A laundry and clothes drying area.
• A boot-cleaning and storage room.

20.3　TEAM MANAGEMENT FACILITIES

This area is not to be confused with the stadium management facilities described in Chapter 19; unless the stadium managers and team managers are the same.

20.3.1　LOCATION

These facilities are usually on the main side of the stadium, close to the administration area (see Chapter 19) but probably at a lower level.

20.3.2　FACILITIES

The rooms will depend largely on the size of the sports club involved, but will probably comprise the following:

• Reception area of approximately 12m² to 15m².
• General office and secretarial area.
• Executive offices with private entrance.
• Board or meeting room of approximately 25m² to 30m², with bar facilities.
• Team manager's office of approximately 18m².
• Assistant team manager's office of approximately 12m².
• Team coach's office of 12m² to 18m².
• Possibly an office for an assistant team coach.
• A chairman's suite connected to the executive offices.

20.4　OFFICIALS' FACILITIES

For every event taking place on the field there will be officials, judges, umpires, linesmen and referees who require separate changing and toilet accommodation. They will also need administrative space which, in the case of smaller stadia, may be shared. Provision will depend on the sport played and the number of games staged in one day.

20.4.1　LOCATION

The rooms described below should be close to the players' dressing rooms, but without direct access. They must be inaccessible to the public and the media, but with direct protected access to the playing area, as described in Section 20.1.2.

20.4.2　FACILITIES AND SCALES OF PROVISION
CHANGING ROOMS

As a general guide, referee and linesmen's changing accommodation should comprise four spaces, allowing 2.5m² per official, with associated lockers, toilets and showers.

A separate area within the room should be provided with a table and chair for writing reports.

The most precise guidance that is available on scales of provision are the FIFA/UEFA recommendations for new football stadia for major matches. While these cannot be directly applied to all stadia, they give a useful starting point.

229

APPEALS ROOM

Every sport is based on a firm set of rules. Players who transgress those rules will have action taken against them by the officials of the sport. To allow this judicial process to take place, an appeals room or court must be provided. The room must accommodate a jury of five or six people, plus two or three other officials. It does not need to be a dedicated space but be one of the other areas in the stadium if suitably located and planned (see Section 19.2.3).

MATCH DELEGATES' ROOM

FIFA and UEFA's recommendations for new stadia for major football matches require a special room for the competition officials who sit on the centre bench of the pitch. This room should be close to the general dressing room area and be at least 16m² in size. Equipment should include:

- One desk.
- Three chairs.
- One clothes locker.
- One telephone.

20.5   MEDICAL EXAMINATION FACILITIES

20.5.1   LOCATION

The accommodation described below should be close to the players' dressing rooms, with easy access to the outside entrance and to the playing area, as described in Section 20.1.2.

20.5.2   FACILITIES AND SCALES OF PROVISION

The specific requirements of local safety authorities and the relevant medical teams will take priority, and must be established as part of the brief. Subject to that, the following advice is given by FIFA and UEFA for new football stadia for major events.

MEDICAL EXAMINATION ROOM

There should be a room of at least 25m², equipped with:

- One examination table 600mm wide, accessible from three sides.

- Two portable stretchers, kept alongside the pitch during games.
- One washbasin.
- One glass cabinet for medications.
- One treatment table.
- One oxygen bottle with mask.
- One blood-pressure gauge.
- One heating apparatus (such as a hotplate) for instruments.
- Possibly some physiotherapy equipment.

See also Section 19.8 which deals with medical facilities for spectators.

RESIDENT DOCTOR'S ROOM

In larger stadia, the team doctor should have his or her own room of 100m² adjacent to the medical examination room, and linked to it internally.

X-RAY ROOM

Where justified, an X-ray room of about 20m² may be provided close to the medical examination room for examination of injuries.

DOPE-TESTING FACILITIES

Stadia used for major competitions will probably require a room of at least 16m², equipped with the following:

- One desk.
- Two chairs.
- One basin.
- One telephone.

Adjacent to this room, with direct private access to it, should be a toilet facility comprising toilet, washbasin and shower. Near the dope-testing room there should be a waiting area with seating for eight people, clothes hanging facilities or lockers for four people, and a refrigerator.

20.6 ANCILLARY FACILITIES

Depending on the size of the stadium, other facilities can be included which will assist in its operation.

- Media interview room: this should be adjacent to the team room, and be supplied with electrical and lighting equipment suitable for TV broadcasting.
- Players' warm-up area and gym for use before the game.
- A field toilet and drinking fountain close to the access route to the pitch.
- Enclosures, or dug-outs, which are covered and have direct access to the appropriate team's changing areas.

20.7   PROVISION FOR DISABLED PEOPLE

Laws such as the Disability Discrimination Act in the UK, and its counterparts in other countries including Australia and the USA, now require all facilities in stadia – including those for players and officials – to be fully accessible to disabled people. For guidance, see Chapter 10.

21

SERVICES

21.1   **LIGHTING SYSTEMS**

21.2   **CLOSED-CIRCUIT TELEVISION SYSTEMS**

21.3   **SOUND SYSTEMS**

21.4   **HEATING AND COOLING SYSTEMS**

21.5   **FIRE DETECTION AND FIGHTING SYSTEMS**

21.6   **POWER SUPPLY AND EVENT CONTINUATION**

21.7   **WATER SUPPLY AND DRAINAGE SERVICES**

21.8   **INFORMATION TECHNOLOGY**

21.1   **LIGHTING SYSTEMS**

233

21.1.1   **INTRODUCTION**

If a stadium is to achieve its full potential use and be operated at night or late afternoon a comprehensive lighting system is essential. Two main types of illumination are needed:

- Lighting of passageways and escape routes so that spectators can enter and leave the stadium safely.
- Lighting the play area so that players and spectators can see the action clearly and without strain. It may be necessary also to illuminate the venue for television cameras, in which case the requirements become more stringent.

Both safety and pitch lighting are required together, since one without the other would be redundant; the only exceptions being:

- Night-time concerts using their own stage lighting systems fed from a power supply on the grounds (which is common practice); or
- Sporting events which finish while there is daylight, but darkness falls before all the spectators have left the grounds (this is most unlikely for major stadia).

In these cases the stadium would need only to supply emergency lighting for spectators.

21.1.2   **EMERGENCY LIGHTING FOR SPECTATORS**

REQUIREMENTS

Emergency lighting must fulfil several functions, primarily to:

- Illuminate escape routes and exits clearly, so that spectators are in no doubt about the correct direction of movement in an emergency, and can move along safely without risk of stumbling and falling even when hurrying and in a panic.

The Beijing Olympic Stadium at night during the 2008 Games.

- Illuminate alarm call points and fire-fighting equipment so that they may be easily located.

Luminaires should be provided along each passageway and escape route so that there are no dark areas, especially on stairs and landings and at emergency doors. In the UK, an illumination level of at least 1 Lux should be provided along the centre line of general-use escape routes. In open areas larger than 60m², an illumination level of 0.5 Lux anywhere in the core area is the minimum; and for permanently unobstructed routes, 0.2 Lux minimum on the centre line.

All such emergency lighting must continue to operate even if the main power system fails, coming on within five seconds of mains failure.

INSTALLATION DESIGN

It is difficult to give recommendations for the spacing of luminaires along the general runs of routes, and an inspection of existing buildings may be the most practical guide. For illumination at critical locations we suggest that luminaires be situated within 2m of all exits and at all points where it is necessary to emphasize the location of potential hazards and safety equipment. Such locations include:

- Along each stair flight to illuminate the nosings.
- At all stair intersections, to illuminate the nosings.
- Near each change of level.
- In front of each exit door.
- In front of each fire door.
- At each exit or safety sign required for safe egress from the stadium.
- Near each fire alarm call-point and each item of fire-fighting equipment.

It may sometimes be difficult to achieve the recommended emergency illumination level of 1 Lux in the large spaces found under stadium structures. Wall-mounted luminaires help overcome this problem, and illuminated signs can make an excellent contribution. Until now such signs (particularly neon signs) have been infrequently used in sports stadia owing to their cost. However the Skydome in Toronto,

Canada, is a striking example of the exploitation of neon advertising signs to create a bright and cheerful atmosphere under an otherwise dark grey structure, and to highlight certain locations.

STAND-BY POWER

Secondary sources of power will be needed in the case of a power failure to keep emergency systems running or to keep the whole event running, see Section 21.6.

**21.1.3   PITCH LIGHTING FOR PLAYERS
              AND VIEWERS**
ILLUMINANCE REQUIREMENTS

If play is to take place at night the sports area should be illuminated to allow players, officials, and those watching both at the grounds and at home on television to see the action clearly. This means that the level of brightness, contrast and glare must be correctly designed over the entire playing area. The most demanding of these requirements is that of colour television transmission, and this specialist area will be discussed later.

The reason we can see any object is because it contrasts with what is behind it in colour or brightness or perhaps both. Colour contrast of a ball and a pitch or an athlete and a running track is largely controlled by the sports governing bodies and therefore is usually out of the control of the designer. An interesting exception to this was the yellow balls and bright clothing introduced by Kerry Packer in Australia some years ago for his night-time cricket World Series. This was a deliberate attempt to make the traditionally white attire and dark red ball more visible to the spectator and hopefully more popular to the public since they would be able to follow the game more easily. It was also essential for the players to see the ball when it was hit high into the night sky. Cricket is traditionally played during the day when the dark ball contrasts against a blue, or at least grey, sky but it would be impossible to see at night. Brightness and glare are therefore the only real controls we have over the visibility of a sport.

Levels of illumination for a sport played at night will generally be lower than those for the same sport played

234

indoors. This is because of better contrast and adaptation when scenes are viewed against a dark night sky. Illumination levels will depend on the particular sport because of the different speeds of action, viewing distances, playing object size, and colour contrasts involved – the faster the object moves the higher the illumination required; and the higher the standards of play the higher the level of illumination required.

Lighting levels will also depend on the size of the venue since those sitting furthest from the action require the greatest level of illumination for them to see to the same standard. The last consideration which may be relevant to a stadium is that our standard of vision deteriorates with age and we require more light to achieve the same level of visibility when we are older. This deterioration can be quite significant, with the illumination levels required by a 60-year-old person possibly four times that for a 20-year-old, simply to achieve the same standard of visibility.

Table 21.1 summarises typical lighting levels, and degree of uniformity, for a variety of sporting types. It is meant only as a general guide; specific up-to-date requirements should always be obtained from recognised International Lighting Standards (in Europe this is BS EN 12193), published Sports Lighting Guides, and recommendations of the particular sporting associations concerned, before commencing design.

All illuminance levels stated are minimum Maintained Average Illuminance (Em). The 'maintained average illuminance' level is the specification level and is inclusive of all depreciation factors that may apply over the periods that occur between planned maintenance. To achieve this a 'maintenance factor' is included in all design calculations. This takes into account light loss from the luminaire due to the accumulation of dirt on light-emitting surfaces, and lamp lumen output deterioration with hours of use.

The cleaning characteristics of the luminaire will have a significant effect on its performance and cleaning interval. Floodlights for stadia systems require a high degree of ingress protection against dust and water (IP65 to IP66) to ensure maximum performance over long maintenance periods between cleaning and re-lamping.

GLARE CONTROL REQUIREMENTS

Player glare for sport is the disabling condition that occurs when an event player views sporting lighting in their primary view angle while participating in the sporting event. When this viewing of the sports lighting exceeds 40 Glare Rating Value it is generally understood that the event player experiences excessive glare and may be unable to perform at their highest level of competition.

Player glare is light density to the viewer eyes and is calculated using the Threshold Increment Program that calculates the glare condition on a scale from 0-100; with 0 being not noticeable to the viewer and 100 as disabling to the viewer.

For overhead aerial sporting events such as tennis, cricket and American baseball a lower rating of 30 is advisable. Additionally special care needs to be taken during the design to avoid to direct line-of-site from the event player to the sports lights from any playing position on the field.

LIGHT SPILL

Spill light is the amount of illumination that falls outside the boundary lines of the sports field or pitch and beyond the boundary lines of the stadium and stadium property line. It is desirable to have illumination beyond the boundary lines of the pitch or field; however, it is not desirable to have illumination outside the boundary lines of the stadium or property. Spill illumination is measured by holding a light meter and aiming the sensor directly at the brightest spot of the stadium. This value is the maximum vertical illumination value being spilled to the environment.

For this discussion we will focus on the illumination outside the stadium; excessive spill illumination to the environment and the surrounding properties is unacceptable. Local government environment regulation may have standards that need to be complied with, though in the absence of these LEED (Leadership in Energy and Environmental Design) guidelines limit the illumination spill light to 6 Lux at the property boundary line.

INDOOR SPORTS LIGHTING RECOMMENDATIONS

Sports	Class	Horizontal	True Vertical	Main Camera Vertical	Uniformity
Basketball	I	2500	1300	1500	.8
	II	1500	900	1000	.7
	III	750	-	-	-
Bowling	I	2500	1300	1500	.8
	II	1500	900	1000	.7
	III	750	-	-	-
Boxing/Wresting	I	4000	1800	2000	.8
	II	2500	1500	1600	.8
	III	1000	-	-	-
Curling	I	2500	1300	1500	.8
	II	1500	900	1000	.7
	III	750	-	-	-
Gymnastics	I	2500	1400	1800	.8
	II	1500	1000	1500	.8
	III	750	-	-	-
Ice Hockey	I	2500	1300	1500	.8
	II	1500	900	1000	.7
	III	750	-	-	-
Indoor Soccer/Football	I	2500	1300	1500	.8
	II	1500	900	1000	.7
	III	750	-	-	-
Tennis/Volleyball	I	4000	1800	2000	.8
	II	2500	1500	1600	.8
	III	750	-	-	-
Table Tennis	I	2000	900	1700	.7
	II	1200	500	900	.7
	III	500	-	-	-

Notes:
1. All calculations and measured values at 1 metre (36" AFF) with .75 maintenance factor.
2. Classes:
   I   National or international broadcasting.
   II   National or club broadcasting.
   III   Recreational training.

Table 21.1

236

OUTDOOR SPORTS LIGHTING RECOMMENDATIONS

Sports	Class	Horizontal	True Vertical	Main Camera Vertical	Uniformity
Baseball	I	2500	1200	1500	.7
	II	1500	900	1000	.65
	III	750	-	-	-
Field Hockey	I	2500	1200	1500	.7
	II	1500	900	1000	.65
	III	750	-	-	-
Football	I	2500	1200	1500	.8
	II	1500	900	1000	.7
	III	750	-	-	-
Soccer	I	4000	1800	2000	.8
	II	2500	1200	1500	.7
	III	750	-	-	-
Lacrosse	I	2000	1000	1200	.8
	II	1000	700	800	.7
	III	750	-	-	-
Rugby	I	2500	1200	1500	.8
	II	1500	900	1000	.7
	III	750	-	-	-
Tennis	I	3500	1400	1800	.8
	II	3000	1200	1500	.8
	III	1500	-	-	-
Track & Field	I	2000	900	1200	.7
	II	1200	500	600	.65
	III	500	-	-	-
Volleyball	I	2000	1000	1200	.8
	II	1000	700	800	.7
	III	750	-	-	-

Notes:
1. All calculations and measured values at 1 metre (36" AFF) with .75 maintenance factor.
2. Classes:
    I   National or international broadcasting.
    II   National or club broadcasting.
    III Recreational training.

Table 21.1

INSTALLATION DESIGN

The correct design sequence is to decide the performance levels that are required (see above) together with cost and other limits, then to get competitive quotations for meeting these requirements, and only at that stage to decide the number and type of lamps, their mounting heights and their spacings. It is a mistake to approach the matter the other way round (as is sometimes done) and to decide at an early design stage the number and the heights of lighting towers, and perhaps even the number and placement of individual luminaires, and then to seek quotations. Alternative lamp types and floodlights will require different spacings and locations to give the same result, and until the luminaires are known the spacings cannot be decided. Subject to that proviso the following general notes may be helpful.

Small stadia are usually lit by a side-lighting system consisting of three or four floodlights located on one side of the pitch mounted at a height of not less than 12m. The angle between the fitting and the pitch centre should be between 20 and 30 degrees to reduce glare, and the angle between the fitting and the side line between 45 and 75 degrees to ensure adequate lighting on players at the touchlines.

Larger stadia may use corner columns or masts, with perhaps a number of fittings along the side(s) so that an optimum illumination can be chosen for any particular type of event. Corner masts are probably the most common system in use. They may be expensive but have the advantage of not obstructing any views to the pitch.

They should be offset at least 5 degrees from the side, and 15 degrees from the end of the field of play, taken from the centre of the respective side or end to ensure that they are outside the principal viewing directions of spectators and players. Typically, mast height should be at least 0.4 times the distance on plan between the mast and the centre of the field, and mounting angles should be as in the previous paragraph to restrict glare. However, in the final evaluation mast height will be greatly influenced by requirements to achieve recommended Glare Rating limits over the playing surface. Corner masts are not regarded as the best lighting arrangement as they create strong shadows on the pitch.

In very large stadia the lighting system will be governed partly by the design of the stadium structure:

- Open stadia will probably use the system described above of four corner masts, about 35m minimum height, possibly supplemented by additional masts around the perimeter if justified by the stadium size. It must be noted that these tall masts can present a major structural and aesthetic design problem, although current floodlight technology has resulted in greatly reduced floodlight quantities which in turn has reduced structural sizes. Where aesthetics are a prime planning consideration, telescopic or retractable masts may offer a solution in difficult circumstances.
- Roofed stadia may have side-lighting in the form of continuous strips mounted along the leading edges of the roofs. These fittings should be mounted at least 30m above the playing surface to reduce the risk of glare, which may be an insurmountable problem because light reaches the spectators at angles near to the horizontal. On the positive side, the increased illumination of the vertical plane associated with roof-edge lighting may be beneficial to television broadcasting. A hybrid solution using both masts and roof-edge side-lighting may offer a solution in some circumstances.

For larger schemes two or three switching levels may be provided to allow different illumination levels for different kinds of event, ranging from training to a full-scale televised match. It may also be necessary for the floodlights to be rotatable by remote control to illuminate different areas of the arena for different types of events. These matters must be clarified with the client at an early stage.

With regard to the structural design of towers, lattice towers are now rarely used. Static masts are cheaper, easier to maintain, and visually less intrusive. Hinged or 'raise and lower' masts facilitate regular cleaning re-lamping and maintenance, all of which are vital if lamp performance is to be maintained. Telescopic (retractable) masts may be suitable where permanent mast structures are prevented by planning regulations, but they are an extremely expensive solution. Where mast floodlight quantities are excessive, and mast heights greater than 45m, internal access structures may be considered.

Floodlighting off grandstand roofs is an alternative to the provision of mast-based systems, and offers the opportunity for a continuous-roof stadium design. However floodlight systems produce a very large roof-edge loading which must be considered at the very outset of the stadium design. Where a stadium roof significantly overhangs spectator areas, extending almost to the pitch edge, it may also be necessary to set-back some of the floodlights beneath the roof edge so as to provide enough vertical illuminance on to players at touchlines for both spectators and camera viewing purposes. Access to the floodlights for maintenance purposes should also be considered, with nosed systems requiring substantial catwalks either above or below the roof edge.

Floodlights are generally located along both main side grandstands, with a limited number permitted along end rooflines so as to restrict glare in the principal playing directions. No floodlighting is permitted within an approximately 15m zone on either side of a line projected along goal axes, to prevent direct glare to goalkeepers in some ball sports, including football and hockey.

21.1.4   PITCH LIGHTING FOR TELEVISION
PITCH HIGH DEFINITION TELEVISION (HDTV)

Due to the constant evolution of camera technology and the desire to produce better quality high definition digital video the sports lighting systems are changing to meet these new demands. Key changes in this evolution are illumination uniformities on the pitch, 'shadow control', pitch vertical and main camera vertical illumination requirements, super-slow-motion video technology, flicker fee environments, and LED lighting.

Uniformities are the illumination variance across the panning ranges of broadcast cameras. With older analogue camera technology these uniformities could vary 40% inside the camera panning ranges without significant degrading of the video quality; however, with the high quality digital video 10% variances are noticeable. Additionally player shadowing on the players and pitch is noticeable;

white colours become whiter and small details on the event participants are lost, similarly darker colours become darker and details are lost. Digital video creates images that focus on the contrast in the panning image and capturing the passion of the sport conflict in faces of the participants and the patrons is extremely critical to the overall success of the broadcast. The goal of the sports lighting is to limit these contrasting conditions, improve uniformities and reduce shadows on the event participants and the pitch around the event players.

Pitch vertical and main camera vertical illumination is the actual illumination the cameras receive during their panning and still-shot positions. It is common for pitch vertical illumination to provide 1,400 Lux with panning uniformity of 10% for all camera positions on the pitch. Additionally it is common to provide 1,800 Lux to the main camera with 20% uniformity. Some events require much more illumination and uniformities whilst other events require less illumination and uniformity. Picking the correct amount of illumination and correct amount of uniformities, and providing the design that complies with international guidelines, is key to the success of a sports stadium.

During the design, super-slow-motion video needs to be included in the process. Slow-motion and super-slow-motion are becoming more important to the broadcast industry due to the demand by the public and the revenue opportunities to broadcast industry. In general European outdoor sports, requirements provide illumination that supports camera frame speed of 600-1000 frames per second (fps). American outdoor and American indoor sport request a frame speed of 600–800 camera fps. The future broadcast industry will be asking for fps up to 1000–1500 fps for the major international events; these new requirements will force new solutions and innovation on the industry.

Flicker free sports broadcast lighting is now the standard request due to super-slow-motion digital video for international world events. Light flicker occurs when the broadcast fps is faster than the line electrical frequency of the ballast that are a part of the High Intensity Discharge (HID) sport lighting fixtures. This flickering condition creates a strobing effect on the event participants creating poor quality

239

digital video. This flickering or strobing condition occurs at camera frame speeds of 500 frames per second. There are several solutions for these issues and the designer needs to be aware of new technologies and new design techniques that avoid flickering during super-slow-motion requirements.

LED (Light Emitting Diodes) are being developed for sports lighting applications. The big difference with LED lighting compared to HID sports lighting are the ballast, lamps, energy consumption, control and colour rating. The LED technologies will solve many of the problems found with the current sport fixture technology. LED technology is being tested now in both outdoor and indoor applications. This technology appears promising; however, it is still a few years away from being readily available and cost competitive for sport facilities. The biggest advantage of the LED products will be the reduction in energy required to produce the lumens needed to illuminate the pitch. We are anticipating a saving of between 30 and 50 per cent of net energy with LED products.

The sports lighting systems for future stadia will have many new opportunities and challenges for innovation, energy sustainability, and production of new video products for the new digital sports fans and media consumers. The sports lighting systems will not merely provide enough illumination for the event; much more will be required. The sports lighting system will be required to enhance the conflict and celebrate the battle in unique ways that will elevate the event to bigger audiences and create more revenue for all parties. The future pitch will be a stage for the most exciting events and conflicts on the planet played out to billions of viewers every week world wide.

INSTALLATION DESIGN

Designing a lighting system that will achieve the above standards requires a great deal of expert knowledge, and the use of extensive computer calculations via sophisticated software. It is strongly recommended that design and installation of sports lighting for colour television (CTV) be carried out with specialist assistance.

Positioning of the lighting system should take into account the fact that television coverage of directional sports will be from one side of the stadium only, otherwise cutting backwards and forwards between camera positions will confuse the viewers. The requirements of secondary, roving, and rail cameras should also be evaluated as broadcasters look to incorporate new camera shots to enhance the TV experience.

Floodlights are increasing in efficiency, making it both cheaper and easier to provide the quantity and quality of light that is required by colour television cameras. This has been made possible by technological advances in High Intensity Discharge (HID) lamp design. Light sources have evolved from enormous tubular and elliptical lamps fitted with large screw threads and poor alignment, into small unjacketed double-ended lamps designed for long life and high performance within sophisticated, compact, and stable optical systems.

Most old lighting towers have therefore been replaced with new lightweight mast structures using only 60 per cent new floodlights, compared with the number in the old installation, but achieving improved lighting levels and greater visual quality.

21.2 CLOSED-CIRCUIT TELEVISION SYSTEMS

Closed-circuit television systems (CCTV) may be used for two purposes in a stadium – for security and crowd control (where its use is becoming ubiquitous), and for informing and entertaining spectators, where its huge potential is not yet fully exploited.

21.2.1 CCTV FOR SECURITY

The need for better control of crowd movement has led to virtually all major stadia now having CCTV installations allowing management to monitor crowd densities, movement patterns and potential trouble spots before, during and after events.

Cameras have become smaller and less obtrusive, so that it is possible to monitor spectators without the latter being aware of the fact and feeling intimidated; picture quality has improved to the point where individual spectators can later be identified from a video recording, particularly if computerised enhancement techniques are

240

applied. A striking example of the degree of miniaturisation already available is a 150mm by 25mm camera fitting into a hollow wicket for close-up action shots of cricket matches – and no doubt even smaller cameras will be available by the time this is published.

Returning to the security aspect: it would be too expensive to place a camera in every corner of the stadium, but a general overview of all areas, plus targeted coverage of all potential trouble-spots must now be regarded as an essential feature of any new stadium design.

In the first instance control personnel should be given a clear view of all spectator approaches to the stadium so that they can identify a potentially troublesome build-up well in advance. As an example the control room of London's Wembley Stadium is linked to cameras at a traffic junction some five miles away where many cars heading for the stadium turn off a major motorway. The police are thus able to identify supporters' coaches and take early precautionary measures if necessary.

Subsequently, they should be able to monitor crowd build-up and behaviour at all areas of dense congregation as spectators move to their seats – for instance entrances to turnstiles and vomitories, concourses, staircases and the like.

SYSTEMS INTEGRATION

The monitoring facilities described above should not be seen in isolation, but in the context of an entire electronic communication system embracing the telephone, public address, crowd surveillance and recording, perimeter access control, general security, fire monitoring and fire alarm, and emergency evacuation systems. Additional aspects such as time and attendance records, parking control, elevator control and the like can also be integrated into the system.

As an example of how such integration may currently operate, an attempted illicit entry into a secure area can be detected by an electronic surveillance system which then activates a recording camera, auto-dials a message to stadium security officers and suggests what steps must be taken, issues a pre-recorded warning to the intruder, sets off an alarm, and makes a video record and computer printout

of the entire sequence of events for future reference. All the correct actions can be taken and a reliable record kept with minimal risk of human error.

Ideally all the services described above should come from a single interconnected source, and it is essential to take expert advice to avoid incompatibilities between sub-systems which ought to be working together to give maximum benefit to the stadium management. For the same reason the information given here should be read in conjunction with other sections of this book such as sound systems (Section 21.3), fire alarm systems (Section 21.5) and so forth.

STAND-BY POWER

A stand-by power system is essential for security services.

21.2.2   CCTV FOR INFORMATION AND ENTERTAINMENT

CCTV offers spectators the possibility of a running commentary on the game, replays and information about the players on the field, highlights from other games, and other possibilities as yet unthought of – all 'narrowcasted' on small personal TV receivers or on huge screens mounted above the pitch.

These are not just gimmicks but an essential element in management's array of techniques to win back spectators from the comfortable alternative of watching sports events free of charge, with close-up shots, action replays and the like in the comfort of their living rooms. The proportion of events being televised increases all the time, enhanced by the spread of cable and satellite television, and stadia must struggle hard to retain their markets.

Some clubs and stadiums now send text, imagery and commentary to mobile phones and devices live during matches as well as afterwards through their websites. As the sophistication of the devices improves the quality and range of the content delivered to spectators in this way will only increase.

There are two technologies available for delivering information by fixed screens within a stadium.

241

22 MAINTENANCE

22.1	INTRODUCTION
22.2	PITCH MAINTENANCE
22.3	STAND MAINTENANCE

22.1 INTRODUCTION

22.1.1 A MAINTENANCE POLICY

Just as a motor car needs to be regularly maintained, so stadium planners should develop a clear maintenance cycle for their building and pitch which can be passed on to the owners in the form of a maintenance manual.

To do this successfully, stadium managers require:
- Well-trained personnel.
- Suitable equipment for these people to operate.
- Supplies of the correct quantity and quality of materials to be used.
- Adequate space in the stadium grounds for storage and workshops.

22.2 PITCH MAINTENANCE

22.2.1 MAINTENANCE OF NATURAL GRASS

In theory, and given proper maintenance, a natural grass pitch will last almost indefinitely. Synthetic surfaces usually need to be replaced every five to 10 years. But in practice, grass pitches can suffer irreparable damage if maltreated. The actual lifetime will depend on factors such as:

- Intensity of wear. This varies enormously. In northern Europe play is limited to a couple of months in summer, giving around 50 hours of use per annum, whilst in southern Europe play is possible all year round, giving 500 or more hours of play per annum.
- Type of usage. The harder the pitch, the more use it can take.

It is essential to follow the procedures briefly outlined below. More detailed guidance will be given by the consultant and specialist suppliers who specified the pitch in the first instance, as discussed in Section 7.1.3.

23

OPERATION AND FUNDING

23.1	**STADIUM FINANCES**
23.2	**CAPITAL COSTS**
23.3	**OPERATING COSTS**
23.4	**INCOME GENERATION**
23.5	**CONTROLLING COSTS AND REVENUES**
23.6	**CONCLUSION**

23.1   STADIUM FINANCES
23.1.1   INTRODUCTION

Stadium economics are such that it is difficult – though not impossible – for a stadium on its own to earn a profit for its owners. With the introduction of the FIFA Fair Play Regulations for soccer clubs, it is now more important than ever that the stadium element of their business maximise the profit-generating opportunities that exist. The starting point for a viable development is a comprehensive feasibility study comprising both the construction of the stadium and its financial operations. This feasibility study will then influence the design, form and content of the final project. It will need to address the following factors:

- Initial capital cost of the project.
- Anticipated operating costs of the stadium.
- Expected income generation.

The notes below deal with each of these in turn, and the advice given is very general. There is so much difference between individual countries, between various types and sizes of stadia, and costs change so much in the space of a few years that specific data in a book such as this would be misleading. We therefore concentrate on principles rather than specifics. In a real project, cost consultants and other specialists would give precise guidance.

23.2   CAPITAL COSTS
23.2.1   COST PER ELEMENT
KEY DRIVERS BEHIND CAPITAL COSTS

When planning a new stadium, it is very important to understand the key drivers behind the capital cost. Stadia are widely appraised on an internationally recognised cost-per-seat basis, benchmarking one facility against another. However, this data

Aviva Stadium Dublin.
Architects: Populous and Scott
Tallon Walker

can be misleading as it gives little indication of the success of the development, with large variances occurring between facilities of similar capacity, often driven by the business needs. For example, a stadium that has been developed with extensive commercial facilities will carry a far greater cost per seat than one that hasn't. But it may deliver a far greater return on investment.

The development of a new stadium will involve many costs additional to the construction costs – land purchase, arrangement of loans, local authority fees and consultancy fees, for example. These will need to be accounted for in the overall financing.

The capital investment cost is a complex equation. It is necessary to have an understanding of what

Figure 23.1
Relationship between stadium capacity and cost per seat.

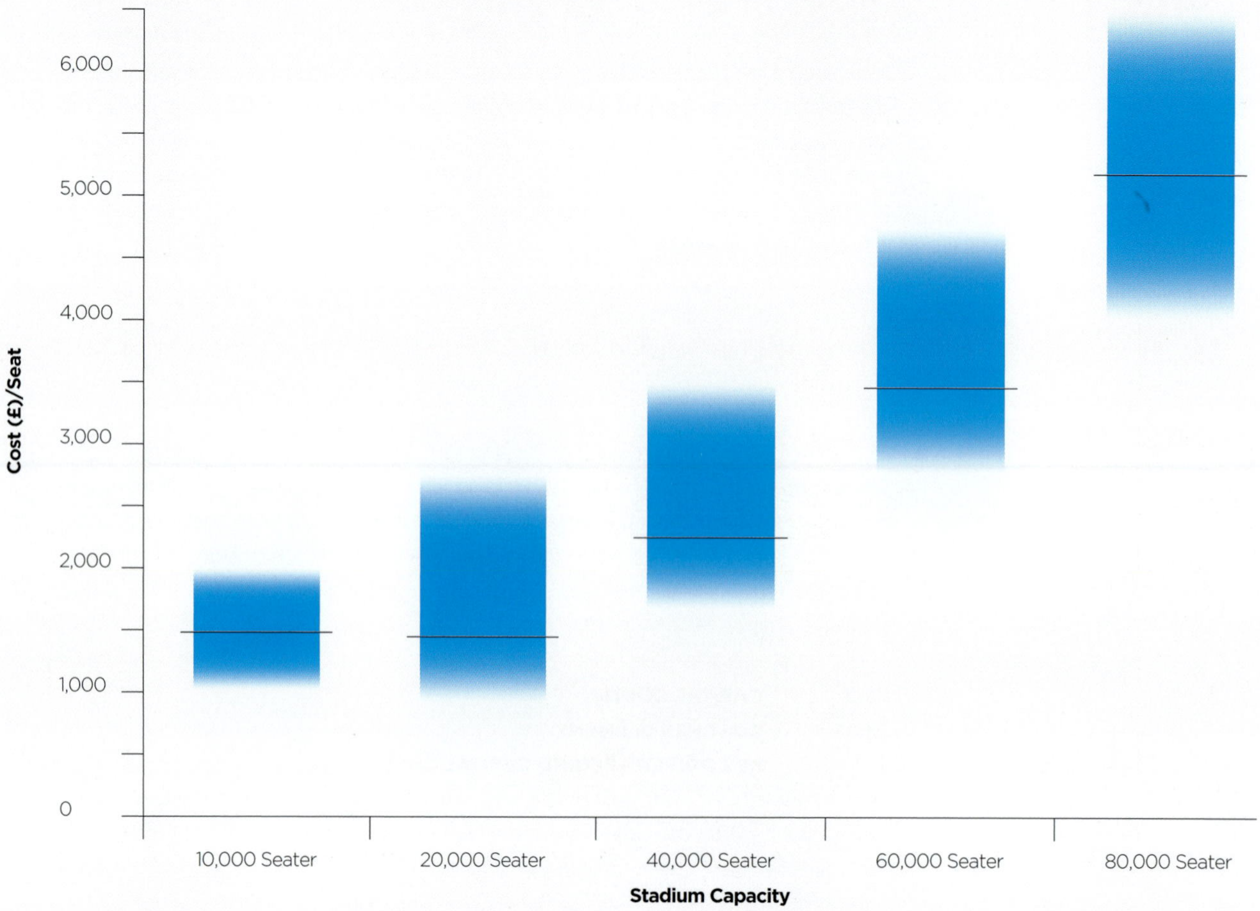

262

the key cost drivers are for any facility. While site-specific issues such as demolitions, power, water and other services connections, external works and contract conditions account for some of the large variances in capital cost between facilities, they do not tell the whole story.

For any project, especially at early feasibility stage, it is important to consider the primary component parts, each of which will influence the capital cost:

a) Event area.
b) Bowl, terracing.
c) Main roof.
d) Accommodation (circulation, hospitality, toilet facilities etc.).
e) Vertical circulation.
f) External envelope.

In the following section the sports business team at Franklin and Andrews, a market leader in stadia cost consultancy, provide an in-depth review of the key influences on the cost of these primary component parts.

EVENT AREA

The event area cost will be influenced by a number of factors, including the local climate conditions and the proposed event calendar. Local climate will determine the heating and irrigation requirements, but more importantly, the proposed event calendar will dictate how the arena floor is constructed. A stadium designed for sports events and other activities, such as the Veltins Arena, in Germany, has a pitch which can slide out of the stadium. and therefore, there is not only the cost of the pitch, but also of a box and moving gear to enable the pitch to slide in and out, and a solid arena floor beneath.

263

Figure 23.2
Comparison of the cost per seat of the accommodation related to different offers to spectators.

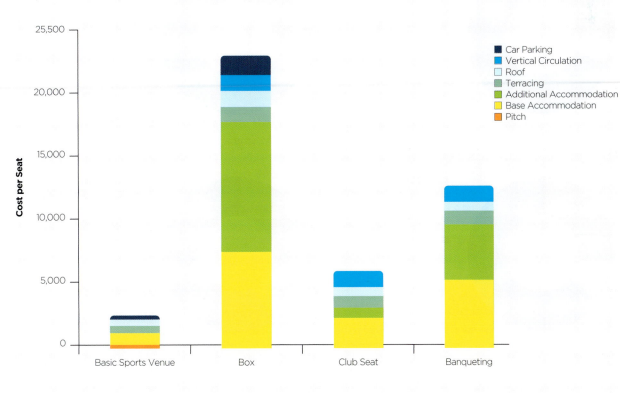

the overall gross internal floor area and output cost of any project. If designed correctly, they can also generate income on non-event days from conference, restaurant and social event use. While additional investment may be required, this is likely to represent a significant part of the revenue stream that will make the project financially sustainable.

Operational areas, i.e. the back of house accommodation that is required to make the facility `tick', also vary from facility to facility: Larger stadia will require larger operational areas to deal with stadium and event management, security, servicing, waste management, media areas etc. While these areas can be designed to the bare minimum, this will invariably result in inflexible and operationally inefficient solutions. On paper, the capital cost of the project may look good, but day-to-day running costs will be increased due to more labour-intensive activities. There will be limits to which other activities can be held there.

Before incorporating it is important to understand the true return on investment equation. For instance, incorporating a number of corporate boxes into a stadium will not just involve building the box, but also increasing the spatial provision in the terracing and the seat quality to improve comfort levels, which in turn can increase the overall area of roof. In addition, extra separate and dedicated circulation will need to be provided, additional operational space (e.g. kitchens) incorporated and finally potentially extra car parking within the external works will need to be provided. In fact, the true cost of incorporating a corporate box can be nearly four times the cost of the box itself. Figure 23.2 identifies the overall typical additional cost of incorporating corporate facilities within a large stadium compared to a basic general admission sports venue.

Participant facilities – i.e. the changing rooms and other areas provided for the athletes – are defined by the proposed stadium use. Today's venues not only have to accommodate the host sport's changing facilities, warm-up areas and lounges, but must also consider requirements for pre-match events, and separate areas for female officials and athletes. For larger-capacity venues, the total areas of these facilities generally increase in size, but not proportionally.

Stadia are large developments with a lot of space beneath the terracing that is often underutilised. This is where non-core facilities come in. Such space can be fitted out with commercial offices, casinos, shops, bars, educational facilities and the like which, in some instances, can be built at a reduced cost due to the sharing of the structure and infrastructure. Obviously the overall area and cost of the development is increased, but adding these elements can attract separate funding, create additional revenue streams and ensure that the development remains active beyond the normal event schedule. All this will assist in ensuring long-term financial sustainability.

When considering whether to incorporate non-core facilities into the fabric of a stadium, it is important to consider the following:

- What are the cost benefits compared to building them as a separate building?
- Will the space be compromised by stadium fabric (e.g. column spacing and only single aspect)?
- Does the space increase in value as a result of being associated with the stadium brand?

VERTICAL CIRCULATION

In larger-capacity stadia, an increasingly greater proportion of the accommodation is located on upper levels. This not only means that the accommodation itself will cost more to build, but it will have a negative impact on the cost of vertical circulation. The design of a 40,000-seat capacity stadium can make it possible for at least 75 per cent of the spectators to reach their concourse without climbing a single step. This percentage is dramatically reduced in a typical 80,000-seat stadium to around 40 per cent. As a result, huge stair cores, banks of lifts and, in some cases, escalators are required to facilitate the safe movement of people, and to ensure the effective operation of the stadium's servicing strategy.

EXTERNAL ENVELOPE

The final building element that will influence the overall cost of a stadium is the external envelope. In addition to providing security and separating the indoor environment of the building from the outdoors, this element along with the main stadium roof can be used to create a unique stadium identity. Whilst additional investment may be required, creating an instantly recognisable stadium can help enormously when negotiating stadium naming-rights deals. Recent examples of where this element has been used to create such instantly recognisable facilities include the Aviva Stadium, in Dublin, and the Allianz Arena, in Munich (see Case studies).

EVERY STADIUM IS UNIQUE

The key to the success of any project is to maximise the potential of the property asset. Focusing purely on revenue generation is not the answer. A project must find the right balance between capital expenditure, revenue generation and operational costs which will generate the greatest operating profit.

The quality and type of materials used for each of the components identified above will not only influence the capital cost and revenue-generating potential but will also influence the operational costs. So it will be important to plan ahead. For instance, what is the proposed design life of the project? Materials should be selected with this in mind to avoid, wherever possible, expensive remedial or replacement works. For example, savings made on the initial cost of the protective treatment applied to roof steels may benefit the initial capital budget; however, the cost of reapplication in 10 to 15 years' time will be very high due to the amount of temporary work associated with the re-application process. It is important to carry out life-cycle costing exercises to determine the most appropriate materials to use and ultimately the most economic whole-life cost solution.

To put this into perspective, occupancy costs

267

Figure 23.4
Diagrammatic cut-away of a stadium identifying the main building elements.

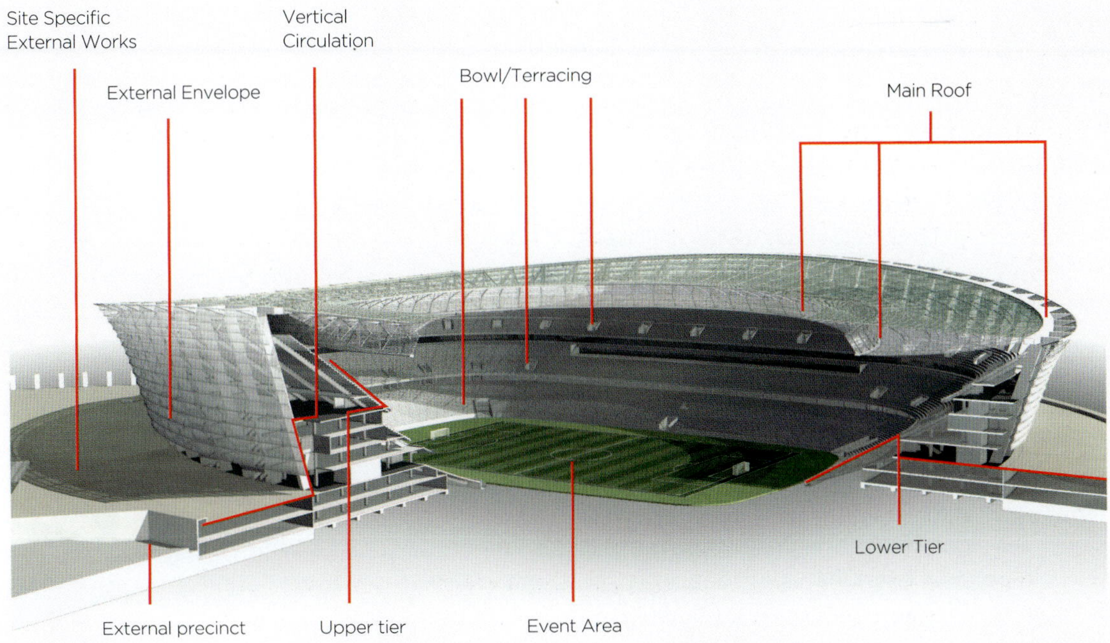

Site Specific
External Works

Vertical
Circulation

External Envelope

Bowl/Terracing

Main Roof

External precinct

Upper tier

Event Area

Lower Tier

Image: GMP

for a building, for example, can be as much as ten times the capital cost over a 25-year lifespan, and therefore significant whole-life cost savings can be made through selective initial investment.

Quality will also influence the demand for the product, and number of spectators. This needs to be reviewed during the briefing process. What market are you trying to sell to? The hospitality facilities may well be adequate to generate revenue on a match day; however, unless they compare favourably with neighbouring competition, it will be harder to generate income during non-event days.

It is important that the scope and brief for each of these components is understood at an early stage so that a realistic budget can be developed by the cost consultant, and incorporated into the business plan to establish whether the proposals deliver the long term return on investment required. One final point to consider is whether the stadium will need to be expanded in the future, on either a permanent or temporary basis. In many cases, the initial stadium brief may reflect the requirements of a one-off or low-frequency event and for the rest of the building's life it may be operating significantly below designed capacity.

In such circumstances it is worthwhile investigating initially building a reduced-capacity stadium which is flexible enough to expand in the future on either a permanent or temporary basis (e.g. overlay).

The latter may be required if the facility is being designed to host a future major event such as the FIFA World Cup or the Olympics, where capacity and accommodation requirements are significantly increased for the few weeks in which the event takes place. The benefits of such an approach include:

1) Reduced initial capital costs.
2) Reduced day-to-day operational costs.
3) Overlay costs are an event cost.
4) Building capacity slightly below market requirements generates demand and can increase sales values.

The downside to designing for future expansion flexibility is that it will involve some additional cost in phase

1, for example future- proofing of the foundations which may never be required, but it is normally cheaper to design the original building to accept future conversions, than to convert a building from scratch at a later date. The conversion process may also have a negative impact on revenue-generating opportunities when the conversion works are taking place. However, in the majority of cases, the benefits far outweigh the negatives.

23.3   OPERATING COSTS
23.3.1   RUNNING COSTS VERSUS CAPITAL COSTS

In the enthusiasm of building a new stadium, the capital costs of the project are usually investigated and planned in great detail while the running costs receive much less attention. This is probably because the latter are harder to quantify at the planning stage, and also because running costs are felt to be a problem for tomorrow rather than today.

This is a counter-productive approach because the running costs over the lifetime of any building usually far exceed the initial construction cost – a trend that is likely to intensify as the costs of energy and labour continue to rise in most countries. The aim should be a stadium proposal that gives value for money not only in terms of initial costs, but also in terms of its whole-life costs. These will include:

- Maintaining the playing surface and the fabric of the stadium in a safe and functionally satisfactory condition year after year.
- Keeping the stadium, playing field and grounds clean.
- The actual operation of the stadium (staffing, lighting and heating, security etc.). The building should be designed in a way that encourages efficiency in these areas.

In all these cases, value for money does not simply mean the lowest cost. It means the lowest cost in maintaining a pleasing, efficient and attractive stadium because it is only by attracting paying customers that the owners can get a return on their investment.

Maintenance and cleaning have been covered in Chapter 22; lighting, security and other services in Chapter 21.

Some notes on staffing follow below. These are very general. Each case must be analysed individually.

23.3.2   STAFFING COSTS

Staffing is a significant factor in the operating policy. There are a number of different categories of staff ranging from well-trained specialists to untrained operatives. A typical list of staff categories includes:

- Administration.
- Stadium maintenance and groundsmen.
- Tradesmen such as electricians, carpenters, gardeners, cleaners and general workmen.
- Auxiliary unqualified workers.
- Additional staff for event days.
- Catering staff.
- Stewards.
- Security personnel.

Adequate accommodation must be provided for all these people and the equipment they need. (See Chapter 19.)

23.4   INCOME GENERATION
23.4.1   SOURCES OF FUNDS

The most common stadia around the world are those fully funded by the community. However, private finance is growing in popularity, with more and more money being generated by the top sports clubs and individuals. In the USA, private financing has usually been limited to the smaller indoor venues, accommodating up to 200 events a year. Large stadia can generally attract only between 20 and 75 event days a year, and are therefore hard pressed to justify the significant financing necessary. This limitation on event days is largely due to the fact that most stadia have an open roof, making them vulnerable to the elements. Also, there are a limited number of events which can attract an audience of 50,000 to 100,000 spectators. These days, pop groups prefer to book a venue for three nights at an arena of 20,000 rather than one night with 60,000. If all three nights do not sell out, they can always cancel the last night rather than go on stage to a half-full stadium lacking in atmosphere.

Completely covered or domed stadia are able to achieve in the order of 200 event days a year. Studies show that up to 250 or even 300 event days are possible.

Stadium funding nowadays is usually a combination of both private and public money, using a number of different methods to balance the finances. We set out below several of these methods, and explain the usual forms they take.

SPONSORSHIP

Private companies justify the injection of capital into a stadium development for a whole range of reasons. Perhaps they simply love the sport, with no need for a return on their investment. Or perhaps it is a planned commercial investment in return for some form of franchise. A major drinks or fast-food company may inject millions in return for its product being sold exclusively in the stadium. See further comment on this in Chapter 25.

ADVERTISING

The greater the number of event days a year at the venue, the more spectators will attend, the greater the value of the advertising rights. If the events are televised, this will also significantly increase the revenue generated. A combination of advertising positions is available around any stadium from fixed display boards on the perimeter of the ground to fixed, movable or digital strip-boards around the outside of the pitch. Front edges of roofs and upper balconies can also be utilised. But the aesthetic balance of the stadium can be ruined if this is not carefully judged. Large video display-boards and colour-matrix scoreboards within the seating bowl, and digital signage and televisions within spectator accommodation can also be used to show advertising before and after play.

SEATING

The most obvious area of revenue generation is selling the seats themselves. A range of standards and positions is important to maximise the return. Private hospitality areas and club enclosures are all part of this range of seats. They have the advantage of usually being paid for in advance. These more private facilities can be a deciding factor in the viability of a

269

new development. In Europe, seat sales tend to account for the major proportion of stadia income, but in the USA, income from seating ranks lower than income from concessions.

An increasingly popular form of financing is the pre-sale of seats for lengthy periods, particularly in the more expensive seating areas of the stadium. With guaranteed income for a fixed period, the stadium owner can borrow money for reconstruction from banks against pre-sold seats. In some circumstances, this long-term season ticket or licence can be mixed with equity in the stadium company to make it more saleable.

NAMED STADIA

There have been many stadia around the world named after the companies that fund them. This can be another form of advertising, but not necessarily. The value of naming-rights deals has increased significantly over the past five years and is now common place across the globe. The USA, which developed the concept, remains ahead of everyone else in terms of the scale of deals agreed with the naming of Metlife Stadium in New York for example worth a reported US$400 million over 25 years.

CONCESSIONS

Selling concessions in a stadium is effectively letting space to the food and beverage industry to sell their goods and merchandise at the grounds. It can be the source of significant revenue, but the concession areas must be well planned at an early stage to ensure they are attractive to prospective concession-holders. A percentage of the sales made is often part of the deal, but this will vary with the venue.

PARKING

Car, bus and bike parking is often limited at a stadium which means the facility can be charged for. Depending on the number of vehicles accommodated, the revenue can be substantial as parking charges are often a quarter to a half of the actual ticket price for the event.

CLUB FUNDING

If a stadium is not actually owned by a club, but by an independent organisation, then the club which uses the facilities can support the venue by injecting initial capital. In return, the club will usually expect some part of the equity of the grounds or a return of the income generated.

LAND DEALS

An increasing number of soccer clubs in the UK are funding themselves through land deals. They may own the ground on which the club sits, but lack the funding to improve their venue. Provided their land is of sufficient value, they can often pay for a new facility on less valuable land by selling their existing site. Land swap can also involve the local authority where an area of land surplus to the authority's needs is sold to the club so that it can move from its original location.

SYNDICATION

This is where a group of companies or individuals come together to fund the development. Their motives can vary, and are not important, provided they have certain similarities in their expectations of the new facility.

LAND DONATION

A public authority may feel there is sufficient benefit to the community in retaining a facility in its area. This will justify providing land for its use. This method of donation is often done because land is the only asset the city owns.

TAX REDUCTIONS

In countries where local taxes are controlled by the local authority, tax breaks can be offered to stadium developers. In the USA, for example, a city authority can reduce or defer its local taxes on a stadium development.

TAX INCREASE

This is the opposite of the above approach. It works only where a city uses revenue from a tax, or introduces a new tax, to pay for a stadium development. A popular method in the USA is the tourist tax, where a percentage is added to hotel bills so that people coming into the city help pay for the facility.

270

GOVERNMENT BONDS

A range of different types of bonds are used in countries where local authorities or central government are allowed to raise them. These might be general obligation bonds where the city sells bonds to finance the construction of a facility and is later paid back via the general city revenue funds. Or they might be revenue bonds which are sold and then paid back from the revenue generated at the facility when it is operational.

TELEVISION

It is most common for TV rights for an event to remain with the event organiser, not the stadium. However, in some instances, the stadium can also be paid to allow certain rights.

CLUB DEBENTURES AND BONDS

A different type of bond is often used in the UK to fund new development. This involves members of the public being offered the right to buy a seat for a fixed period of time. The period can last from just a few years to as many as 125 years – as offered recently by a number of soccer clubs. This method of funding allows the club to finance new development and still maintain future income from seat sales.

GRANTS

By far the most attractive method of funding, as far as the developer is concerned, is a direct grant from a city or local authority. A grant may be offered for a number of reasons and can be very substantial. Florida, in the USA, for example, is reported to be offering $30 million for a professional team to move into the state. Grants can also take the form of specific financial assistance with areas such as road systems, drainage and general infrastructure. This can be significant at the early stages of development.

BETTING REVENUE

Sometimes this is a politically sensitive subject, but the betting revenue which accrues from sport is enormous, and continues to grow largely due to the increased accessibility of online betting. Although largely generated from horse racing, all sports promote some degree of betting. In countries where it is possible to reinvest a proportion of the profits, the sports facilities will benefit. In the USA, betting on American football and baseball is illegal. But in the UK and a number of other countries, betting on all sports is legal. It is not uncommon to find betting outlets at soccer stadia.

OUTSIDE INCOME

Income can be generated to help finance a project from outside the main operating area of the development. This usually involves the joint development of the stadium with other, perhaps more financially viable activities. These are sometimes referred to as 'enabling developments'. They can range from directly related activities, such as sports and health clubs, to completely unrelated activities, such as offices and residential accommodation. Such developments may not be possible in isolation but by combining with a stadium, they can increase their value and chances of securing a successful planning application. In some instances it may be beneficial to complete some or all of this development first in order to improve overall project cash flow.

NON-EVENT DAY ACTIVITIES

Although they are unlikely to be a major contributor to overall financing, the letting of the stadium's club areas, restaurants and boxes for conferences, weddings and parties can assist the whole financial picture. The frequency of these activities is likely to increase if the stadium is built adjacent to a complementary enabling development.

23.5   CONTROLLING COSTS AND REVENUES
23.5.1   TYPICAL HEADINGS

If the feasibility study indicates that all the above factors can be balanced to give a financially sustainable project, the next step is to ensure effective financial control in all parts of the facility. This includes the careful recording and checking of all transactions for both income and expenditure. It is important that the individual sources of income and expenditure are identified to allow their assessment at a later date.

We list below typical headings for these individual categories. Some carry very much more weight than others. The outgoing cost of financing the capital can account for as much as 70 per cent of the total.

271

INCOME

1   Spectator attendance.
2   Visitors to the ground on non-match days.
3   Club income from membership.
4   Advertising revenue.
5   Television revenue.
6   Ground rental for events.
7   Naming rights.
8   Car parking.
9   Leasing of commercial space.
10 Food and beverage sales.

EXPENDITURE

1   Staff costs.
2   Administration costs.
3   Maintenance expenses.
4   Public relations.
5   Operation costs.
6   Fuel and energy.
7   Machinery and repairs.
8   Events costs.
9   Taxation (if applicable).
10 Financing and depreciation.

23.5.2   CLUB PARTICIPATION POLICY

An important aspect of operational policy relates to the players who use a stadium owned and run by a club. The skill of the players, managers and trainers largely dictates the success of the team, and the success of the team in turn determines the financial strength of the club. A significant factor in this equation is the cost of buying athletes in professional sport, and the cost of training them. The league system is ideal for training as it gives all clubs a chance to find new and promising players who they can train to their financial benefit. But the North American college system is probably even better as it effectively pushes the cost of training on to the educational system. The cost of training players in American football and baseball is therefore relatively low.

It also benefits the financial stability of a sport to limit the number of teams who can take part, although this is against the principles of most amateur sports since they believe in as wide an involvement as possible. Rugby union, in the UK, for example, has around 2,000 registered clubs. The UK's Football League, meanwhile, is having a hard time preventing their league reducing from approximately 60 clubs. The theory is that if the number of top clubs is reduced, and the number of spectators at least stays the same, then there will be more spectators at the clubs who do survive. If you eliminate your competitors and thereby increase your market share, it is inevitable that sport becomes a market place when the financial risks and profits are so high.

One of the reasons for the perceived success of American sport is that the governing bodies of American football and baseball limit the number of clubs they allow to play in their competition by not granting playing franchises to new clubs. This has increased demand for the clubs who do have playing franchises since major cities value the recognition and financial advantages a major league club brings to their community. Having a team based in a city can add cultural perspectives to the community, and increase secondary spending from out-of-town fans on restaurants and hotels in the city. This situation puts the sports club in a very strong position to negotiate the terms of their moving to a city or their continued presence in a city. It is not uncommon for a club to have a new stadium built for it by the city authorities, or to be offered cash to relocate.

23.6   CONCLUSION

Stadia must be designed to an exacting set of financial controls in terms of both their initial capital cost and their ongoing operating costs. Maximum revenue potential must be built into the design. This is the key consideration for all developments but for stadia, the finances are often tougher than with other types of development. Therefore there is less room to make mistakes in the financial planning. Modern, safe, efficient and beautiful new stadia are possible, but if they are to survive anywhere near as long as those that our ancestors built, they must also prove themselves on the balance sheet.

24   SUSTAINABLE DESIGN

24.1	WHAT IS SUSTAINABLE DESIGN?
24.2	RE-USE
24.3	REDUCE
24.4	RECYCLE
24.5	PLANTING AND GREEN ROOFS
24.6	CERTIFICATION
24.7	FUTURE TECHNOLOGIES

24.1   WHAT IS SUSTAINABLE DESIGN?

Sustainable design, also known as environmentally sustainable development (ESD), is an increasingly important consideration in building construction. It is one of the dominant issues of our time.

The most widely quoted definition of sustainable development is from the Brundtland Commission of 1987: 'Sustainable development meets the needs of the present generation without compromising the ability of future generations to meet their own needs.'

Sustainable design recognises the interdependence of the built and natural environments. It seeks to harness natural energy from biological and renewable processes, eliminate reliance on fossil fuels and avoid the use of toxic materials. Another aim is to improve resource efficiency.

It is the responsibility of designers to create buildings which protect and potentially enhance the environment.

THE IOC

The International Olympic Committee (IOC) regards environmental issues as a priority. It is one of three policy objectives, alongside sport and culture.

As societies around the world have become increasingly conscious of environmental threats and challenges, so too has the Olympic movement. It is now the case that the Olympic Games cannot ignore the expectations of the public, and the needs of the planet. It must support not just environmental protection, but also sustainable development.

Many matters need to be considered. They include location and landscape. They determine not only the environmental impact, but also accessibility, proximity to users and visual impact. They include construction which can cause nuisance and can environmentally damage resources if not properly planned. And they include energy which can deplete resources, and increase air pollution, global warming and risks to human health.

The Copper Box, the handball arena for the London 2012 Olympics, showing natural light tubes in the soffit. Architects: Make and Populous.

Figure 24.1
Predicted global surface warming, based on the Intergovernmental Panel on Climate Change (4th Assessment Report)

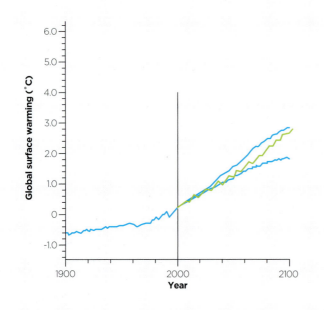

The London 2012 facilities are claimed to be the most sustainable of all modern Olympic Games.

Sustainability will be an enormously important issue for the future. Projections show huge effects on the planet caused by an increase in the planet's temperature. An increase in temperature is set to continue as the table below indicates.

In developed countries roughly one half of the energy used by society is from the construction and operation of buildings. This results in carbon dioxide emissions which are harmful to the planet. Figure 24.2 shows the typical consumption for countries by sector in the developed world (based on UK statistics).

Building designers need to deal with the matter in two parts: the amount of energy needed in the construction of the building, and the amount of energy required for its use.

There are three key factors in minimising the quantity of materials used in the construction, and reducing the environmental impact of sports and entertainment venues worldwide:

RE-USE
REDUCE
RECYCLE

Figure 24.2
Diagram showing the typical national consumption of energy by sector.

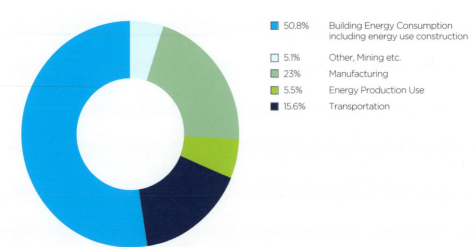

50.8%	Building Energy Consumption including energy use construction
5.1%	Other, Mining etc.
23%	Manufacturing
5.5%	Energy Production Use
15.6%	Transportation

24.2   RE-USE

When planning a new building, the first thing to investigate is whether an existing building can be re-used, refurbished or even given a radical redesign.

RE-USE: WIMBLEDON

The redevelopment of Wimbledon's Centre Court is a great example of a sports venue that has been given a radical redesign. The owners, The All England Lawn Tennis Club, realised that to maintain the status of Wimbledon's prestigious tennis tournament, they needed to improve their facilities. But rather than knock down their existing Centre Court, they decided to make a range of improvements to it, including a new retractable roof. Around 75 per cent of the stadium has been re-used, and much of the original 1922 design has remained (see Case studies).

Other facilities at Wimbledon in need of upgrading will benefit from this blend of heritage and innovation.

RE-USE: TRANSPORT

Whenever possible, existing transport infrastructure should be used. The potential legacy of new infrastructure should be planned for.

Occasionally it is the local transportation rather than the actual stadium itself which is the most important feature of a redevelopment. In the 1990s, England's Football Association looked at several potential sites for their new national stadium. However, one of their existing stadium's strongest points was its public transport system that had been developed over the previous 80 years. In terms of sustainability, it was far better to rebuild Wembley where it was, rather than relocate and be forced to construct brand new transport links.

A new rail line was built for the Sydney 2000 Olympic Games. It linked the city centre with Homebush Bay, home to a number of key Olympic facilities such as the main stadium, the swimming centre, the media centre, the athletes' village and the hockey, tennis and basketball venues.

In Beijing, use was made of existing university facilities that were already well served by public transport. A massive investment in the Chinese capital's transport system enabled several key projects to be completed including:

- A new terminal building and a third runway for the international airport.
- An additional fifth and sixth ring on the road network.
- Four new metro lines for Beijing Metro, including a direct link between the city centre and the airport.

RE-USE: TEMPORARY STRUCTURES

Temporary structures are particularly useful for cities staging major one-off sports events such as the Olympic Games.

There are many forms a temporary structure can take. These include:

Temporary structures used only for a major sports event and then later dismantled. Several of these were built in London for the 2012 Olympic Games.

Temporary modular grandstand structures added to an existing sports venue to cater for a one-off influx of spectators. Similarly, the main stadium for the 2014 Asian Games in the South Korean city of Incheon will initially hold 70,000 spectators, before shrinking to a capacity of 30,000 afterwards and becoming a park for the local community. The Hypo-Arena, in the Austrian city of Klagenfurt, catered for 32,000 football fans during the 2008 European Football Championships. Now the event is over, it may be reduced in size. The ANZ Stadium in Sydney featured temporary stands for the 2000 Olympic Games that gave it a capacity of 115,000. When they were removed after the event then it reduced to 80,000 (see Case studies).

Temporary facilities designed to be later reassembled and re-used elsewhere. The temporary stand at the Sydney Aquatic Centre, for the 2000 Olympic Games, for example, was later reconstructed as part of Wollongong Showground, just south of Sydney.

The London 2012 Stadium was designed for a capacity of 80,000 for the Olympic events. This allowed the possibility for the upper tier structure to be removed after the Games, leaving a reduced capacity of 25,000 (see Case studies).

24.3   REDUCE

Sports stadia are huge pieces in the overall infrastructure of a city. When it comes to sustainable design, their use of energy is a major issue. The industry must learn to reduce the energy used in their initial construction – the so-called embodied energy – and to later re-use the building materials in future projects.

Operational energy – The energy used in heating, lighting and cooling a building.

Embodied energy – The energy used in the materials and construction of new buildings.

REDUCE: EMBODIED ENERGY

278

In office buildings, most of the energy expended is operational energy, used to heat, cool and illuminate the interior. It is a similar case in concert arenas. The O2 Arena, in London, for example, is used as much as 200 days a year.

But when it comes to stadia, usage is on a much lower scale. The energy used to build a stadium – the embodied energy – far outweighs the operational energy used over its lifetime. Most stadia are designed to last 50 years, but many are used for only 18 months of those 50 years. Once they reach the end of their useful lives, they then require huge amounts of energy in demolition – far more than typical office buildings do.

This is why lean design of stadia and the considered use of materials in construction or refurbishment are so important.

Source materials used in the construction of buildings should be selected according to their life-cycle cost and likely environmental impact. Consideration should be given to factors such as energy used and pollution generated during extraction, processing, manufacture, transport, treatment and disposal of these materials. It is a good idea to consider the life of the materials to be used in construction in order to extend the period before replacement is needed. Materials which are produced using toxic substances should be avoided.

The design of stadia and arenas should incorporate flexibility for multi-purpose use.

The stadia or arenas can also be linked with other facilities such as retail and conferences.

London's O2 Arena has become the world's most popular entertainment venue, selling 2.34 million tickets in 2010. It is crucial that venues such as this are designed to stage all types of music, sports and entertainment, in order that the embodied energy used to construct them is not wasted.

REDUCE: OPERATIONAL USE

The stadia we design need to be more flexible so they can stage all types of events, and operate at least 80 days a year. A stadium that can welcome sports as disparate as rugby or athletics, and stage pop concerts or large meetings, will be a more sustainable building over its life thanks to a more efficient use of its embodied energy.

Another solution is to design two venues within one and thereby satisfy the needs of several stakeholders. This prevents unnecessary construction, shares embodied energy and maximises revenue.

Every facility should be used as much as possible. Multi-purpose stadia and arenas should also include other non-sport functions and facilities that have a symbiotic relationship with the sport function. Hotels, for example, where hotel rooms are private viewing boxes, or conference space, educational facilities, community facilities etc.

REDUCE: SUSTAINABLE STRUCTURES
EFFICIENT DESIGN

When it comes to developing sustainable structures, the most crucial aspect is efficient design. Innovative lightweight structures will reduce the amount of building material required, and make use of materials that produce less carbon dioxide during their manufacture. This reduces both the overall embodied energy and the financial costs. The less material and the simpler the designs, the more you save in energy and money.

SUSTAINABLE MATERIALS

Wood, for example, is much easier to manipulate than steel. It can always be sourced locally, and developed into clever but simple structural solutions. The building materials with the greatest amount of embodied energy in them are aluminium and stainless steel. The latter contains six times

Figure 24.3
Comparison of the whole-life energy use of stadia and other building types.

more than reinforced concrete, for example. When it comes to carbon dioxide emissions, both aluminium and steel are major culprits.

The choice of building material for sports venues depends on several factors: size, capacity, location and use. Despite containing less embodied energy, concrete is not always the best choice since it is so much heavier than a steel structure of similar strength. By far the greatest amount of embodied energy is in the foundations and superstructure, rather than in the cladding, so it is important for designers and engineers to use little steel or concrete in these areas.

RECYCLED MATERIALS

Increased use of recycled materials is essential to reduce the embodied energy in the building fabric.

TRANSPORTATION

The transportation of building materials from source to construction site is often overlooked. Shipping timber by sea from Canada across the Atlantic Ocean to the UK, for example, uses less embodied energy than transporting timber the short distance by road from the north to the south of the UK. Sea freight uses the least embodied energy, while air freight uses the most.

TOPOGRAPHY

It is important to make use of the existing topography of the construction site as much as possible. This may include building terracing onto the natural slope of the land.

Lightweight and efficient structures mean less material used in the structure. This, in turn, means fewer

25

BRAND ACTIVATION

25.1   MAXIMISING REVENUE

25.2   TIME, NOT SPACE

25.3   BRAND ACTIVATION THROUGH INTEGRATION: THE FAN EXPERIENCE

25.4   MARRYING TEAM BRAND WITH COMMERCIAL IDENTITIES

25.5   THE PROCESS

In the stadia business, revenue is generated primarily from three sources:

287

• ticket sales
• broadcasting rights
• sponsorship

Nowadays sponsors are looking for far wider and more sophisticated ways to engage with audiences than mere static adverts on a wall. Outside the seating bowl and its concourses, every part of a building is defined by commerciality. So how do you marry design with the need for revenue?

25.1   MAXIMISING REVENUE

The first and most obvious point is to optimise the design to appeal to the relevant company or customer. A city law firm might want to see a wood-panelled suite, for example, whereas a digital start-up company would be looking for a more high-tech solution. Of course, for most commercial buildings, there's more than one company to consider. The O2 Arena, for example, has a naming rights partner with huge collateral, but beneath that the building provides the canvas for up to ten founding partners and almost 100 suite-holders, each seeking return on their investments. For the designer, the goal is to create unique opportunities for all sponsorship partners, without drowning them out with other advertising noise. It's crucial that the presence or impact of one branded opportunity doesn't reduce the value of another.

25.2   TIME, NOT SPACE

It used to be the case that advertising – as far as buildings were concerned – was sign writing: simply a slogan occupying physical space. It was fixed and hard to change. Nowadays, technology allows all sorts of ways to advertise. Consider New York City's Times Square – the flashing and blinking of hundreds of slogans, each given their allotted

Emirates Stadium London. The identities of the club and its major sponsor, Emirates Airlines, designed in concert around the venue. Architects: Populous

time in rotation. This is a much more malleable form of branding. Major sponsors, or founding partners, can be given longer and more frequent time in the spotlight, whilst those with less equity still have an opportunity to have their name seen.

This concept of time doesn't just apply to names flashing up, or ticker-tape messages. Temporary pop-up advertising structures are an increasingly popular branding solution. Physically, particularly with stadia, it's impossible to allot permanent space to every brand. The building would need to be limitless. By creating temporary pods or pop-ups, you allow brands a presence, and give fans an essential point of focus, without being committed to a permanent structure. This also enhances the fan zone experience. By giving brands the option to re-site themselves outside a stadium or arena, they are able to continue interacting with the fans long after the end of an event. This interaction can then be tailored to the particular event and its audience.

25.3   BRAND ACTIVATION THROUGH INTEGRATION: THE FAN EXPERIENCE

We don't do advertising anymore. We just do cool stuff.
Simon Pestridge, Nike UK Marketing Director
(*Revolution* magazine)

This begs the question: how do our buildings become part of the cool stuff? Or, to put it another way, how do you create an experience?

To do this, it's important to understand a brand. What is the brand's DNA? And how can you integrate that into a building so that fans or visitors interact with the brand in a three-dimensional way, and so that the positive experience they enjoy on seeing their favourite band or team play is extended to positive feelings about the brand?

Consider London's O2 Arena. On the exterior of the building, the distinctive blue branding is bold, without being overwhelming. Inside, the colour continues, subliminally reminding event-goers who the venue sponsor is. From the way-finding signage and the lighting, to the food and drink concessions, the identity of communications company O2 flows through the building like blood through a body.

25.4   MARRYING TEAM BRAND WITH COMMERCIAL IDENTITIES

The Emirates Stadium, home of Arsenal Football Club, in London, is another example of imaginative brand activation. The large concrete letters spelling Arsenal at the entrance act as an anti-terrorist vehicle barrier, a meeting point and a climbing frame for local children. At the same time they embed the club in the community. The club's identity is carefully balanced with that of the major naming-rights sponsor, Emirates – a key consideration in many modern stadia.

In the past decade, sports teams have become brands in their own right. Industry pioneers such as Karen Brady have extended the brand of football clubs such as Birmingham City through innovative community promotions. For example, Arsenal have eight million fans on Facebook, but only 60,000 seats in their ground. In the United States, only seven per cent of National Football League fans have ever set foot in an NFL stadium. The world of social media, loyalty cards and mobile messaging has broadened the fan experience far beyond buying a ticket, leaving home and travelling to a match.

This has to be considered when designing sporting stadia. The identity of the club has to stay strong and legible because it's this identity that the commercial brands want to be associated with in the first place. Co-branding is the ultimate aim: a perfect marriage between the sponsor and the owner.

25.5   THE PROCESS

At the start of the design process, a stadium's future sponsor or naming-rights partner is, in all likelihood, unknown. Thus you're creating a blank canvas to which you can apply a number of treatments, all with the aim of attracting different sponsors. The space outside the building will also be key; and the internal and external elements need to work together. Much like building a Formula 1 car, experts work on each component to create something that, as a whole, works perfectly, giving the event-goer a seamless brand experience.

01

APPENDIX: STADIA BRIEFING GUIDE

General design information

Status of commission	Feasibility study Outline design Full design Working drawings Supervision	Previous studies Board requirements Local authority needs
Finances	Financial constraints Maximum costs Revenue potential	Present income Projected income
Programme	Planning timetable Building start date Target completion date Close season consideration	Determine phasing Determine financing

Project objectives

Compactness	Provide good visibility Minimum viewing distances	Running track included Additional sports
Catering	Participants Spectators Family provision Private boxes Hospitality suites Club facilities Administrators	
Convenience	Accessible to transport Location in city	
Comfort	Inviting environment Easily understood Clear signposting	
Flexibility	Arrangement of spaces Juxtaposition of spaces Relationship of spaces	
Economics	Initial capital expenditure Annual maintenance costs	

Project parameters

Client's requirements	Accommodation schedule	Participants Spectators Administrators
Traffic movement	Car, bus, pedestrian, rail	Public and private vehicles Inside and outside stadia
Ground capacity	Seated and standing	Consider trends Design to be convertible
Site services Phased development	Present and future Options with flexibility	Service phasing Pattern of use Phased financing
Safety and control	Police and stewarding	

02

Since publication of the first edition of this book, there have been huge developments in giant screens and electronic scoreboards. Indeed, they have become a necessary feature in modern stadia and technology. They are also discussed in the Chapter on Services, Section 21.2.2.

Larger stadia will often use the large screen colour video display (LSVD), but there are options for stadia with more modest budgets to use limited video capability, providing text information and high-quality graphics. For those stadia considering investing in this type of technology, early dialogue with manufacturers and suppliers is advisable. The following notes offer brief guidance:

LSVD can represent a major capital outlay and should be carefully selected to suit the needs and light conditions of the stadium, as well as the budget the client has available. Considerations also need to be given to the integration of the scoreboards, the video production room and the LSVD, as the specification and performance of one of these elements can have an effect on the others.

Video screens can now form part of larger integrated systems to transmit pictures to smaller screens around sports buildings through wireless signals to phones or other hand-held devices and onto the internet.

Certain systems are sold with some accompanying video editing software, but in other cases an editing suite may be required to provide the content shown on the screen.

The expertise of the simple scoreboard companies is usually not applicable to the LSVD companies, and vice versa. In order to secure the best value for each particular stadium, it should be considered whether high definition (or even very high definition) is required. For example, scoreboards need relatively low-tech light bulbs, whereas using the same technology to replay action from a cricket match would be inappropriate.

TECHNOLOGY

LED technology has overtaken all others for large screens and now offers high-resolution, fast-refresh rates, sufficient brightness to be viewed in sunlight and reduced energy usage.

The screen is made up of three base colours: red, blue and green. When combined, these colours can produce the 16.7 million colours theoretically possible.

LIFE CYCLE

While the life-cycle costing of screens is important, their longevity is less important in a stadium situation. Most stadia will only use their screen for around 250 hours per year. Since most LED screens have a lifespan of approximately 100,000 hours, this is not a major consideration. The cost of maintenance, refurbishment and operation is, however, a key component in the life-cycle analysis. A decision also has to be made about how long the screen will remain cutting-edge, and how long before it becomes obsolete.

QUALITY

The quality of the screen image is mainly determined by the quality of the LEDs used for the pixels, and the pixel pitch of the screen. Generally, the smaller the pitch (i.e. the closer together the pixels are to each other), the better the image will be. A resolution of 576 x 720 is suggested as a minimum. The video processor is also of high importance for the quality of the image. The control system should at least be ready for HD-SDI signals. The pixel pitch has been reduced over the last few years, and today the typical range of pixels used for stadium installations is 16mm, 20mm or 26mm.

SCREEN SIZE AND POSITION

The size of a screen for any given location is ideally determined by its height, which should be three to five per cent of the maximum viewing distance from the screen. The screen itself should have a proportion of four units in width by three units in height. (Preferably 16 units wide by nine units high.) Therefore, in a stadium where the maximum viewing distance is 200m, the screen should be 6m high and 8m or 10m wide. This would produce a screen of 48m² or 60m², which, if it was LED, would weigh around 3.5 tonnes. It should be noted that screens also have a minimum viewing distance of around 8m. It is obviously necessary for screens to be visible to all spectators. Viewing angles should not be less than 140° horizontally (-70°/+70°), and 60° vertically (-30°/+30°).

Other ways of showing moving images are becoming available thanks to more powerful projectors, and LED in strips or curved screens that can be mounted in various imaginative ways around the building and the development of more powerful projectors.

COST

After all considerations have been taken into account, it is the available budget that will be the main determinant in the selection of a screen. Manufacturers should be contacted about prices, but it is important to note that comparative costs should include the supporting structure, electricity supply and control software. Some manufacturers will offer deals for the supply of large screens together with other electrical equipment, or if the cost can be set against advertising revenue.

SCREEN COMPANIES

It seems there are over 4,000 screen companies currently in existence but probably only 20 to 30 who could be considered major players.

PROGRAMME

The procurement strategy may consider a hire arrangement which can be very attractive if use is low. This might be a single package, or split into two or three packages. Lead times are around one month to develop an invitation to tender; one month for the companies to respond; four to five months for manufacturing; and a final month for installation.

03

APPENDIX: CASE STUDIES

INTRODUCTION

The following case studies are examples of stadia design from all over the world. They are listed in an alphabetical sequence. The examples have been chosen to illustrate different responses to the design challenges, which reflect location, climate and circumstance. They also reflect different uses: some are multi-purpose, some are sport specific. Many incorporate technical innovation, and some have opening and closing roofs. Most of the examples are large in scale: it is felt that these produce the real design challenges for the designers. Some respond to their site situation, but all have something interesting to say about stadium design.

01.	ALLIANZ ARENA	MUNICH, GERMANY
02.	AMSTERDAM ARENA	AMSTERDAM, NETHERLANDS
03.	ANZ STADIUM	SYDNEY, AUSTRALIA
04.	ARIZONA CARDINALS STADIUM	PHOENIX, USA
05.	ASCOT RACECOURSE	ASCOT, UK
06.	ASTANA STADIUM	ASTANA, KAZAKHSTAN
07.	AT&T PARK	SAN FRANCISCO, USA
08.	AVIVA STADIUM	DUBLIN, IRELAND
09.	BRAGA MUNICIPAL STADIUM	BRAGA, PORTUGAL
10.	COWBOYS STADIUM	DALLAS, USA
11.	DONBASS ARENA	DONETSK, UKRAINE
12.	EMIRATES STADIUM	LONDON, UK
13.	FORSYTH-BARR STADIUM	DUNEDIN, NEW ZEALAND
14.	GREENPOINT STADIUM	CAPE TOWN, SOUTH AFRICA
15.	HEINZ FIELD	PITTSBURGH, USA
16.	MARLINS PARK	MIAMI, USA
17.	MELBOURNE CRICKET GROUND	MELBOURNE, AUSTRALIA
18.	TELSTRA DOME	MELBOURNE, AUSTRALIA
19.	NANJING SPORTS PARK	NANJING, CHINA
20.	OITA STADIUM	OITA, JAPAN
21.	OLYMPIC STADIUM	LONDON, UK
22.	THE OVAL	LONDON, UK
23.	RELIANT STADIUM	HOUSTON, USA
24.	SALZBURG STADIUM	SALZBURG, AUSTRIA
25.	SOCCER CITY	JOHANNESBURG, SOUTH AFRICA
26.	SOLDIER FIELD	CHICAGO, USA
27.	STADE DE FRANCE	PARIS, FRANCE
28.	STATTEGG SPORTS AND LEISURE FACILITY	GRAZ, AUSTRIA
29.	WEMBLEY STADIUM	LONDON, UK
30.	WESTPAC STADIUM	WELLINGTON, NEW ZEALAND
31.	WIMBLEDON AELTC: CENTRE COURT	LONDON, UK

01. ALLIANZ ARENA MUNICH, GERMANY

Completed in 2005, the Allianz Arena was designed by Herzog & De Meuron to host the opening game of the FIFA World Cup 2006. It is home to two local soccer clubs, FC Bayern and TSV 1860. The architecture of the 60,000-seat stadium is distinguished, above all, by its unique skin. This is a translucent luminous body consisting of large shimmering white, diamond-shaped ETFE cushions, each of which can be illuminated separately in white, red or light blue, the colours of the two clubs. The colours of the cushions can be controlled digitally so that the home team playing in the stadium can be identified from the outside. The outer enclosures of the stadium are multilayer, pneumatic structures. At every corner a pumping station maintains the internal air pressure within the pneumatic elements. The changing appearance of the stadium enhances its attraction as an urban monument even for people who are not interested in soccer.

The design concept is based on three principles. Firstly, the presence of the stadium as an illuminated body that can change its appearance. Secondly, to have fans arrive procession-like in a landscaped area. And thirdly, to develop a crater-like interior of the stadium itself.

Both the shell and the structural skeleton of the stadium are designed throughout to implement these three key concepts. Hence, the main stairs along the outside of the shell follow the line of greatest slope underscoring the procession-like approach of visitors to the stadium. As a huge luminous body, the stadium marks a new location in the open landscape to the north between the airport and downtown Munich.

The car parks are laid out between the underground station and the stadium so as to create an artificial landscape for the arrival and departure of the fans. Since only soccer will be played at the stadium, the seating is directly adjacent to the pitch, and each of the three tiers is as close as possible to the action.

302

Architects: Herzog
& De Meuron

02. AMSTERDAM ARENA AMSTERDAM, NETHERLANDS

Completed in 1996, Amsterdam ArenA was the first European stadium to be built with a retractable roof. It opens and closes within 25 minutes. The state-of-the-art 52,000-seat stadium, which can be increased to 68,000 seats for concerts, is the home of the Ajax Football Club, as well as the stage for a range of very successful entertainment events. The stadium hosts more than 70 major events every year, including concerts, dance parties, religious meetings, product presentations and other sporting events such as international matches of the Dutch national soccer team and American football. The Amsterdam ArenA has a wide range of corporate facilities including a Royal Suite, VIP lounges and 16 hospitality rooms which can seat 2,500, as well as 2,000 business seats.

The stadium is located in the east of Amsterdam and is accessed by several metro and railway stations.

There is also a large car park for 2,000 cars under the stadium, and 12,000 car parking spaces within walking distance of the arena. The arena is continuously upgrading its facilities such as a new sound system, and more escalators and elevators for the long climb from the underground parking to the second tier. The roof is based on two large arches with two longitudinal beams corresponding to the playing field's rectangle fixed to them. Semi-transparent panels are connected to the arch. It is these panels which open and close to provide the retractable roof.

The arena has two large video screens and an internal pay system with smart cards acting as an electronic purse. Supporting facilities include a museum and fan shop.

303

Architects: Robert Schuurman & Sjoerd Soeters

03. ANZ STADIUM SYDNEY, AUSTRALIA

ANZ Stadium (formerly Stadium Australia and Telstra Stadium) was the largest Olympic stadium ever built. During the main ceremonies of the Sydney 2000 Olympic Games it hosted 110,000 people. It is both durable and adaptable, a powerful icon on the Sydney landscape. It has since been reconfigured to 80,000 seats, with a rectangular pitch added, to suit rugby league, rugby union and soccer. It is also used for concerts, exhibitions and public gatherings. The philosophy behind the stadium is to provide a flexible, multi-functional and economically viable venue with widespread appeal.

One of the main design features is the translucent saddle-shaped stadium roof which is 58m (or 16 storeys) above the arena. It is a hyperbolic paraboloid, which not only offers protection to twice the number of spectators when compared to stadia with cantilever roofs of a similar form, but allows

rainwater to be siphoned off into tanks to irrigate the pitch. The roof slopes down towards the pitch, enhancing the intense atmosphere and optimising stadium acoustics. The roof is supported by the seating structure and two 295m-long trusses.

Spectators have access to the stands via four helical ramps, escalators and lifts. The stadium's circulation routes for spectators, athletes and services personnel were designed never to cross for reasons of security, convenience and efficiency.

The stadium is environmentally sustainable. Passive design measures include ventilation, natural cooling and heating. Rainwater is recycled from the roof and used to irrigate the pitch.

Architects: Populous and Bligh Voller Nield

04. ARIZONA CARDINALS STADIUM
PHOENIX, USA

The Arizona Cardinals Stadium is a 65,000-seat stadium located in the Phoenix suburb of Glendale, in Arizona.

The project sports an opening roof to shelter spectators from the desert sun. Additionally, as a first for North America, the stadium contains a moveable playing field. The field resides outdoors most of the time, rolling into the stadium on rails for use during American football games and other sporting events. This provides the grass with the sunshine it needs to grow, and also allows the building to function as a venue for trade shows, concerts or other events on non-game days.

The basic form of the stadium pays tribute to its surroundings, taking the shape of a barrel cactus. The outer skin features dramatic vertical slots that alternate with large, smooth panels, creating a beacon whose colour and light reflect the brilliant Arizona desert sky. This mixture of steel decking, glass, stucco and a fabric roof creates sweeping lines and a sense of texture in the design.

In addition to housing the Arizona Cardinals American football team, the stadium hosted the 2008 Super Bowl.

Architects: Populous
with Eisenmann
Architects

305

05. ASCOT RACECOURSE ASCOT, UK

Top-class thoroughbreds and world-class jockeys compete for some of the highest accolades in horse racing against the stunning new backdrop of this grandstand, completed in 2006. As elegant as the fashions on the field, and as exciting as the action on the track, the new Ascot Racecourse provides the essential requisites for a satisfying racing experience: aesthetics, style, taste, simplicity and clarity.

The new 30,000-seat grandstand is perched on the brow of a hill with panoramic views of the course to the north and Windsor Great Park beyond.

The 480-metre grandstand takes the form of a shallow-arched hyperbolic paraboloid, conceptualised as 'a building between trees'. A slight curve on plan embraces the racecourse.

The new stands, with their lofty, elegant and structured architecture, form a backdrop to the parade ring, the outdoor public spaces and social activities. The combination of large-scale dramatic new stands, the buildings retained at the site

edge, and major public outdoor lawn spaces distinguished by mature deciduous trees, all provide the race-goer with a variety of different spatial experiences. This much-loved characteristic experience of the Ascot Racecourse has been preserved to enhance the uplifting spaces created in the new buildings.

Running the length of the building, the internal galleria both separates and connects the viewing and dining functions. The design of the southern elevation to the galleria brings natural light into the covered concourse, providing even-tempered environmental shelter at the heart of the building.

The grounds of Ascot Racecourse have numerous superb trees which inspired the soaring steel structure of the cathedral-like galleria. The large atrium acts as an environmental lung for the grandstand, which is topped by a lightweight glass and steel roof. Sailing over the whole building are the dramatic form and lines of the roof's light, sweeping canopy.

306

Architects: Populous

307

Architects: Populous
in collaboration with
Tabanlioglu Architects

06. ASTANA ASTANA, KAZAKHSTAN

The Astana Stadium is a 32,500-seat venue located in the
new sports campus of the Kazakhstan capital, Astana.

It has an opening roof, and is fully air-conditioned to
mitigate the extremes of the local climate. The pitch is turfed
to FIFA standards.

This is the first modern stadium project in Kazakhstan, and
the first stadium in any former Soviet Union country with an
opening roof.

It was opened by the president of Kazakhstan on 3 July
2009 and, two years later, hosted the opening ceremony of
the 2011 Asian Winter Games.

The stadium is conceived as a multi-functional venue for
soccer and other sporting events, as well as grand shows and
large-scale cultural ceremonies. Its form was generated by
the need to create an efficient enclosure and to ensure a
simple opening roof design. The overall form is cylindrical
with the roof moving horizontally across the short east-west
axis. Primary and secondary trusses connect to quadruped
columns in the stadium bowl. The moving roof elements are
clad with clear polycarbonate, and a roof light encircles the
stadium all the way around the perimeter, coinciding with the
structure of the perimeter truss and the wall structure. In this
way, the structural design of the stadium is highlighted so
that spectators can have a sense of how the building works.

07. AT&T PARK, SAN FRANCISCO, USA

The site for AT&T Park has it all: San Francisco's skyline, the hills of the East Bay and vivid ocean sunsets over the Golden Gate. The ballpark takes every advantage of its spectacular location, creating a seamless relationship with the city and turning the bay into an inimitable design feature. The *San Francisco Chronicle* called it 'reassuring proof that cities can still glow'.

Spectators commonly arrive using public transport. The journey becomes part of the experience, from a lively streetcar ride to a scenic ferry trip, or an invigorating amble down Second Street. Upon arrival, visitors are greeted with a composition of steel, concrete and brick. Heroic in scale and proportion, the ballpark's rugged face recaptures the spirit of the grand old game, and the South of Market context. Flanked by clock towers, this face engages the city street network and the neighbourhood's scale.

Recalling the language of the ubiquitous waterfront pier buildings, larger than life portals allow the public to glimpse the verdant playing field without a ticket. This gesture of owner and architect collaboration is perhaps the most compelling example of the effort to combine the building, the game and the city as one.

Architects: Populous

308

08. AVIVA STADIUM DUBLIN, IRELAND

The new 50,000-seat Aviva stadium was opened in 2010 to replace the Lansdowne Road stadium where the first game of international rugby was played in Ireland in 1876. The new building was developed by the Football Association of Ireland and the Irish Rugby Football Union as the new home for their national teams, whilst also being flexible enough to host concerts on the pitch, conferences and social events in the lounges and concourses.

The site is close to the centre of the city, with a railway running through it, surrounded by residential properties on three sides, and a river on the fourth side. The complicated site conditions led the design team to create a building responsive to the requirements of the land and its surroundings. A curvilinear shape,

and a roof that drops to the south and drops more dramatically to the north, allows light to the nearby houses. Covered in polycarbonate panels, the roof and walls of the stadium allow plenty of light onto the pitch and into the spaces surrounding it.

This is an environmentally friendly stadium. Energy use was reduced during construction, and measures have been included to lower energy consumption during the life of the building. The mechanical systems include hot water heated by waste heat from the generators, whilst rainwater is recycled to irrigate the pitch. Its location in the city, with no parking on site for spectators, means that car travel is reduced. Spectators reach the stadium either on foot or via public transport.

Architects: Populous and Scott Tallon Walker

310

Architects: Souto Moura
– Arquitectos

09. BRAGA MUNICIPAL STADIUM
BRAGA, PORTUGAL

Braga Municipal Stadium is situated within the Dume Sports Park on the northern slope of Monte Castro, in Portugal. The stadium, built for the 2004 UEFA European Football Championship, has two unusual features. It has been integrated into its rocky surroundings, and it features only two stands, located along the sides of the pitch.

The location was chosen to avoid making a dam along the water's edge in the valley. The two stands, each accommodating 15,000 spectators, are very different. The West Stand was dug into the rock after 1,000,000m³ of granite were removed from the hillside. It is accessed from above at a height of 40m. The entrance offers expansive views across the stadium and the surrounding countryside. Inside there are spacious access and concourse areas as well as extensive VIP areas, including a two-storey underground car park beneath the pitch, a separate entrance and catering facilities.

The East Stand is a free-standing, solid reinforced concrete building, accessed via eight ramps which lead to an ambulatory serving the lower tier, with stairs to the upper tier. Both stands are fully covered with strongly projecting roofs, connected with ropes and modelled on the ancient bridges of the Peruvian Incas.

10. COWBOYS STADIUM DALLAS, USA

Deeply concerned at the adverse impact of television on fan attendance, the stadium owner for the Dallas Cowboys NFL team challenged the architects to deliver a facility within which the 'real time/real place' experience of viewers would be superior in all aspects to that of home viewing. HKS responded with a design that effectively 'fuses' three building genres (stadium/auditorium/cinema) into a new stadium typology.

The new stadium for the Dallas Cowboys in Arlington, Texas, was opened in 2009. It is the largest domed stadium in the world with a capacity of 110,000 including 80,000 seats, plus decks and terraces at the ends for standing spectators. It has an opening roof and opening ends walls and is fully air-conditioned internally.

Spectators watch the events live whilst simultaneously viewing action 'close-ups' on the 55 metre wide/15 metre high centre-hung screens which also provide complementary information (personal player histories etc.) and action replays as the event proceeds. Over 3,000 LCD screens within VIP and concourse areas ensure fans remain involved and informed wherever they are within the stadium.

The stadium is also designed to accommodate multiple other sporting events, concerts and conferences as a basis for securing supplementary revenues. These range from traditional conventions and trade fairs to motocross, and from rodeo shows to soccer, pop-concerts, 'popera' and opera.

In the spirit of the Greek and Roman traditions of 'civitas' and public place making, leading contemporary artists were commissioned to create major installations throughout the public areas of the venue. Priceless and permanent, they are an expression of the civic value attached to the stadium

Architects: HKS

11. DONBASS ARENA DONETSK, UKRAINE

This stadium, for local team Shaktar Donetsk, seats 52,500 people, and opened in August 2009, to coincide with Ukrainian Miners' day. It is situated in a region famous for mining.

Construction began on 27 June 2006. Around US$400 million was spent constructing it, and also the surrounding landscape. Ukraine's first UEFA Five Star Stadium, it was a host venue for the 2012 UEFA European Football Championship.

It was conceived as a 'jewel in the park', namely Donetsk's Leninsky Komosol Park, a site of major cultural importance. It is also known locally as the 'Diamond of Donetsk'.

The arena has a distinctive jewel-like shape, with a 24,000m² glazed facade, intended to evoke a diamond when lit from within at night.

The roof design is partly a solution to the geotechnical challenges of the four mines and two fault lines in the area. It slopes from north to south so as to allow optimal sunlight and ventilation to the natural grass pitch.

Besides sporting events, the venue also hosts concerts and shows. There are cafes and restaurants on site, as well as a club museum and brand shop. The stadium has over 1,000 car parking spaces (245 are underground), and 45 corporate boxes that can accommodate 830 people. It has received several awards, including: the 2009 Top Construction Site award by Donetsk Design & Construction Club, the 2009 Best International Mobotix Project award, and the 2009 Best Construction in Ukraine prize.

312

Architects: Arup

12. EMIRATES STADIUM LONDON, UK

Emirates Stadium is a striking addition to the civic architecture of Islington, in north London, and an excellent example of a stadium acting as a tool for urban regeneration. On a former brownfield site defined by railway lines on two of its boundaries, this 60,000m², 60,000-seat state-of-the-art stadium replaced the revered Highbury Stadium. The design reflects the demanding nature of the site and rises dramatically behind Victorian terraces, revealing itself in unusual, unexpected vistas that create a striking juxtaposition of scale. Two new bridges link the stadium with the adjacent neighbourhoods.

It has an elliptical form with eight cores around the circumference. Steel tripods support the two primary trusses, resulting in a clean-edged roofline. The materials give a clear reading of the building's function. Toughened glass plank façades at podium level respond to the more robust environment of large crowds, while overlapping glazed and woven-steel mesh screens articulate the exposed concrete of the vertical circulation cores at higher level. A metallic under-clad roof seemingly floats above the exposed concrete seating bowl. Undulating glazing shelters the rear of the upper tier.

The stadium provides an upper and lower tier of general admission seating, with a range of positions for disabled spectators. In between these levels are the corporate and executive box facilities. The Club Level provides a unique mix of restaurant and networking bar spaces, plus dedicated bowl seating, with 150 executive boxes and an exclusive private members' club above.

Emirates Stadium was the catalyst for an integrated urban planning exercise to regenerate a deprived, underutilised area stretching west from the existing stadium. One of Britain's largest regeneration projects, it will see the construction of over 2,000 new homes, including key worker and social housing, and create over 1,800 new jobs.

By adopting a series of green measures integral to the design – for example, using passive environmental systems to heat and cool the building – the stadium also helps to redevelop the area in a forward-looking and sustainable way.

Architects: Populous

13. FORSYTH-BARR STADIUM
DUNEDIN, NEW ZEALAND

Located in the city of Dunedin, on New Zealand's South Island, this innovative building is the most southerly professional sports stadium in the world. It has a notoriously cold, wet and windy climate. Completed for the Rugby World Cup, in 2011, to replace the existing Carisbrook Stadium, it has 20,000 permanent and 11,000 temporary seats. This meant that after the tournament it became the largest indoor venue in the country, and was used for concerts and festivals as well as rugby and soccer.

This is the only stadium in the world to have a natural grass pitch grown under a fully enclosed roof of ETFE. It's a new prototype for stadia in cooler climates. The stands are on the two long sides, with the end walls and roof designed to maximise the amount of sunlight reaching the grass. The pitch construction, maintenance regime, ventilation and light conditions were thoroughly modelled and studied before construction. An experimental enclosure was set up to test the growth of grass under a sample roof, and out in the open. The turf under the ETFE was found to be stronger.

Architects: Populous in association with Jasmax

315

14. GREENPOINT STADIUM CAPE TOWN, SOUTH AFRICA

The skyline of Cape Town is dominated by Table Mountain, Signal Hill and the Atlantic Ocean. Greenpoint Stadium forms a landmark at the foot of Signal Hill, and fits respectfully into its environment. The challenge was to create a standalone building in this unique location that enriches rather than mars the world-famous picture-postcard setting.

Together with the horizontal line of Table Mountain and the rounded top of Signal Hill, the curving contours of the stadium act as a kind of bottom note in a harmonious triad. Lightweight in concept, the circular stadium comes across as unobtrusive and respectful of its surroundings. Its appearance varies greatly with the typical lighting conditions of the area. With its translucent external skin, it reacts to different weather and daylight conditions at different times of the day or seasons, and diverse lighting effects give it a sculptural look.

This design concept was combined with the purely functional requirements. For spectators, it provides a logical but sensory structure, and inside the stadium engenders a terrific atmosphere during soccer and rugby matches and concerts alike. The stadium provides seats for 68,000 spectators, arranged on three tiers, 2,400 of them for business and a further 2,500 in boxes. Broad access promenades on Levels 2 and 6 form 'lobbies' round the stadium arena, allowing visitors freedom of movement, a pleasant environment to linger in and ease of orientation round the stadium. The pitch is visible from the 'lobby'. The upper 'lobby' at a height of 25m offers a panoramic view over Green Point Common, the city and the ocean.

Architects: gmp-von Gerkan, Marg und Partner-Architects

The parabolic profile of the stands gives all spectators an optimal view of the pitch. The strongly curving outline of the top tier contrasting with the more muted curves of the roof edge is a result of their functional geometry. During the 2010 World Cup temporary rows of seating were installed on either side of the top tier, but these were replaced later by event suites and club rooms. This reduced the seating capacity from 68,000 to 55,000 but increased the number of rentable areas, so as to contribute to the commercial viability of the stadium post-World Cup.

17. MELBOURNE CRICKET GROUND
MELBOURNE, AUSTRALIA

One of the largest-capacity sporting venues in the world, Melbourne Cricket Ground (MCG) is over 150 years old. It has great historic and spiritual significance as the home of Australian cricket and Australian Rules football. It was the main venue for the 1956 Olympic Games and, in March 2006, hosted the opening and closing ceremonies and the athletics for the Commonwealth Games.

The MCG has undergone a number of transformations. The latest, a AUD$435 million remodelling, completed in March 2006, involved a 60 per cent redevelopment of the ground, transforming the stadium into a modern world-class facility. Populous was commissioned to provide full architectural services as part of MCG5 Sports Architects*.

The new stadium is open and transparent, with views back to the city and into the Yarra

Park. The design took care to ensure patrons felt a connection to the city which is within walking distance. Each of the three new entrances features a grand glass atrium, serviced by escalators taking patrons to the upper levels. The new hybrid roof is constructed of metal and glass. Sightlines from all 100,000 seats are uninterrupted, with the new structure much closer to the field of play than the stands it replaces. 80 per cent of the seats are under cover.

Another major feature of the redevelopment is the relocation and expansion of the stadium's heritage facilities, with a precinct for museums and entertainment which is open seven days a week. The museums include the Australian Gallery of Sport and Olympic Museum, the Sport Australia Hall of Fame and the Australian Cricket Hall of Fame.

*MCG5, a joint venture between Populous, Daryl Jackson, Hassell, Cox Architects and TS&E, provided full architectural services

18. TELSTRA DOME
MELBOURNE, AUSTRALIA

Telstra Dome, formerly Colonial Stadium, is set in the redeveloped Docklands precinct immediately adjacent to Melbourne's central business district. The AUD$430 million integrated urban stadium development, which opened in 2000, was designed to be flexible, allowing it to attract a full range of sports and entertainment events.

The multi-functional four-tier stadium features a fully closing roof, moveable spectator tiers and a natural turf playing surface. It provides uncompromised sightlines and proximity to the playing surface, with 52,000 seats for oval pitch-based sports, and over 49,000 for rectangular pitch-based sports.

Sophisticated moving-tier technology allows the lower section of the stadium seating to be reconfigured, drawing spectators up to 18m closer to the action when hosting soccer or rugby

The roof, in its retracted position, provides an opening of 160m by 100m, while still maintaining roof protection to 98 per cent of the patrons in the spectator stands. The roof can be closed in 20 minutes.

Another key feature is a ring road located at basement level connecting all back-of-house facilities, and allowing independent servicing without disruption to match-day patrons. There are 67 luxury suites and 12,500 membership seats with separate dining and bar facilities, plus a four-tier spectator bowl, all overlooking the playing surface with views back to the city.

Architects: Telstra Dome was designed by a joint venture of Populous, Bligh Voller Nield and Daryl Jackson Pty Ltd.

319

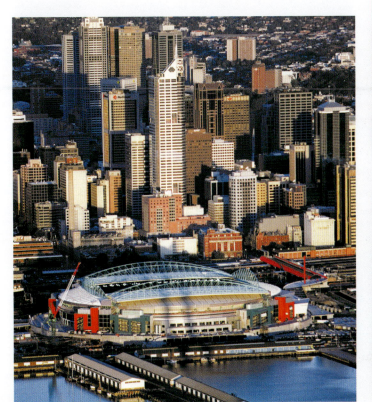

19. NANJING SPORTS PARK NANJING, CHINA

The Nanjing Sports Park, one of the largest athletic venue projects ever completed in Asia, was designed and built for the 10th China National Games, held in the ancient Chinese capital in October 2005. Populous was the architect for the masterplan and all buildings, designing all stages from beginning to completion of the project.

The US$285 million sports park includes a 60,000-seat stadium, 11,000-seat arena, swimming pool, tennis centre, media centre and outdoor facilities for baseball, softball, hockey and basketball.

The sports park forms the centrepiece of a new downtown precinct development to the west of Nanjing, and marks a new generation of stadia, illustrating the significance of sport as a catalyst for urban development. The Chinese government used the National Games as a precursor to the Beijing Olympics to gain as much experience as possible about how

facilities work for a major event. The primary concept of the sports park was to create what they called a 'people's palace', a combination of world-standard sporting facilities with the main stadium as the centrepiece within a recreational park. The sports buildings are grouped closely together with 35 per cent of the precinct dedicated to parkland.

The sports complex incorporates a number of new design features and represents a leap forward in interconnectivity. All facilities were designed concurrently and in record time to allow the greatest possibilities for interconnection and design harmony, and also to enable maximum efficiency for both major event and everyday use. Access to the buildings is by an elevated podium so that the park can be used regardless of whether events are taking place in the sports buildings. Spectators can circulate between the facilities, via the podium, without needing to enter the park area.

Architects: Populous

20. OITA STADIUM OITA, JAPAN

The Oita Stadium, in southwest Japan, was built for the 2002 FIFA World Cup. Designed by Kisho Kurokawa and the Takenaka Corporation, it is affectionately known as the Big Eye because, with its retractable roof, it resembles a large eye and eyelid.

The stadium is extremely versatile. As well as providing a home for soccer and rugby, it can host international athletics and a range of entertainment events such as rock concerts. The closing roof and a movable seating tier, which can be installed in the front section, help create maximum atmosphere.

Oita Stadium is designed as a simple geometric sphere, based on ancient Japanese symbolism. The gentle curvature not only blends in with the surrounding landscape, but also provides a perfect base for a retractable roof. The elliptical shape at the opening portions of the roof has a north-south axis, and is designed to allow maximum sunlight into the rectangular natural grass pitch. The use of Teflon in the movable roof panels also allows sunlight to reach the grass when the roof is closed. When open, some main beams remain exposed over the central area.

The Oita Stadium is part of a large-scale versatile sports park for the people of Oita Prefecture. The total land is 255ha. As well as the stadium, the masterplan includes an arena, training centre, pool, parkland and facilities for soccer, rugby, softball, baseball, gateball and tennis.

The use of deliberate gaps between the seats and the roof gives natural ventilation to the stadium. It also means patrons do not feel enclosed since they can look out on the mountains beyond. The Oita Stadium installed the world's first mobile camera, which meant images could be sent around the world.

321

Architects: Kisho Kurokawa
architect and associates

21. OLYMPIC STADIUM, LONDON , UK

Embrace the temporary. This was the philosophy Populous adopted for the architectural design of London's Olympic Stadium. The unprecedented brief called for an 80,000-capacity stadium to host the athletics competition and the opening and closing ceremonies of the Olympic and Paralympic Games. But, after the Games, it had to be scaled down to a smaller 25,000-capacity venue. This meant that within the larger venue there could be a smaller permanent facility. However, surrounding the larger venue there would be the temporary facilities needed just for the Games.

The triangular stadium site, bounded by rivers on two sides, and a public footpath on the third, is located at the southern end of the new Olympic park. The fact that it's an island allowed the designers to separate the venue perimeter from the stadium structure, so that once spectators cross the bridges over the rivers and have their tickets checked, they are inside the venue. This allows the stadium perimeter itself to be permeable and easily negotiated, something that is particularly important for a stadium where all spectators will be visiting for the first time.

The levels of the site were manipulated so that the spectator circulation around the building could be separated from the level below where the athletes warm up and meet the media, and where other back-of-house activities take place. The permanent 25,000 seats are provided in the lower tier, accessed from the podium. Most of the remaining seats are within the upper tier, reached by simple staircases that radiate around the building. As hospitality facilities are provided elsewhere in the park during the Games, the stadium has a modestly sized accommodation for the Olympic family and heads of state, taking the form of lounges and a 400-cover dining suite located within the west stand, with direct access to seats in the mid tier. This simple arrangement has allowed a surprisingly compact seating bowl to be created, in an elliptical shape around the athletics field of play. Taking inspiration from the 2012 Games logo, a striking pattern has been created with the seats using black fragments on a white background.

The roof is a very lightweight tensile fabric design which appears to hover over the upper tier, surrounded by a white tubular steel truss, supported on diagonal columns which contrast against the black-painted steel that supports the upper tier. This composition has already become a symbol of the success of London's Olympic project.

Surrounding the stadium is the wrap. This provides the all-important threshold between the garden party atmosphere of the outer podium and the intensity of the seating bowl. 360 strips of white tensile fabric, each twisting by 90 degrees, reach down to the podium to allow spectators to pass through. It's a lightweight envelope to match the lightest Olympic stadium ever built.

322

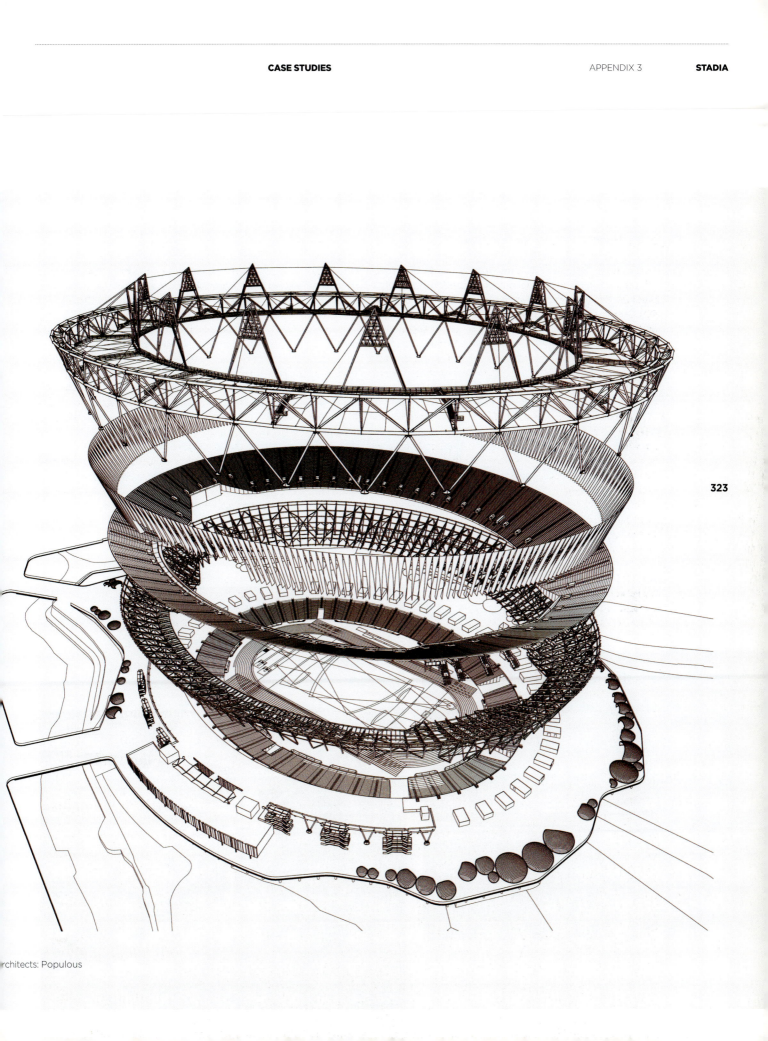

323

chitects: Populous

22. THE OVAL LONDON, UK

Surrey County Cricket Club had an ambition, in 1995, to preserve the status of the 125-year-old Oval as one of the finest cricket grounds in the world. In June 2005, this ambition was realised when the stadium opened following an eye-catching facelift to host the final Ashes Test where England was at last victorious.

The Oval has been transformed, boasting a brand new four-tier 23,000-capacity structure, known as the OCS Stand. Geometrically bold with futuristic curves in white steel, the stylish new stand is truly iconic, elegantly harmonising with the imposing Victorian appearance of the Pavilion. The dramatic sweeping form of the new roof has been composed to act as a foil to the gas holders which form the backdrop at this end.

The OCS Stand has been designed to dramatically improve the match-day experience. Spectators are brought closer to the action than ever before, and presented with the added luxury of more legroom. Acoustic consideration was also important. The stand now reflects the noise back into the ground to create a more vibrant atmosphere.

A further feature of the redevelopment is the 183m external living wall, which supports a variety of climbing plants, adding to the summer ambience of the external concourse, and bringing the seasons into the urban fabric of the area. The tapering timber louvre screen also helps restrict overlooking from the adjacent residential accommodation, and dissipates traffic noise from the main end.

The Oval is a stadium fit for the 21st century, providing spectator terracing, a press centre, broadcasting suite and corporate hospitality facilities. Open all year, the stadium can host everything from conferences and board meetings to weddings.

324

Populous provided the concept design for the Oval. MillerSport provided detailed design.

23. RELIANT STADIUM HOUSTON, USA

Houston is an epicentre of technology, industry and space exploration. Reliant Stadium is designed to embody the city's visionary spirit and the uniquely Texan sense of pioneering and adventure.

The 70,000-seat stadium features a retractable fabric roof which combines with expansive areas of glazing to provide a sense of transparency. The stadium's sliding roof panels are made of steel-hinged frames wrapped in translucent Ultralox fabric, which allows in natural daylight. The bright, open-air feel of the facility's concourses and gathering spaces generate the feel of an outdoor stadium with the comforts of climate control necessary for Houston's extreme weather.

Home of the Houston Texans NFL franchise, Reliant Stadium offers an intimacy and compactness similar to a large indoor arena. All seating levels are designed to be as close to the field as possible. A palletised natural grass field provides the optimum playing surface for American football and soccer, while allowing flexibility for rodeos and other events.

The interiors of the facility have also been designed with the region in mind. The careful use of frosted glass and brushed aluminium with stained woods, rich leathers and cattle brands evokes the blend of Houston's sleek modernism and Texas' rugged sense of history and heritage.

325

Architects: Populous

24. SALZBURG STADIUM SALZBURG, AUSTRIA

The Salzburg Stadium, in Austria, opened in 2003. The 16,500-seat venue, designed mainly for soccer, has been integrated into its surroundings in the immediate vicinity of Klessheim Castle, designed by Fischer von Erlach in 1694. This has had a significant impact on the design of the stadium.

The heights of the surrounding buildings and the fact that the stadium is so close to the castle has resulted in a design concept in which the building height of the stadium has been kept to a minimum. As a result, the soccer field was dug into the topography. Hence, what is seen from the outside is the shape of a slightly slanted, uniform building, with a semi-transparent light roof, supported by an intricate steel-frame structure.

The low building height has created great atmosphere inside the stadium, enhanced by the design of a continuous seating bowl. The concourse has been positioned at entrance level. The stadium was designed to be multi-functional and has already been used for a range of events including concerts and motocross meetings. It was expanded to a 32,000-seat capacity for the 2008 UEFA European Football Championship.

Architects: Schuster Architekten

25. SOCCER CITY STADIUM
JOHANNESBURG, SOUTH AFRICA

Soccer City Stadium, located near Soweto, in Johannesburg, seated 88,600 for the 2010 FIFA World Cup. It was the venue for the opening and closing matches.

The previous 1980s structure of the FND Stadium was almost entirely demolished to make way for the new stadium. This was not the original intent but, during construction, it was decided to almost totally rebuild the stadium.

Some aspects of the original stadium were retained, and the geometry of the bowl was modified to improve sightlines, with a unique split-level lower tier and concourse introduced for the first time in a large soccer stadium project.

The stadium external envelope was determined after intense consultation with local cultural leaders. It resembles a pot, or calabash, in the local idiom. This reading has been adopted widely and was evident during the opening ceremony of the FIFA World Cup.

The seating bowl is designed to be as open as possible, yet it retains a strong intimacy, despite its size. A double-layer tensile fabric roof covers the upper half of the stadium. The roof structure rests on super-columns featured in the perimeter atrium, which is enhanced with a continuous roof light.

The main vertical circulation ramps are entirely contained within the calabash so that spectators get a sense of the drama of the large roofed atria spaces within. Lower level concourses are open to the bowl and to the perimeter so that the space seems to flow directly from inside to outside, and the spectator has a sense of the stadium's entirety.

Architects: Populous in collaboration with BUEP Architects

26. SOLDIER FIELD CHICAGO, USA

After years of political wrangling, the Chicago Bears and their fans are finally enjoying their new state-of-the-art 63,000-seat stadium. Named the 'best damn new stadium, period' by GQ magazine, this venue and its 17 new acres of parkland is changing the face of sports architecture. Wood + Zapata, working in close collaboration with the team's owners, developed a scheme that saves the classic colonnades of

Soldier Field, while providing one of the most exciting luxury skybox configurations in American football, with 120 luxury suites, 9,000 partially covered club seats, and two cantilevered LCD video boards, one in each end zone. The regular seats offer a superior view of the playing field, due to their proximity, and also offer fans incomparable views of both downtown Chicago and Lake Michigan.

Architects: Wood + Zapata. Lohan Caprile Goettsch Architects

27. STADE DE FRANCE PARIS, FRANCE

The cities of antiquity have demonstrated that stadia were, and still are, magnificent urban objects. The Stade de France, built in the heart of Saint Denis, a district close to Paris, provides public open spaces for the local inhabitants with a roof that seems to offer shelter to the neighbouring districts. From the very top it offers panoramic views over the town, with, in the distance, the monuments of the Sacré Coeur and the Saint Denis Basilica.

The imposing Stade de France is distinguishable by its great elliptical disc, the high-tech roof of the stadium, elevated 43m into the air. The disc is supported by 18 steel masts, placed at 45m from each other and following the curve of the nearby Saint-Denis Canal.

The multi-functional 80,000-seat stadium, built originally for the final of the 1998 FIFA World Cup, is designed for both football and rugby, because of the elliptical shape of the tiered seating. It naturally provides a convergence of the spectators' view towards the pitch, and more particularly, towards the goals. But it is also adaptable to a wide range of athletic events. The 25,000 seats of the first ring terraces are mobile, and can be mechanically pulled back 15m, rolling on a cushion of air, steel and Teflon rollers.

The roof has a total surface of more than 6ha, weighs as much as the Eiffel Tower, and houses all the lighting and acoustical functions. Its interior edge of glass also works as a filter of natural light, and can be used as a backdrop for a variety of special lighting effects.

Architects: Aymeric Zublena, Michel Macary, Michel Regembal & Claude Constantini

28. STATTEGG SPORTS FACILITY GRAZ, AUSTRIA

Stattegg sports facility, on the outskirts of Graz, is a model complex, built on the basis of a study on multi-functional leisure and sports facilities with an integrated energy strategy. The project is the combination of a wooden module system with versatile rooms that can be used in a number of different ways.

Because of the difficult topography, and poor orientation of the existing sports ground, and the incorrect position of the clubhouse, the site was completely reorganised. The new two-storey stadium with solar panels on its roof is now situated along the southwest side of the pitch. The stand is triangular in shape, reflecting the wedge shape of the site – wide at the entrance area that all visitors have to pass through, and narrower towards the rear. The façade facing away from the pitch resembles a residential building, and blends in with the surrounding architecture.

The players' changing rooms and toilets are located on the lower floor, and the upper floor has been designed so that virtually all functional units have at least two uses. In the centre is the restaurant area, which takes the form of a free-standing red cube inserted beneath the large stadium roof. The kitchen, serving hatch and toilets of the sports bistro can also be used during matches, while the soccer club-room is available as a restaurant extension. The two offices adjoining this, and the associated infrastructure, are shared by several different sports clubs.

Simple, confidently used and often brightly coloured materials make the building an inviting new village centre. The good-looking, cost-effective facility has been extremely well received by the Stattegg community.

Architects: Hohensinn Architektur

Wembley Stadium was designed by the World Stadium Team (WST), a joint venture between Populous and Foster & Partners

29. WEMBLEY STADIUM LONDON, UK

The 90,000-seat state-of-the-art Wembley Stadium, which opened in 2007, has built upon its past heritage to become the world's most dynamic stadium. Designed to the highest specifications, using the latest technology and offering every fan an unrivalled match-day experience, the stadium continues its renowned status as the Venue of Legends.

Replacing the famous Twin Towers is a wonder of modern architecture. When our first sketches of an arch hit the tracing paper, one could see the magic in that form. Rising 133m, the Wembley Stadium arch not only provides London with an iconic landmark, but holds a crucial function in supporting the 7,000-tonne steel roof structure, eliminating the need for pillars.

The roof has retractable panels to allow light and air onto the pitch, maintaining the quality of the famous Wembley Stadium turf. Between events, the roof can be left open, but can be moved to cover all the seats within 50 minutes, ensuring fans are sheltered during an event.

Stadium facilities have been designed to maximise spectator comfort and enjoyment. The quality of seats and the space allowed has improved dramatically. Seating provisions for disabled spectators have been greatly improved, increasing from 100 to 310.

The geometry of the seating bowl, designed as a single form rather than four separate stands, ensures that spectators have an unobstructed view from each of the three tiers. Careful attention has been paid to the acoustics which enhance the noise from fans on match days and create a legendary atmosphere. The famous Wembley Roar has not been forgotten.

Although designed primarily for rugby, soccer and concerts, the new stadium is capable of hosting world-class athletics events by means of a platform adaptation. With the platform in place, the stadium seating reduces to 67,000.

30. WESTPAC STADIUM WELLINGTON, NEW ZEALAND

Sited on disused railway yards on the edge of Wellington Harbour, the 34,500-seat Westpac Stadium is a modern purpose-built cricket ground. It is also the home of New Zealand's other main sporting code, rugby. The stadium has taken a leading role in the redevelopment of the surrounding area.

The project provided a unique opportunity to develop a world-class cricket venue as a whole entity rather than adding to an existing facility in a piecemeal fashion. The design demonstrates a minimalist approach, with the cricket arena cut back to the tightest possible configuration, allowing the stadium to also accommodate rugby without placing the spectators too far from the pitch. The bowl design includes a complete oval lower tier, with separate box level seating for 2,600, to the underside of the roof, giving dramatic and unobstructed views of the whole arena. The complete enclosure of the field with the oval seating bowl provides an ideal amphitheatre for the action of the sporting arena.

The building's external skin of horizontally striated reflective metal cladding has created a large sculptural landmark on the northern edge of the city's central business district. The concourse areas include gallery spaces providing seven-day-a-week entertainment, cultural and exhibition space serving the community. The stadium also includes offices, a sports-medicine facility, cricket academy and a cricket museum.

It opened in early January 2000, and has been awarded the New Zealand Institute of Architects (NZIA) Resene National Award for Design and the Royal Australian Institute of Architects International Building Award.

Westpac Stadium was designed in a joint venture between Populous and Bligh Voller Nield in association with Warren and Mahoney

31. WIMBLEDON AELTC CENTRE COURT LONDON, UK

Wimbledon is one of the world's most recognisable and evocative sports arenas, with a history of more than 120 years. Almost every summer, however, the prestigious outdoor grass-court Grand Slam tournament has to deal with the frustrations of the occasionally inclement British weather.

Until recently, the Australian Open was the only Grand Slam tennis event with a retractable roof. It was important for Wimbledon to move with the times and protect its position at the top of world venues. The organisers also needed to ensure their huge TV audiences had tennis to watch so as to ensure the event's long-term financial viability. The Centre Court stayed where it was. It was simply remodelled to bring the 1922 building into the 21st century.

The design of the innovative hydraulically-operated roof (a folding fabric concertina) evolved after a scientifically demanding process. Measuring 65m by 70m, the structure works on a principle similar to an umbrella, with metal ribs supporting a translucent fabric.

A key element of the design is to allow natural light to reach the grass, while an airflow system removes condensation from within the bowl to provide the optimum internal environment for the comfort of spectators and players when the roof is closed.

The addition of six rows of seating to the upper tier on three sides allowed increased capacity on Centre Court from 13,800 to 15,000 spectators. New wider seats were installed, as well as extra stairs and lifts to provide greater spectator comfort. To allow for the new seating, new media facilities and commentary boxes replaced those in the upper tier. They were located in a similar position at the back of the seating bowl.

333

Architects: Populous

Note: page numbers in italics refer to figures; page numbers in bold refer to tables.

A

access roads, 41
activity areas *see* playing areas
administrative operations, 215-222
advertising, 269, 287-288
    boards and signs, 97, 234, 269
air-supported roofs, 65
Alberta, McMahon stadium, 131
American football, 12-14
    pitch layout and dimensions, 87
    preferred viewing positions, *134*
    viewing distances, *135*
amphitheatres, 3-5
Amsterdam ArenA, 66, 303
angle of rake for viewing tiers, 141-143
Ann Arbor, Michigan Stadium, 13
anti-graffiti coatings, 57
anti-terrorism measures, 34, 71-75
appeals room, 230
architectural form and structure, 49-68
Arizona, Cardinals Stadium, 305
Arles amphitheatre, 5
artificial surfaces, 77, 79, 81-83
artificial turf, 81-82, 256-257
Ascot Racecourse, 306
Astana Stadium, Kazakhstan, 307
Athens
    ancient Greek stadia, 2-3
    Olympic stadium (1896), 6
    Olympic stadium (2004), 11, 21, 52
athletes, 16-17
athletics
    orientation of playing areas, 29, *30*
    track and field layout and dimensions, 94, *95*
    viewing distances, *135*
Atlanta, Olympic stadium (1996), 11
attendance, 127-128
audio systems, 242-246
Australian rules football, **88**, *134*
automatic vending machines, 186-188

B

Baltimore, Oriole Park, 34
Barcelona
    Noucamp Stadium, 204, 205
    Olympic stadia and arenas (1992), 11
Bari Stadium, 49, 54
bars *see* catering
baseball, 12-14
    pitch layout and dimensions, 92
    preferred viewing positions, *134*
    viewing distances, *135*
Beijing Olympic Stadium, 11, *232*
Berlin Olympic stadium (1936), 6-7, *7*
betting revenue, 271
bicycles, 42
board rooms, 216

box enclosures, 160-161
Bradford
    Odsal Stadium, 79
    Valley Parade stadium, 18, 30, 55
Braga Municipal Stadium, Portugal, 310
brand activation, 287-288
brickwork, 55
broadcasting *see* media
building maintenance and services rooms, 218
bullring method, 116
bus parking, 42
Byzantium Hippodrome, 6

C

cable net structures, 63-64
canopies *see* roofs
cantilever structures, 61-62
capacity of grounds, 127-128
Cape Town, Greenpoint Stadium, 315
capital costs, 131
Cardiff, Millennium Stadium, 35, 66, *135*
cars *see* parking areas
catchment area, 35, 130
catenary cable structures, 63
catering, 183-192, *see also* private viewing and facilities
    disabled people, 123
    media, 211
cat's cradle fence, *111*, 112
Cheltenham racecourse, 41, 186, 203
Chicago
    Comiskey Park Baseball Stadium, 13
    Soldier Field, 328
circulation, 73, 167-180
    disabled access, 123
closed-circuit television (CCTV), 240-241
club debentures and bonds, 271
club enclosures, 162-163
club funding, 270
coach parking, 42
colours
    in materials, 54
    of seating, 151
commentators' cabins, 210
communications technology, 249-252
compression/tension ring structures, 62-63
computer equipment rooms, 218
concerts, 106
concourses, 57
concrete shell structures, 62
concrete structures, 54-55
conference rooms, 211-212
Constantinople stadium, 18
control rooms, 73, 216-218
costs
    capital, 131
    operating, 268-269
cricket, 15, 93
crowd control, 109-116, 178

D

Dallas, Cowboys Stadium, 311
delivery facilities, 43
Delphi stadium, 3
directors' lounges, 163
disabled access, 53
disabled spectators, 119-124
    parking provision, 42
    seating, 128-129, 155
    toilets, 199-200
display screens, 217-218, 242, 297-298
domed stadia, 68
Donetsk, Donbass Arena, 312
drainage, playing areas, 80
Dublin, Aviva Stadium, 12, *144*, *260*, 309
Dunedin, N.Z., Forsyth-Barr Stadium, *281*, 314

E

economic considerations, 17-18, 21-22, 261-268
Edinburgh, Murrayfield rugby stadium, 61, 131
egress from stadia, 175-176, *177*
    disabled people, 124
electronic scoreboards, 297-298
elevators, 180
emergency exit, 175-176
emergency lighting, 233-234
enclosure
    complete, 65, 68
    degree of, 58
energy conservation, 278, 280-282, *284*
entrances, 169-171, 176, 178
    disabled access, 122-123
Ephesus stadium, 3
Epidauros stadium, 3
Epsom Downs racecourse, 57
escalators, *166*, 179
event days, typical, **102**
executive suites, 161-162
expansion, staged, 131, 268

F

fast-food kiosks, 188
fences, 110-112
financial viability, 17-18, 21-22, 261-268
fire detection and fighting, 246-247
fire safety zoning, 30-32
fireproof construction and materials, 55, **150**, 151
first aid facilities, 221-222
flammability of seating, 151
football *see* soccer

G

Gaelic football, 89
gates and turnstiles *see* entrances
Gelsenkirchen, Veltins arena, 56
glare control (lighting), 235
Glasgow, Ibrox Park, 18, 61
glass, safety, 73-74
goal post structures, 60-61
Goodwood Racecourse, 65
government bonds, 271

336

grants, 271
grass surfaces, 56, 68, 78-80, 255-256
Graz, Austria, Stattegg sports facility, 330
ground capacity, 127-128
guest rooms, 163

H
heating and cooling systems, 246
history of stadia, 2-15
hockey pitches, 90
Hong Kong stadium, 46, 60
horse-racing *see* racecourses
Houston
    Astrodome, 38, 68, 77
    Minute Maid stadium, 13
    Reliant Stadium, 325
Huddersfield, Galpharm Stadium, 39, 131, *136*, 159
hurling pitches, 91

I
illumination *see* lighting
income, 269-271
Indianapolis, RCA Dome, 65, 68, 100, 102
information systems, 40, 217-218, 241-242, 249-252
in-town stadia, 38, 52
inward movement into stadia *see* entrances
irrigation of grass, 80-81, 256

J
Johannesburg, Soccer City Stadium, 327

K
Kansas, Harry S Truman sports complex, *13*, 14, 103, 105, 179
kiosks, 44
kitchens, 160, *161*, 186, 188
Kuala Lumpur, Selangor Turf Club, 179

L
land availability and cost, 39
landscaping, 44-46
lawn tennis, 14-15
    court layout and dimensions, *96*, **97**
    orientation of courts, 29
    playing surfaces, **78**
    viewing distances and positions, *133*, *134*
lay-by areas on circulation routes, 174, *175*
layout for circulation, 168
lifts, 180
light spill, 235
lighting, 44, 233-240, 280
location of stadia, 38-39
London
    Emirates Stadium, *136*, *156*, 160, *286*, 313
    Lord's Cricket Ground, 15, 51, 64, 68
    O2 arena, *182*
    Olympic stadium (1908), 6
    Olympic stadium (1948), 7
    Olympic Stadium (2012), 11, *26*, *27*, *274*, 322-323
    Oval Cricket Ground, 15, 324

Queens Park Rangers stadium, 160
Stamford Bridge football stadium, 62
Tottenham FC stadium, 160
Twickenham Rugby Football Ground, 12, 131, 205
Wembley Stadium, *76*, *111*, *118*, *134*, 159-160, *166*, 331
White City, 6, *7*
Wimbledon AELTC Centre Court, 14, 66, *67*, 277, 333

M
Madrid, Zarzuela racetrack, 54, 62
Manchester City FC ground, 53
Manchester United FC stadium, 205, 256
markings on pitches, 81, 83
Marylebone Cricket Club *see* London: Lord's Cricket Ground
masterplanning, 27-35
materials
    for seating, **150**, 151
    for stadia, 53-55
    sustainable design, 278-289, *282-283*
media, facilities for, 43, 207-213
medical facilities, 221-222, 230
Melbourne
    Cricket Ground, *161*, 318
    Etihad Stadium, *104*, 105
    Rod Laver Arena, *14*, 14-15
    Telstra Dome, 319
members' enclosures *see* private viewing and facilities
membrane structures, 64-65
Mexico City
    Aztec Stadium, 8, 11, 131, 135
    Olympic Stadium (1968), 8, 10
Miami
    Marlins Park, *300*, 317
    Orange Bowl, 13
    Sun Life stadium, 53, 103, 105, 179
Milan, San Siro Stadium, 53, 65-66, 78, 179
Milwaukee, Miller Park (Brewer) baseball stadium, 66
Minneapolis, Hubert H. Humphrey Metrodome, 68
moats, 112-116
Monte-Carlo, Louis IV Stadium, 40, 52
Montreal, Olympic stadia and arenas (1976), 11, 66
motorcycles, 42
movable seating, 103, 105-106
multi-purpose uses, 22, 99-106
    viewing distances and positions, 136-137
Munich
    Allianz Arena, 302
    Olympic Stadium (1972), *10*, 11, *48*, 63-64, *135*
museum spaces, 205

N
Nanjing
    Sports Park, 320

Youth Olympics, *33*
natural grass surfaces, 56, 68, 78-80, 255-256
New Haven
    Hockey rink, 63
    Yale Bowl, 13
New Orleans, Louisiana Superdome, 13, 68
New York
    Flushing Meadows, 14, 15
    John Shea Stadium, 13
    Yankee Stadium, 13
Nimes amphitheatre, 5

O
office accommodation, 216
officials, facilities for, 43, 229
Oita Stadium, 66, 321
Olympia stadium, 3
Olympic stadia, 6-11
open sites, 38
opening roofs, 66
operating costs, 268-272
orientation of playing areas, 29
out-of-town stadia, 38
outwood movement from stadia *see* egress from stadia

P
Paris
    Parc des Princes, 51, 61
    Roland Garros stadium, 15
    Stade de France, 12, 105, 265, 329
parking areas, 40-45
    disabled people, 122
    media, 209
    security implications, 72
Pasadena, Rose Bowl, 13
pedestrian routes, 43-44, 167-180
Peloponnesus stadium, 3
perimeter fences, 110-112
Pessimus Hippodrome, 6
pitch replacement concept, 79
pitches *see* playing areas
Pittsburgh, Heinz Field, *2*, 316
planning, 37-46
planting *see* landscaping
players, facilities for, 43, 225-231
playing areas
    dimensions and layout, 83-96
    lighting, 234-240
    maintenance, 255-257
    orientation, 29, *30*
    perimeter fences, 110-112
    pitch markings, 81, 83
    protective coverings, 83
    shared uses, 103
    surround, 96-97
playing surfaces, 16-17, 55-56, 77-83
police, facilities for, 219-220
polymeric surfaces, 82-83, 257
Pontiac, Silverdome, 45, 65, 68
pop-music concerts *see* concerts
Popplewell Inquiry into stadium safety, 18

337

post and beam structures, 60
power supplies, 247–248
press see media
private viewing and facilities, 157–164
programme sales, 204
protective coverings, 83
public transport, 40
Pula amphitheatre, 5

Q

queue management, 178

R

racecourses, 41, 57, 65, 186, 203, 306
rain, shelter from, 58–59
rake, angle of, 141–143
ramps, 53, 57, 179
refreshment facilities see catering
renewable energy, 282
retail sales, 203–205
retractable seating, 103, 105–106
Rio de Janeiro, Maracana Municipal stadium, 12
riser heights, 137–143
Riyadh Stadium, 65
Rome
    ancient circuses, 5–6
    Colosseum, 3, 4, 5, 49, 109
    Olympic stadia and arenas (1960), 7–8, 8,
        8, 9, 54, 62, 63
roofs, 51, 58–66, 131–132, 265
    coverings, 66–68
    opening, 66
routes see circulation
rugby, 12
    orientation of pitch, 29
    pitch layout and dimensions, 85–86
    viewing distances and positions, 133, 134, 135

S

safe areas, 32, 174
safety, 18
    circulation, 167–169
    crowd control, 109–116, 178
    perimeter fences, 110–112
    seating, 143, 145–146
    zoning, 30–32, 168–169
St Louis, Busch Stadium, 13
Salzburg Stadium, 326
San Francisco, AT&T Park, 308
scoreboards, 242, 297–298
screens, display, 217–218, 242, 297–298
seating
    capacity, 29, 127–128
    colours, 151
    design, 24, 145–155
    dimensional standards, **149**
    dimensions, 152–154, **153**
    disabled spectators, 155
    fixings, 154–155
    flammability, 151
    geometry, 56–57

materials and finishes, 151
    movable and retractable, 103, 105–106
    private facilities, 157–159
    range of viewing standards, **158**
    retractable and movable, 103, 105–106, 149
    versus standing accommodation, 129–130
    types, 146–150
seating times, **146**
Seattle
    Husky Stadium, 61
    Safeco Field baseball stadium, 66
security, 34, 71–75, 219–220
    CCTV, 240–241
Seoul, Olympic stadia and arenas (1988), 12, 51,
    53, 62
service and delivery facilities, 43
services, 233–252
shared uses see multi-purpose uses
Sheffield
    Don Valley Stadium, 65, 68
    Hillsborough Stadium, 18, 38, 110, 184, 221
shelter provided by roofs, 58–59
shops, 204–205
sightlines, 136, 137–143
    perimeter fences and moats, 110–116
signage, 174
    disabled spectators, 124
    parking, 44
Silverstone motor racing circuit, 41, 185
site boundary planting, 46
snack-bar kiosks, 188
soccer, 11–12
    orientation of pitch, 29
    pitch layout and dimensions, 84
    viewing distances and positions, 133, 134,
        135, 136
sound systems, 242–246
souvenir shops, 204
space frames, 65–66
special events, 32–33, 101–102, **102**
spectators, 15–16, see also disabled
        spectators; stands
    ground capacity, 127–128
Split stadium, 68
sponsors' lounges, 164
sponsorship, 269, 287–288
sprinkler systems, 55
staged expansion, 131, 268
stairs, 57, 173, 178–179
stand-by power, 247–248
standing areas, 129–130
stands, see also seating
    angle of rake for, 141–143
    degree of enclosure, 58, 59
    entrances, 171–174
    geometry, 56–57
    maintenance, 257–258
    viewing angles and sightlines, 137–141
steel structures, 55
sterile zones, 168
stewards, provision for, 218–219

structural systems, 60–66
subdivision of stadia, 168
sun, protection from, 58
surface finishes, 53–54, 57–58
surfaces, playing see playing surfaces
Surrey County Cricket Club see London: Oval
        Cricket Ground
sustainable design, 275–286
Sydney
    ANZ Stadium see Olympic stadia and
        arenas (2000), 126
    Olympic stadia and arenas (2000), 11, 36,
        46, 51, 68, 127, 277, 282, 304
    Sydney Football Stadium, 52
synthetic turf, 81, 82

T

tax concessions, 270
Taylor report on stadium safety, 18, 38, 221
technology, 23–24
television, see also media
        lighting for, 239–240
temporary events management, 218
temporary structures, 50–51, 277
tennis see lawn tennis
tension structures, 63–65
terrorism, 34, 71–75
Thebes stadium, 3
ticket sales, 203–204
    disabled people, 122
timed exit analysis, 175–176, 177
toilet and washing facilities, 195–201
    administrative staff, 221
    disabled people, 124, 199–200
    media, 211
    players, 227, 229
    private, 160
Tokyo
    'Big Egg', 65
    Jingu National Stadium, 8, 9
    Olympic stadia and arenas (1964), 8, 9, 51,
        54, 63
Toronto, Skydome, 38, 102, 105, 164, 204,
    219–220, **220**, 234
tourism, 34–35
transport issues, 39–40, 277
turf see grass surfaces

U

Ulleval stadium, 82
urban sites, 38, 52

V

Vancouver, BC Place, 65
vending machines, 186–188
ventilation, 73, 246
Verona amphitheatre, 5
video displays, 217–218, 242, 297–298
Vienna, Prater Stadium, 53, 55, 62, 63
viewing, 127–143, see also sightlines
    angles and sightlines, 137–141

disabled spectators, 123
exploiting the corners, 133
optimum viewing distance, 132, *133, 135*
preferred locations, 132, *134*
VIPs *see* private viewing and facilities
visitor centres, 205
visitors' rooms, 163

W

washing facilities *see* toilet and washing
    facilities
water supply, 248, 282
Wellington, N.Z., Westpac Stadium, 332
wheelchair users, *see also* disabled spectators
    provision for, 128–129
wind, shelter from, 58–59
wind uplift, roof design for, 60

Z

zoning, parking, 43
zoning, safety, 30–32, 168–169